Negotiating in Times of Conflict

Gilead Sher and Anat Kurz, Editors

Negotiating in Times of Conflict

Gilead Sher and Anat Kurz, Editors

iNSS
המכון למחקרי ביטחון לאומי
THE INSTITUTE FOR NATIONAL SECURITY STUDIES
INCORPORATING THE JAFFEE   TEL AVIV UNIVERSITY
CENTER FOR STRATEGIC STUDIES   אוניברסיטת תל־אביב

משא ומתן בעת סכסוך

גלעד שר וענת קורץ, עורכים

Graphic design: Michal Semo-Kovetz and Yael Bieber
Cover design: Tali Niv-Dolinsky
Printing: Elinir

Institute for National Security Studies (a public benefit company)
40 Haim Levanon Street
POB 39950
Ramat Aviv
Tel Aviv 6997556
Israel

Tel. +972-3-640-0400
Fax. +972-3-744-7590

E-mail: info@inss.org.il
http:// www.inss.org.il

ISBN: 978-965-550-574-0

Contents

Introduction

"There is no easy way," Senator George J. Mitchell

While in the summer of 2014 we at the editorial board were busy reviewing the set of articles by the contributors to this volume, Israel and Hamas were engaged in yet another bloody round of hostilities. Provisional ceasefires collapsed one after another. For over seven weeks, Israeli civilians faced the reality of relentless rocket, mortar, and missile fire from the Gaza Strip by Hamas and Palestinian Islamic Jihad. In Gaza, one of the poorest and most densely populated areas in the world, massive destruction as well as the number of direct and collateral deaths and casualties accumulated as Israel resorted to an all-out military campaign – Operation Protective Edge – in an effort to bring the fire from the Strip to a halt.

When blood is spilled, people are filled with vengeance and anger, along with despair, bereavement, mistrust, and frustration. This moment is a golden opportunity for hate-driven extremists, yet even for the non-radical person, emotions run high and harsh rhetoric tends to eclipse hope and calls for a diplomatic resolution. However, we suggest that there might be ways to resolve, or at least to mitigate, even complex, violent, and protracted conflicts between communities and nations, the Israeli-Palestinian conflict among them. The articles collected here explore this potential for conflict resolution.

When we first decided to publish this volume, we contacted prominent researchers and practitioners from around the globe with specializations in a variety of different conflict arenas. Interestingly, several dominant themes and recommendations for negotiating in times of conflict recurred in many papers. Perhaps this is not surprising, as in attempts to manage conflicts throughout history and throughout the world, the same mistakes have been made time and again – mistakes that too often result in futile efforts, widespread fatalities, and horrendous suffering. In light of this, the importance of taking on board the experiences of conflict resolution analysts and practitioners cannot be underestimated. We hope that the lessons presented in this publication provide valuable material for policymakers, mediators, and negotiators who strive to avoid pitfalls in their quest for peace and aim to create a tolerable if not promising future for those embroiled in conflict and war.

The articles herein focus on elements and policies equipped to facilitate alleviation of tension and contribute to peacemaking efforts within the context of negotiation strategy. The lessons and policy recommendations for the most part were based on specific cases that were then translated into general terms. Much emphasis falls on inclusiveness as a key negotiating strategy, the potentially supportive role of international actors, and the psychological dimension of conflicts and conflict resolution. Additional lessons concern the challenge of paving the way for negotiations, where rival parties face a deadlock. Many of the articles touch upon several of these aspects, and together reflect with three principal themes: general approaches to negotiations, case studies, and the Israeli-Palestinian conflict.

The section dedicated to the Israeli-Palestinian conflict reflects the particular interest at INSS and its Center for Applied Negotiations (CAN) in enriching the discourse on managing and advancing a resolution of this complex issue and on guiding associated peace-oriented policy. In light of this underlying logic, general conclusions that are specifically relevant to Israeli-Palestinian peacemaking efforts are underlined in the context of this introductory, integrative essay.

A Focal Negotiating Strategy: Inclusiveness

A significant lesson that emerged repeatedly from the analyses and conflict resolution accounts stresses the importance of inclusiveness. Many authors advocate making an effort to include as many influential actors as possible into a peace process, even those who are considered as spoilers of the process or armed non-state insurgent groups, i.e., terrorist organizations – though this would not be unconditional inclusion and must be based on their readiness to discuss terms for an end to violence. The main message from these papers is that whatever the challenges, the more inclusive the peace process, the more successful it is likely to be. Trying to marginalize spoiler groups and other problematic constituents rarely works, and in many cases only bolsters the group one is seeking to sideline. Talking to and including groups in the process is nearly always recommended: it will not always succeed, but it will succeed often enough to be worthwhile.

In his essay, Erik Solheim asserts that history shows that governments in many cases end up talking to those they once branded as terrorists, so they may as well try earlier. Several groups that were once deemed spoilers have been convinced to lay down their arms and adopt a political approach. Solheim explains that talking to terrorists or rebel factions does not mean giving in, but is rather an attempt to avoid violence if there is even a slim chance of reaching agreement by bringing up issues of conflict and perceived wrong and injustice. In other words, speaking with such groups does not mean that their violence is condoned.

While negotiations are often seen as comprising two opposing parties, the reality is far more complex. Breakaway factions, diaspora communities, interest groups, and an array of third parties all have an influential role in negotiations that must be fully understood and addressed. Thus, Miriam Fendius Elman urges policymakers to include into the peace process, as early on as possible, constituencies known as spoilers who attempt to undermine the negotiations. Elman explains that while governments work to integrate their spoilers into the peace process, they must not shy away from taking a swift and decisive response if violence should occur. Cracking down on spoiler violence sends a message to the other side that leaders are serious about peace.

In their chapter, Benedetta Berti, Ariel Heifetz Knobel, and Gary Mason present a case study on intra-party loyalist negotiations in Northern Ireland. They argue that for inter-party peace negotiations to succeed, consensus must be built internally. The authors contend that the peace agreement in Northern Ireland was reached once the importance of keeping combatant communities on board the peace process was finally understood. Prisoners were consulted before political decisions were taken, and ex-prisoners played an important role as internal agents of change, as they began pursuing nonviolent strategies. Leaders must offer alternative ways, other than violence, for groups to demonstrate loyalty.

In the chapter that follows, Gallia Lindenstrauss draws insights relevant to the role played by the diaspora in the negotiations between Turkey and Armenia in 2009-2010. She argues that major developments in peace negotiations in the homeland can force the diaspora to reflect on its identity, causing resentment and even leading to actions against such developments that may inspire hardliners in the conflict arena and hence complicate efforts to embark on the path toward conflict resolution. At the same time, she explains, diaspora communities can also contribute to peaceful resolution of conflicts, for instance, by supporting moderates in the state of origin and participating in problem-solving workshops. Lindenstrauss recommends that leaders positively engage with diasporas by actively informing diaspora leaders in real time about major policy shifts – if possible, involving diaspora leaders themselves in the peace negotiations, and helping the diaspora to create a "new identity" in the post-conflict period to ease tensions related to the fear of losing one's identity. Lindenstrauss' conclusion should be seriously considered by Israeli and Palestinian peace negotiators aiming to advance a solution to one of the core contentious issues, namely, the Palestinian refugees.

Focusing on the Israeli-Palestinian sphere of conflict, Anat Kurz argues that a unified Palestinian representation is a vital Israeli interest, in addition to being a primary Palestinian interest unto itself. Indeed, the rivalry between Fatah and Hamas, which touches upon many issues – not all of them directly associated with the Israeli-Palestinian conflict – is far from exhausted. Its intensity was further exposed in the summer of 2014, against the backdrop of the military campaign between Israel and Hamas. At the same time, Kurz contends that the logic underlying the likely benefits of unifying the Palestinian political arena for the Palestinians, Israel, and especially the peace process between the two peoples is still valid. More specifically, it is suggested that concrete efforts toward integration of Hamas in the Palestinian Authority may over time not only decrease the intensity of the power struggle between the two leading Palestinian parties, but could also reduce motivation in the ranks of Hamas' military wing to trigger repeated cycles of violence with Israel and hence diminish the party's significance as a spoiler. She concludes that in order to facilitate such an eventuality, Israel should abandon its opposition to Palestinian inter-party accommodation attempts and even make an active effort to enhance intra-Palestinian institutional cooperation. This would serve as a means to encourage the creation of a broadly-based Palestinian representation that will be an accountable party for negotiating an end of violence and an end-state solution to the conflict.

An additional lesson particularly relevant to conflicts involving inter-religious themes and tension is offered by Trond Bakkevig, who explains how religious dialogue can often clear the way for political dialogue and thus should be included in a negotiation process. Religious leaders can play a role in assisting negotiations and peace building. Religious leaders also often have increased influence during crisis situations and war, not only because many conflicts have a religious basis, but also because religion becomes a source of strength for those suffering. At such times religious leaders have the power to intensify conflicts, for example, by stressing exclusive ownership of places and narratives. Conversely, these leaders can seek a common vision for such places and narratives, appreciating that of others while still demanding respect for their own. This conclusion is also relevant to the Israeli-Palestinian conflict, which against the backdrop of the rise of political Islam throughout the Middle East and in the Israeli-Palestinian arena, has become ever rifer with religiously-related tension.

In the chapter that follows, James Sebenius urges negotiators to advance their own interests by helping the other party address its internal problems. Negotiators would do well to help the other side attractively frame the deal for their own constituents; this might mean providing the ingredients for the other side to make an acceptance speech about why conceding to the deal you want is smart and in their interests. Being able to provide such assistance requires a deep understanding of the context in which the other side is enmeshed: the web of favorable and opposing constituencies as well as their relationships, perceptions, and sensitivities. Clearly, this recommendation is in line with Kurz's discussion on the inter-party strife in the Palestinian arena and its relevance to the Israeli-Palestinian conflict.

Louis Kriesberg supports helping the other side bring its constituents on board. Kriesberg warns that types of coercion that are violent, humiliating, and convey threats to collective survival will likely provoke resistance, not compliance. He also maintains that too great an asymmetry between adversaries, particularly when it is based on military strength, can interfere with reaching an equitable agreement. Overwhelming military strength does not necessarily translate into strength at the negotiating table. Kriesberg's conclusion seems to apply to a variety of asymmetric conflicts.

International Support

Throughout history, international actors proved time and again that they can instigate conflicts between other parties and hinder their path to peace, as a means to advance their own interests at the expense of the security and wellbeing of those directly involved in hostilities. However, as shown by many successful peacemaking processes, regional and international parties can also play a constructive role in mediating agreements and monitoring compliance with the negotiated stipulations as means to enhance their sustainability.

Patrick Hajayandi attributes the success of the Arusha peace accords largely to the combined efforts of internal, regional, and international actors. The UN, the Carter Foundation, and the Organization of African Union all played a role in trying to resolve the Burundi conflict in a power sharing process. The regional leaders took ownership of the negotiation process with the support of the international community. International leaders and mediator Nelson Mandela also exercised a great deal of pressure on the conflicting parties, successfully urging them to look for alternatives to violence.

In addition, smart diplomacy is at least as important as military intervention for saving lives. This issue is discussed in the chapter by Alan J. Kuperman, which describes how diplomats threatened the rebels with prosecution unless they halted their offensive, and peacekeeping forces were deployed to prevent their advance. In addition, the international community refrained from demands that Liberia's leaders surrender all power or face quick elections or prosecution. Instead, international negotiators promised asylum to Liberia's president and a share of power to his political circle, thereby averting a potentially violent backlash from the regime.

The benefit of a well-crafted multilateral approach is underscored in the chapter by Marc Finaud, who highlights the role of the international community as a crucial factor in sustaining the agreement. This ceasefire understanding was supervised by the Israel-Lebanon Monitoring Group, co-chaired by the U.S. and France, with the participation of Israel, Syria, and Lebanon. Finaud provides an in-depth analysis of how the monitoring group functioned and extracts recommendations for constructing successful agreement implementation models. Clearly, however, the sustainability of any ceasefire is dependent first and foremost on the interests of the parties to the conflict. When circumstances change, interests shift and the rivals find themselves engaged again in war, and the effectiveness of any international monitoring tends to be significantly reduced, if not lose meaning altogether. This eventuality was registered repeatedly in the context of Israel-Hizbollah conflict – most recently in the summer of 2006.

The Psychological Dimension

The psychological dimension is widely considered to be one of the "soft" yet focal features of conflict situations and peace processes. Dealing with this dimension is challenging and particularly intriguing, due to the problematic isolation of its factors from the "hard" attributes and characteristics of the conflict. Nevertheless, in this volume a serious effort was made in two articles to address this theoretical and practical challenge.

Ruthie Pliskin, Eran Halperin, and Daniel Bar-Tal maintain that a new peace-supporting repertoire must be created that stresses the need to resolve conflicts peacefully, humanize the enemy, and challenge the perception of conflicts as a zero-sum game. Advancing this goal should involve both bottom-up and top-down processes. Focusing on the top-down evolution of psychological change that results in policy modification, the authors contend that change often begins when leaders realize that they – as well as their country – are likely to lose more from the continuation of conflict than by making concessions for peace. A case in point concerns changes registered among Israeli policymakers. Those who moved toward supporting conflict resolution often cited reasons for the shift in terms of future economic, demographic, or strategic losses if conflict continues.

A complementary approach is offered by Byron Bland and Lee Ross, who assert that the real barrier to peace is fear that if the other side were to reach its goal, the future for one's own side would be unbearable. They provide a new paradigm for structuring negotiation processes: the Four-Question Framework developed by the Stanford Center on International Conflict and Negotiation. Emphasizing the psychological elements involved in perceptions of conflict and conflict resolution, this framework tackles problematic issues by structuring peace processes around questions relating to a bearable shared future, trustworthiness, loss acceptance, and justice. This approach aspires to allow for reshaping relationships to achieve more positive interactions and greater trust. Taking the Israeli-Palestinian conflict as an example, Bland and Ross explain how advancing agreements on the most contentious issues – borders, the holy places, refugees – would be easier when addressed through this framework.

This case, however, needs further corroboration, and for the time being, examples referring to the Israeli-Palestinian conflict remain at the theoretical level since the two parties find it hard to agree on peace terms and even on terms of reference for getting negotiations back on track. This makes the question of what should be done when conditions for concrete negotiations are not ripe all the more urgent and relevant.

When Conditions for Negotiations are not Ripe

Robert H. Mnookin suggests that the conflict cannot at present be solved by negotiations, even though there are a number of possible agreements that would better serve the interests of the majority of Israelis and Palestinians than the continued conflict. Mnookin sets out what such an agreement for a solution could look like as it addresses the core issues of conflict: territory, Jerusalem, settlements, security, and refugees. The lack of resolution is not simply because actors are "irrational," he explains, but rather because of a range of strategic, psychological, relational, and institutional barriers. Like Bland and Ross, he suggests it may be possible to overcome these barriers by working on relational issues. Drawing on Gilead Sher's approach to advancement of the two-state solution, he also recommends considering unilateral Israeli moves to withdraw from Palestinian territory in order to best serve both sides' interests. Finally, he posits that another possibility might relate to strong-arm mediation, perhaps led by the U.S., combined with enough carrots and sticks to help both sides reach an agreement.

Gilead Sher advocates complementing a negotiation process, and eventually replacing it, by constructive unilateral steps that are in line with the final objective of the negotiations. He suggests that the Israeli government should begin a process of taking independent steps toward turning the two-state solution into a reality. The same applies for the Palestinian leadership. Even though the author contends that a negotiated settlement is the best way to resolve the Israeli-Palestinian conflict, he urges leaders to examine constructive alternatives, when negotiations appear to be failing. This paper recommends that Israel adopt a policy of withdrawal from areas in the West Bank, translate the two-state solution into a reality, and secure Israel's future as a Jewish, democratic state, which in turn will help it facilitate its integration in the region. Sher highlights the need for this disengagement to be gradual and coordinated among regional and international actors relevant to the quest for Israeli-Palestinian peace, to avoid the pitfalls of the Gaza withdrawal, which occurred before suitable and comprehensive policies were outlined.

This edited volume reflects a large and committed team effort. First and foremost, we would like to thank the contributing authors for sharing their rich experience and providing valuable insights, furthering the field of negotiations and conflict resolution. Special thanks go to Moshe Grundman, Director of INSS Publications, Yael Basford of the INSS editorial staff, and Judith Rosen, Editor at INSS; Shlomo Brom and Mark A. Heller, INSS senior research fellows; and the staff of the Center for Applied Negotiations (CAN) at INSS, including Amit Barkan, Liran Ofek, Deborah Shulman, and Farah Yousef, all of whom offered extensive help in preparing the volume.

Gilead Sher and Anat Kurz
April 2015

Always Try Engagement

Erik Solheim

What do Yasir Arafat, Menachem Begin, Nelson Mandela, and Meles Zenawi have in common? They were all considered terrorists in their time.

It is commonly said that one man's terrorist is another man's freedom fighter. While any attack on innocent civilians must be condemned, many individuals affiliated with terrorists or terrorist groups are reasonable people. Quite a few even evolve to become heads of state. When discussing the issue of engaging terrorists, one must ask: what is the rational thing to do if your own daughter is kidnapped by a militant group? Should talks be encouraged if it increases the likelihood of release and improves her well-being? Is it reasonable to try to find out how she is treated and on what terms she is being held? Conversely, should any communication be excluded as a matter of principle? Is it rational to oppose anything less than an unconditional release to uphold a principle of never speaking to terrorists? To put it bluntly: would you let such principles take command? This essay argues that it is right to try to talk to terrorists. The strong opposition to the idea of talking to terrorists is somewhat surprising, since negotiation arguably seems to be the common sense position.

Always Try Talks

At the Oslo Forum, the biggest global gathering of peace negotiators, the participants once discussed whether invitations should be extended to "pure" terrorists like Osama bin Laden. The majority view seemed to be: yes, it is worth trying.

Talking is a practical approach rather than a moral conviction or ideological doctrine; it is a principle based on the notion that armed conflict is so devastating that any alternative is nearly always preferable. Wars usually cause death and suffering while destroying economies. In December 2013, the young state of South Sudan broke down due to a power struggle between President Salva Kiir and Vice President Riek Machar. The country imploded in ethnic violence. Tens of thousands of people were killed, nearly two million were displaced, and the country was left in a humanitarian crisis. The two leaders, who once fought together for independence in the Sudanese civil war, became sworn enemies, and much of what they once fought for and built up together was lost. They both craved power, and it is difficult to imagine that it would not have been better for everyone if they had managed to reach a negotiated outcome.

The African Development Bank has estimated that the economic costs of conflict in Africa are equivalent to 35 years of development. In 1980, Liberia was among the most prosperous states in Africa, with a national income of $1269 per person. After years of conflict and war, it declined by around 90 percent and was down to $163 when Ellen Johnson Sirleaf was elected to pick up the pieces in 2005.[1]

The only alternatives to negotiations are outright military victories or stalemates with endless spirals of violence and revenge. Due to the extremely high human and economic cost of conflict, anything that can be done to avoid conflict is worth trying.

Engaging with an enemy is difficult, but negotiated agreements can only be reached if enemies talk to each other. Dialogue does not mean giving in and forsaking one's beliefs. Dialogue merely means talking to a hostage taker before taking action if there is any chance of success. Engagement does not necessarily mean that the threat of force should be taken off the table, but it is worthwhile if it can help prevent, stop, or shorten wars. Though engagement and conflict prevention are considered difficult and costly, they should essentially be compared to the cost of conflict.

A policy of never engaging with brutal dictators, terrorist leaders, or warlords can be difficult to carry out. History shows that in many cases governments end up talking to those they once branded as terrorists. A policy of always trying to talk would be more consistent. Talking to the Taliban right after the allied invasion of Afghanistan in 2001 could have resulted in a negotiated solution when the Taliban was at its weakest. Instead, the idea of talking to the Taliban only gained traction after they had regained their strength.

The International Criminal Court's Darfur genocide charges against Sudanese President Omar al-Bashir made it difficult for the international community to engage with him during the peace negotiations with South Sudan. In the end, he let South Sudan go ahead and establish the new nation in 2011. Many American envoys consequently wanted to reward Sudan for this through reduced sanctions and increased contact. However, none were able to carry this policy through in Washington.[2] Omar al-Bashir is still an influential man in the region and has met with his South Sudanese counterpart Salva Kiir during the course of the ongoing Ethiopian-led negotiations. A policy of holding leaders accountable for crimes is obviously important, but talking to al-Bashir was also necessary for those wanting to create lasting peace in the region.

Counter Argument: Munich

A common example used by those opposed to engagement with terrorists and dictators is the 1938 Munich Agreement between Chamberlain and Hitler. It is argued that Chamberlain's peace efforts in Munich led to appeasement; dialogue is said to have only encouraged and emboldened Hitler. Once again, this argument should be further examined.

One may argue that Chamberlain's biggest mistake was speaking to Hitler and trying to negotiate a peaceful solution. However, negotiating to avoid the potential horrors of war was surely worth trying. Chamberlain should not be judged by history for talking to Hitler, but rather for what he said; by giving up Czechoslovakia, Chamberlain indicated his desperation to accommodate Hitler at the expense of his principles. Hitler obviously understood and reacted to this weakness. Therefore, Chamberlain's biggest mistake was giving in to Hitler, not the mere act of engagement.

Another example is Sarajevo. In 1914, the major European states stumbled into an unwanted war. Leaders with narrow visions were unable to consider their adversaries' perspective. The leaders brought upon the world a war much longer and bloodier than anyone could have anticipated. The First World War took a great toll on all parties, and there was hardly anyone who gained. Three empires went under, while Communism and Nazism flourished.

It is hard to imagine that the First World War could not have been avoided through negotiations. Preferable outcomes may have been achieved if visionary and flexible leaders had really tried.

Counter Argument: Evil

In the aftermath of the 9/11 terrorist attacks, President George Bush said, "No nation can negotiate with terrorists, for there is no way to make peace with those whose only goal is death."[3] Vice President Dick Cheney came out even more forcefully stating that, "We don't negotiate with evil; we defeat it."[4] Bush and Cheney's remarks reflect the position according to which dialogue is hopeless and no settlement is feasible, as terrorists are perceived as mad psychopaths and irrational evil-doers.

This is, quite simply, wrong. In any case, one would have to speak to terrorists to verify or reject the notion of "evil terrorist." It is probably true that some terrorists will stop at nothing and must be defeated militarily. But many others are rational actors seeking power and influence through violent means. Several terrorist groups have been convinced to lay down their arms and integrate into democratic politics.

The U.S., on many occasions, talked to terrorists and even provided mediators to negotiate with them. Northern Ireland is one of many examples. Another example is the Nepali Maoists who were once condemned by most diplomats as "mad terrorists" beyond reason. This image was proven wrong when mediators spoke to Nepali Maoist leaders Prachanda and Baburam Bhtattarai in India, leading to a breakthrough in the negotiations. Later, these leaders returned to Kathmandu as democratic politicians after 20 years of conflict, finally winning the 2008 election. Both later became Prime Ministers of their country.

Prior to this summit, the U.S. and many other nations refused any contact with them. However, a meeting between the American ambassador to Nepal and the Maoists, which was held in the Norwegian embassy in Kathmandu, was a crucial first step. Through talks, it quickly became apparent that the Maoists were not as crazy as their reputation may have suggested.[5]

Counter Argument: Do Not Reward Terrorists

The third argument against talking to terrorists emphasizes the fear that speaking to perpetrators of violence may be seen as rewarding such behavior.

Some may question the value of engaging violent actors while ignoring a peaceful opposition; they may claim that if arms and a history of violence are a prerequisite for engaging in negotiations, more groups may be encouraged to arm themselves. There is some truth to this assertion, and the argument should not be dismissed. However, the unfortunate reality is that peace processes must involve those who command the arms. The potential benefits of talking must be weighed against the cost of not doing so.

It can be argued that all relevant parties should be included in the talks, regardless of the basis of their relevance and influence. The more inclusive the peace process, the more successful it is likely to be. In South Africa, Nelson Mandela brought everyone into one "big tent." Even white fascists advocating for continuation of apartheid and black extremists who wanted to expel all the whites out of South Africa were invited. Their views were heard, but the voices of progressive whites accepting the tide of history and blacks preaching reconciliation were the dominant force leading the negotiations.

Mediators faced this dilemma from the very beginning during the peace negotiations in Sri Lanka. The Tamil Tigers claimed to be the sole representative of the Tamil people. They insisted on talks being an exclusive exercise between themselves and the government of Sri Lanka. This inevitably excluded many other relevant groups. Most importantly, it excluded the Muslim community and the Sinhala opposition party. But it also excluded Tamils who were opposed to the Tigers and Tamils who agreed politically with Tigers but did not support violence. Negotiators constantly tried to make the peace processes more inclusive, but with little success. Both the Tamil Tigers and the government accepted that negotiations were solely for the two entities that commanded an armed force.

Peace processes ought to be as inclusive as possible. It is extremely important to try to involve those with broad public support but no army. However, at the end of the day, peace is about keeping weapons off the playing field. Generals and guerrilla commanders are normally more important in this regard than civil society activists. If terrorists win huge concessions after taking up arms, others may indeed be tempted. But once again, talking is not the same as giving in to unreasonable demands.

Counter Argument: Do Not Legitimize Terrorists
Those opposed to talking often stress the fear of legitimizing terrorists. This argument is not without merit; there will often be many cameras present

when talks are initiated with terrorists. They will be given a platform from which to speak to the media. They may be seen from a more sympathetic angle and possibly given an opportunity to mobilize further support.

This was the main argument throughout the peace process in Sri Lanka. Critics argued that the dialogue with Tamil Tiger leader Prabhakaran was providing him legitimacy and respect. Consequently, at times the government of Sri Lanka was reluctant to allow any contact with him. The Norwegian negotiators in Sri Lanka became the only non-Tamils speaking to him. In essence, contact with Prabhakaran became a reward for "good behavior" on his part.

In the end, this isolation probably became the main obstacle for the peace process. It was only Prabhakaran who could make peace, not Tamil farmers or the rank and file of the Tamil Tigers. But he was isolated and knew very little of the wider world outside of Sri Lanka. The peace process would have benefitted from wider engagement with Prabhakaran. The international community should have overwhelmed him with visits, explaining what he could potentially achieve for the Tamil people and where the limits were drawn. International leaders could have legitimized Singhalese views in the eyes of the Tamils and vice versa.

Isolated and with little contact outside the Tamil world, the Tamil Tigers made huge political and military mistakes. These mistakes, combined with a new and more aggressive approach with fewer restrictions on killing innocent civilians from the government in the capital Colombo, became a major reason for the downward slide of the peace process after 2004-2005. It is possible that those mistakes could have been avoided through more international contact and warnings to Prabhakaran from visiting ministers and diplomats. Few Tamils were able to give unwanted advice to the leader. The international community could have done that.[6]

Awarding terrorists legitimacy is a real concern. But this risk must be weighed against the benefits of talking. Providing legitimacy to valid points of view can be a good thing.

Counter Argument: Terrorists Refuse to Talk
Just as many states refuse to talk to terrorists, many terrorist groups refuse to talk to states. A strong stance against talking is in many cases a public

position taken by the parties to a conflict, while in reality they are indirectly or directly engaging in other ways. However, in some conflicts it is an absolute position. How does one engage with terrorists if they themselves refuse to engage with you?

The most obvious solution is to explore the possibility of a third party mediator. One must accept that it can take time to prepare the ground for talks. But no conflict is static. Those who refuse to talk today may be compelled or feel forced to talk to each other further down the road. The key is to build broad networks and identify negotiators to whom states and terrorist groups may be willing to speak. Religious networks, tribal structures, civil society activists, and business leaders can be efficient intermediaries.

Prior to the "Anbar Awakening" (a Sunni movement that had risen in Iraq in 2006), terrorism was on the rise and Iraq was on the verge of full scale sectarian and civil war. By reaching out to tribal leaders and Sunni groups, U.S. General Petraeus was able to build alliances to combat foreign and al-Qaeda fighters while reducing violence. The "Anbar Awakening" was established through a local tribal leader who rallied other tribal leaders to fight and secure their communities while negotiating with the Americans for support. Many of the Sunni groups were involved in direct conflict with American soldiers, and it would have been very difficult to establish such an alliance without a mediator who understood tribal codes and concerns.[7]

States and terrorists often refuse to engage in deliberations, but that can change quickly. The Taliban in Afghanistan refused to negotiate in general, and the U.S. and many other states refused to talk to the Taliban. However, gradually everyone understood such a rigid approach did not work. Informal talks are a good way of building networks and preparing the grounds for the day when the warring parties are persuaded to talk. Religious, tribal, and business leaders can all play an important role as both informal and formal mediators of talks when parties to a conflict have rejected talks.

Engage on Behalf of the Powerless

Negotiators facing moral qualms about whether or not to talk to terrorists or violent leaders should ask themselves one simple question: what do those suffering from the oppressing policies or the bloodshed want to achieve? Talking to a dictator who is persecuting his people and ruining an entire country can feel futile. This was the sense when meeting Zimbabwean President Mugabe at his presidential palace in Harare. The once great freedom fighter was leading his country towards economic ruin and sending people to their deaths.

Most Western governments had a policy of isolating Mugabe. Even dialogue-preaching Norwegian colleagues questioned the purpose of talking to a man who had shown little interest in bringing his country forward. One particular meeting took place at the request of Tendai Biti, the Minister of Finance from the Democratic Movement. Only a few months earlier Biti had suffered beatings by the Mugabe regime and taken refuge in the Norwegian embassy. He pleaded for Norwegian ministers to meet Mugabe. The reason was that the weak coalition government needed to find a way forward and that path entailed showing Mugabe sufficient respect. The idea was to encourage him to walk along with the coalition government and not turn his back on them.[8]

Still, most Western countries refused to talk to Mugabe and they insisted that it was a matter of principle. A fair enough principle, but it is not Western heads of state or newspaper editors who suffer under Mugabe. It is important to remember that the ten million Zimbabweans living in extreme poverty suffer the most. The democratic forces like Biti and then-Prime Minister Tsvangirai were forced to deal with Mugabe every day and they believed that engagement was the right way forward.

Speaking with brutal leaders can raise a variety of moral dilemmas and personal qualms. However, a negotiation is not about the mediator's personal feelings or preferences. Conflict mediation is about setting it right for the victims of wrongs. It is about those who do not have a seat at the table, but are living with conflict and violence every day.

Engage Because Leaders are Isolated

Merely trying to engage with others can provide insights that lead to solutions and help avoid mistakes. This is one of the most underestimated reasons for the efficacy of deliberations; leaders may appear crazy and often act in ways that defy logic, but this erratic behavior can be explained by the fact that they are isolated and misinformed. Many presidents and guerrilla leaders have never heard anything but praise. They are seemingly revered and may even see themselves as God's gift to the Tamils, Singhalese, Zimbabweans, Sudanese, Iraqis, or humanity. They are constantly told that a greater, wiser, braver, and more benevolent leader never walked this earth. Such isolated leaders can easily become deluded.

There is no doubt that Saddam Hussein completely misinterpreted the military and political situation in both wars involving the U.S. Saddam's advisors were no more than petrified minions whose main objective was to try to figure out what Saddam most wanted to hear. Cases like Saddam's Iraq or North Korea are extreme. But this problem is much wider than we tend to anticipate, even in more democratic societies.

Mediators are often the only ones with nothing to lose from telling the truth. The peace mediator can be the only party with the ability to tell a leader that he or she is completely misinformed about what the international community believes, unrealistic in their goals, or plain wrong about the strength of the country or organization's military force.

The first crisis for the new state of South Sudan referred to sharing oil revenues with neighboring Sudan, which still controlled all the pipelines bringing oil to world markets. SPLM, the ruling party and former guerrilla group, wanted to stop the oil flow through the north and have China build a new pipeline to the sea across Kenya. The idea of cutting off Sudan in the north was hugely popular in the south. There was full support of this decision in the government. Only foreigners could tell them this was plainly irrational as oil revenues account for 98 percent of the South Sudanese budget. The government could not provide education, health services, and roads without the income from oil. People tend to take to the streets and rebel when governments stop providing services. It was equally unreasonable to think that the government could ask China to build anything after having berated them in the media, threatened to stop the flow of oil destined for China, and unilaterally raised tensions with China. Indeed, negotiators were able to get an oil revenue sharing deal six months later.[9]

Furthermore, the world is often equally misinformed about the intentions of secretive governments or the true nature of guerrilla movements. Talking can prevent such misunderstanding and identify possible solutions. Conflicts are rarely about what the leaders of conflicting parties say in public. Leaders often make grand statements about historical injustice, national security, or the wellbeing of the people. But leaders are more often concerned with their own wellbeing rather than with the noble cause they claim to front.

Talking through others is always an option. One of the main duties during the Sri Lanka peace negotiations was to channel messages and information back and forth between the Tamil Tigers, India, and the U.S. Both nations had proscribed the Tamil Tigers and did not want to engage directly. But both were eager to establish an indirect channel through Norway. Americans preferred to relate to the Tamil Tigers behind the scenes. There were also secret meetings between India and the Tamil Tigers. Then American deputy secretary of state Richard Armitage even came to Norway and shook the hands of the Tamil Tiger chief ideologue Anton Balasingham. The only condition was: no photos.

Engage Because You Can Resolve "Minor" Issues

Not all engagements lead to declarations of peace, democratic breakthroughs, and high profile signing ceremonies. Some engagements lead to better conditions for prisoners or easier access for humanitarian workers. A few released prisoners of war mean everything to their families. Red Cross access to the rest means a lot to those who remain. No one who has seen the joy in the eyes of a mother getting her son back would disregard such victories as "minor" issues.

Success breeds success in peace talks. Any little agreement on a specific issue may bring the entire process forward. However, there are equally many smaller issues that can threaten to unravel the entire process. It usually takes a long time and many small victories before the larger issues can be resolved.

Engage Because Success is Possible

There are many great success stories in the last decades, resolved through mediation and engagement: Nepal, El Salvador, and Mozambique, to mention a few. Both Colombia and the Philippines seem to be on the verge of triumph and peace as well.

The guerrilla leaders of the Free Aceh Movement (GAM) in 2001 were living in modest apartments in a working class district outside of Stockholm, Sweden. The Aceh conflict seemed intractable and it did not appear likely that they would ever return to their homes in Indonesia. However, the conflict was peacefully resolved four years later thanks to the mediations by Finnish President Ahtisaari, the foresight of Indonesian President Yudhoyono, and the persistence and flexibility of GAM leaders. The GAM leaders returned from Stockholm and ended up elected leaders of the province. It was even more impressive when the Indonesian government and GAM pulled off the development miracle in Aceh, one of the most successful reconstruction efforts following a natural disaster anywhere in the world. Around 200,000 people died in Aceh during the Asian 2004 tsunami and much was destroyed, but today the province is a model of reconstruction.

Another example of a peace miracle is Myanmar. Many people in the West became "Burma activists" after the violent crackdown on democracy activists and Aung San Suu Kyi in Myanmar in 1988-90. There was broad public support for a boycott of the military government. This strategy was increasingly questioned during the 1990s; in Norway, for instance, some were beginning to argue that engagement was more likely to succeed than isolation. Although criticized by activists and questioned by some allies, from 2005 the Norwegian government slowly began establishing links to the military junta.

Myanmar's turn towards democracy was motivated by nationalism. The military leaders realized how underdeveloped Myanmar had become compared to neighboring Thailand and China. They decided to open the gates, and provide for development, economic growth, and prosperity. The nationalists also understood that national security is vulnerable when you only have one friend in the world, namely China. Myanmar's isolation slowed down the reform process. It would probably have happened faster with more engagement earlier on.

Conclusion: Talking is Worth Trying

Talking to terrorists may be meaningless, but we will never know unless someone tries. We may demonize each other but most humans are basically the same. Those involved in war and peace may agree that the process is haphazard and subject to factors such as mood and personality.

The fact that Jonathan Powell, the lead British negotiator, initiated peace talks with the IRA in a small farmhouse somewhere in Northern Ireland rather than the grand halls of London was probably influential. Food was a recurring problem during the peace process between the Tamil Tigers and the government in Sri Lanka. Not everyone loves salmon, reindeer, and potatoes as much as Norwegians, and even $1000 plates of Japanese delicacies can be a bad substitute for rice and curry in the eyes of Tamils or Singhalese. Issues related to venue, food, the shape of the negotiation table, or the set-up of chairs are crucial; pragmatism, hospitality, and flexibility may contribute to success. Solutions to conflicts do not only come from rigorous analysis, brilliant strategies, or flawless organizations. Breakthroughs can happen in chaotic exchanges of text messages or over a drink in the early hours of the morning. Talking is important because people start conflicts and only people can end them. Talking is the only way to find out whether the person sitting across is indeed a demon or a rational person worth talking to.

In conclusion, talking is worth trying because it can resolve conflicts and war. Talking is the most consistent policy. Talks will not always succeed, but talking will not make matters worse unless one gives in to unreasonable demands. Talks will succeed often enough to be worthwhile and are worth trying to avoid something as horrible as war, even if there is just a miniscule chance of success.

Notes

1   M. Ncube, B. Jones, and Z. Bicaba, *Estimating the Economic Cost of Fragility in Africa, Working Paper Series* No. 197 (Tunisia: African Development Bank, 2014), p. 24.
2   Erik Solheim, *Politikk er å Ville* (Politics is Wanting) (Oslo: Cappelen Damm, 2013), p. 88.
3   G. Bush, "Remarks on the Situation in the Middle East, April 4, 2002," *Public Papers of the Presidents of the United States 2002*, Book 1, p. 546, ISBN: 9780160723193.
4   M. B. Reiss, *Negotiating with Evil: When to Talk to Terrorists* (New York: Open Road Integrated Media, 2010), p. 19.
5   Solheim, *Politikk er å Ville*, p. 97.
6   Ibid.
7   Greg Bruno, "Backgrounder: Finding a Place for the 'Sons of Iraq,'" Council on Foreign Relations, 2009, http://www.cfr.org/iraq/finding-place-sons-iraq/p16088.
8   Solheim, *Politikk er å Ville*, p. 80.
9   Ibid., p. 87.

Obstructing the Spoilers of Peace

Miriam Fendius Elman

Peace processes invariably generate spoilers – dissatisfied constituencies that attempt to foil the negotiating process or prevent the successful implementation of a peace agreement preferred by the central government and a majority of the public. Dissenters against government-led negotiations may use violent or nonviolent means to derail peace processes. In democratic settings where opponents of peace agreements lack the capacity to use force, they may instead try to manipulate existing institutions, legal mechanisms, or media outlets to undermine the prospects for reconciliation. Preventing spoilers from derailing negotiations requires different strategies, depending on whether spoilers employ violent or nonviolent tactics and whether they operate in democratic or non-democratic settings. Democratic states face greater difficulties in peacemaking than do their non-democratic counterparts, since leaders have a limited ability to repress discourses that reject peace efforts. The use of force and other coercive measures to marginalize spoilers are not trouble-free options, nor is it possible for democratic governments to fully control the media or educational outlets. In other words, spoilers can be especially difficult to manage in democratic settings because a culture of peaceful conflict resolution limits the ability of governments to impose their preferences on citizens. At the same time, those societal groups that seek to derail an active peace process preferred by the societal majority and the government also cannot easily use violence to promote their interests.

In negotiations between adversaries engaged in protracted conflicts, governments and third party mediators must manage spoilers better when they first emerge.[1] Policymakers operating in democratic settings can overcome the challenges to successful peacemaking that are presented by spoilers by seeking their inclusion in the peace process early on, and initiating a dialogue with potential spoilers so that their interests can be more accurately gauged and addressed during the negotiation process. Negotiators on the opposing side should bear in mind that specific concessions can be especially useful if they make it easier for their counterpart's government to convince potential spoilers that they have a stake in the peace. Third party mediators can also help to transform spoilers into stakeholders by working with both sides to conceptualize innovative and creative options for integrating dissident domestic parties into a concrete plan for conflict resolution. However, if minority actors resort to violence, governments involved in negotiations must stop spoiler violence in its tracks. A swift and decisive response to spoiling sends a powerful message to the opposing side regarding the government's commitment to conflict resolution. Because spoilers can point to ongoing violence as a way to undermine public consensus for peace, negotiators committed to resolving protracted conflicts must handle these situations with great care.

The Dynamics of Spoiling

It goes without saying that in most cases of armed conflict, whether civil or international, the preferred outcome of the conflicting sides is not to negotiate reconciliation but to impose their own terms on a final settlement. Approximately 85 percent of civil wars end in the military victory of one side over the other. In the remaining 15 percent, warring factions come to the negotiation table because they recognize that they could not achieve a decisive military victory.[2] Yet as Matthew Hoddie and Caroline A. Hartzell note, "The recurrence of civil wars points to the fact that there are often powerful opponents of peace seeking to derail the settlement process if given the opportunity."[3] Thus, in many cases peace settlements are default outcomes, though former warring parties may spoil a negotiated peace once their military capacity for fighting has been restored. And if the expected payoffs from peacemaking do not materialize, they may calculate that the payoffs from renewed violent engagement are higher than maintaining the peace.

The case of Angola's civil wars in the 1990s is instructive here. After Angola's independence from Portugal in 1975, several independence movements, including the Union for Total Independence of Angola (UNITA) and the Popular Movement for the Liberation of Angola (MPLA), fought a long war of attrition for most of the 1980s with generous support from South Africa and Cuba, respectively. With the end of the Cold War, this patronage plummeted and the impetus for peace grew. The result was the UN-sponsored 1991 Bicesse Peace Accords. Yet Jonas Savimbi, leader of the UNITA rebel group, reneged on two separate peace agreements once he realized that his political power would be diminished in a post-conflict, democratized Angola. As long as Savimbi thought UNITA would do well in the elections, he was willing to adhere to the peace process. After being defeated at the polls, all bets were off. As Savimbi failed to get the majority of the votes in the 1992 presidential election, he reignited the war.

Thus, Savimbi signed a peace agreement in 1991, but he never gave up on the military option. He made sure that he had the capacity to continue funding a war option if he needed to, by seizing diamond mines before the agreement was signed and dragging his feet on demobilizing UNITA's armed forces and integrating the remainder into a new national Angolan army. Savimbi only returned to the negotiation table when UNITA's military gains against government MPLA forces began to evaporate. When the military option became less tenable for Savimbi, he agreed to sit down with the MPLA, and a state of non-war was restored with the Lusaka Protocol in 1994. By then, however, 300,000 Angolans had died in the worst fighting since Angola's independence.[4]

The Angolan case is an empirical example of a general finding: peacemaking is always a process of managing potential spoilers. If one side believes that it has the capacity to achieve a better deal than the one on the table, it is more likely to resort to spoiling behavior. Similarly, if former enemies think that under the terms of a peace deal they are being undermined, they are also likely to renege on the deal. Challenges to peace processes emerge when one or both sides of the conflict doubt that their rivals will fulfill the commitments specified in the agreement. While observers often claim that peace agreements fall apart because of lack of trust and mutual suspicion, what this in fact means is that at least one side is wary of fulfilling its own obligations while the other side is not. Preventing spoiling, therefore, requires that the custodians of peace build into an agreement both "fear reducing provisions" (reassurance) and "cost increasing provisions" (deterrence).[5] To better handle spoiling, signatories and third party mediators need to put disincentives in place that discourage reneging on the agreement. They also need to change the payoffs associated with continued cooperation. In general, peace agreements should increase the costs of returning to violence and increase the benefits of peace for the majority of both societies.

Spoilers of Peace: Defining a Concept

In recent years, a growing body of work has considered the impact of spoilers on negotiation outcomes.[6] According to a seminal study by Stephen John Stedman, "Peacemaking is a risky business… the greatest source of risk comes from spoilers – leaders and parties who believe that peace emerging from negotiations threatens their power, worldview, and interests, and use violence to undermine attempts to achieve it."[7] For Stedman, spoilers can only exist when there is an actual or existing peace to spoil: when an agreement has been signed, or at the very least, when former warring parties have publicly committed themselves to a peaceful settlement. He also suggests that spoilers can be either insiders or outsiders. That is, they can be signatories to the agreements themselves, or they can be excluded from the forum of peace negotiations. A key component of Stedman's conceptualization of spoilers is that not all parties, or even factions within parties, will benefit equally from a peace deal. Spoilers are often driven by a principled rejection of the terms of the agreement. Even when actors use violence, it is important not to lose sight of the (often legitimate) criticism of the peace process. Because peace agreements tend to produce winners and losers, unless handled correctly, these dissenters can become actors that derail the peace.

A problematic aspect of Stedman's definition is that it focuses on spoilers (as a noun), and not on spoiling actions (spoiling as a verb). Labeling groups or individuals as spoilers inserts bias because it can be a means for excluding specific groups from the negotiation process. Also questionable is Stedman's assertion that violence is a necessary feature of spoiling, as this ignores the fact that spoilers may use nonviolent methods. In democratizing and quasi democratic political space, it will be more common to see spoilers using violence. In these contexts, the state is weak and lacks a monopoly on the use of force; different parties may retain armed forces and militias because a nationalized military has yet to be established. The rule of law and formal governance institutions will also be less entrenched than in mature democracies, and a culture of resolving state-societal conflicts via peaceful methods will not yet be ingrained. These features make it likely that potential spoilers will put far less faith in the democratic process, and will be more likely to fall back on armed force as a spoiling option. By contrast, in mature democracies, spoiling generally occurs when dissenters against a peace process foil the majority's interest in sustaining the peace by working within the system. Accordingly, spoilers are best defined as either individual political actors or political groups that use violence or nonviolent means to undermine a peace process preferred by both the central government and the majority of society and, in so doing, jeopardize peace efforts. Important to note is that spoilers are typically marginalized from the peace process itself. While there are internal spoilers – those signatories who wind up reneging – peace processes are typically spoiled by actors that have never been given the opportunity to become stakeholders of the peace.

In sum, "spoiling a peace process involves adopting policies that scuttle conflict resolution efforts when the latter are preferred by a majority of the public. In this sense, spoilers defy not only the authority of the government, but also the national consensus."[8] As Oded Haklai notes, "Spoilers are dissenters from a government-led peace process who sometimes contest the right of the central government to represent the polity and its population in the conflict. Accordingly, when the central government is not formally involved in a peace process, opponents of compromises do not constitute spoilers."[9]

Preventing and Managing Peace Spoiling: Risks and Opportunities

Spoilers and "oversold" agreements. Spoiling is typically a small-group phenomenon. While spoilers can generate a mass following, all spoilers need the support and complicity of a much larger part of society. It follows that peace agreements must be "sold" appropriately so that critics cannot present the agreement as a sham. This, in turn, requires that the agreement not be presented to the public as more than it really is. Too often, peace agreements are pitched to the public as "end of conflict" deals, yet this only raises the public's expectation that their interests will be fully realized. When presumed outcomes fail to materialize, expectations are dashed. Spoilers can then more easily muscle into the discourse to highlight the discrepancy between the agreement and the reality of the situation. Even if there have been mutual concessions and positive developments, spoilers will always be able to point to the cup half empty.

A good example of this dynamic is the rise in attacks by Chechen insurgents into regions of Russia between 1996 and 1999, and the Russian military invasion of Chechnya as a counter-terror response in October 1999. Ironically, the ratcheting up of the Russo-Chechen conflict in this time period occurred after the Russians and Chechens had signed the August 1996 Khasavyurt Agreement, negotiated by General Lebed on behalf of then-Russian President Yeltsin and Aslan Mashkadov, leader of the insurgent movement who would later become the President of Chechnya. The agreement was followed by a treaty between Yeltsin and Mashkadov in May 1997. Yet as one commentator noted, "In some ways, the peace process culminated in a more horrifying situation in Chechnya than had existed before the process started."[10]

The 1996 peace agreement had only three provisions: that both sides renounce the use of force; agree to construct their relations in accordance with international law; and continue further negotiations. The issue of the status of Chechnya was left out, yet most Chechens believed that the agreement and subsequent treaty were in fact offering de facto recognition of Chechen independence. Yeltsin, however, had no such view of the peace agreements. Recognition of Chechen independence would have required revisions of the Russian constitution and would have inevitably limited the extensive powers of the presidency and weakened Yeltsin's political power. In fact, Yeltsin had only pushed for a peace accord in 1996 because public opinion polls showed dissatisfaction among the Russian public for the war in Chechnya and elections were looming. In effect, the 1996 and 1997 agreements, despite all their fanfare, represented a premature peace; it was politically expedient to get a ceasefire, but the quickly drafted and adopted agreements did not go far enough in addressing the core issues between the two groups.

In the interest of stopping the immediate violence, neither side insisted on solving the permanent issue of Chechnya's status. This rush to agreement allowed the parties to declare the war over, based on very little negotiation. The vagueness meant that the public could interpret the agreement in different ways. The Chechens expected an improvement in the political and economic situation, but Yeltsin and the Russian government never proceeded with the necessary follow-up negotiations, thus weakening the position of Mashkadov. When the promised results of the peace process did not materialize, Mashkadov found it harder and harder to control the Chechen warlords. Basayev, a veteran of the first Chechen war, emerged to lead a new insurgency that actively used violence to sabotage the peace process. As more and more Chechens lost patience with, and faith in, the peace, Basayev continued to gain strength. Meanwhile, the peace agreements signed by the Russians and Chechens had promised the Russian people protection from terrorist attacks. The Russian public was willing to back a new military strategy advanced by Putin, who campaigned in 1999 on the promise to deal with Chechen violence. The societal majority backed Putin because their expectations had been dashed, that is, the promises of safety had not been met.[11]

The demise of the Israeli-Palestinian peace process in the 1990s offers another example of how spoilers can be empowered when negotiators "oversell" peace agreements as offering far more than they can deliver. Palestinians assumed that the 1993 Oslo agreement would lead to the end of Israeli occupation and a sovereign Palestinian state. Given dashed Palestinian expectations, the expansion of existing Israeli settlements in the West Bank, East Jerusalem, and Gaza during the Oslo years had a volatile impact. While settlement growth was not a violation of the Oslo Accords, the perceived deepening of Israeli occupation undermined support for the peace process by creating a gap between what Palestinians believed that the Oslo agreements were supposed to give them, and what they actually got. Critics of Oslo regularly pointed to Israeli land expropriation as "proof that the Palestinians were being shortchanged by the Oslo process."[12] To be sure, Israel redeployed under the terms of the Oslo I and II agreements, and the newly created Palestinian Authority offered self-governance to hundreds of thousands of Palestinians living in West Bank cities and towns. Yet despite these positive changes, spoilers could always point to Israel's continued control over Palestinian life. As Jeremy Pressman notes, "Popular Palestinian discontent grew during the Oslo peace process because the reality on the ground did not match expectations created by the peace agreements."[13]

Unmet expectations on the Israeli side likewise contributed to Oslo's failure by empowering peace critics who insisted that Oslo was a sham. The Israeli public expected that the Oslo peace agreements would mean an end to Palestinian violence. The immense gap between these expectations and the dire reality (terrorist attacks intensified during the 1990s) had a devastating impact on Israeli public opinion and galvanized spoilers who had long held the peace process in contempt. Here too, the situation could have been framed in a more positive light. By the mid-1990s, coordinated Israeli and Palestinian counter-terrorism operations resulted in a significant suppression of Hamas and Islamic Jihad – hundreds of operatives from these rejectionist groups were jailed and nearly two dozen of their leaders were killed.[14] Yet continued terrorist attacks made it easy for Oslo's critics to delegitimize the Palestinian Authority precisely because Israelis had presumed that the peace agreements of 1993 and 1995 would mean an end to terrorism. As Eisenberg and Caplan note, "Ongoing terrorism and Arafat's ambivalence played into the hands of Oslo's detractors."[15]

These examples of spoiling in the Russo-Chechen and Israeli-Palestinian cases suggest that one way to prevent and manage spoilers is to avoid overselling a peace agreement. Peace agreements forged via the big fanfare of public, high profile peace summits often raise unrealistic expectations that can be exploited by spoilers. By contrast, incremental change that builds mutual trust through tit-for-tat concessions is a harder process for spoilers to derail because such incrementalism does not bill itself to be anything more than it is – tentative, cautious, yet deliberate steps away from violent conflict toward a more constructive phase of the conflict. To be effective, however, negotiators must utilize media and educational outlets to launch a public relations campaign that presents these incremental moves as positive steps forward.

Including potential spoilers in the peace process. Central to the prevention of spoiling is to ascertain which actors should be suppressed and which should be integrated into the peace process. To be sure, some domestic political actors will never support peacemaking with the adversary and will always be unwaveringly opposed to a peace settlement, no matter what its conditions or circumstances. It is important to identify these actors early on in the process, and impede their ability to renew violence or dominate the discourse regarding the value of a peace deal. Here, a central government committed to peacemaking must avoid appearing weak, neutral, or inconsistent; early in the post-peace process it needs to confront such spoilers, raising the costs for those actors who refuse to engage in peacemaking. However, it is also critical that these actors not be conflated with the larger majority. In fact, these actors need to be removed from other potential spoilers that may still be convinced of the merits of a peace agreement. Unfortunately, what often happens is that in dealing with would-be spoilers, states pursue policies that target the majority as well. These sorts of dragnets are the scourge of peace processes and make it that much more likely that spoilers will prevail. In nondemocratic settings, but especially in democratic states, there are drawbacks in using force to deter and compel spoilers, as this can run the risk of radicalizing moderates and the larger society.

One important means of handling spoiling is to bring would-be spoilers into the peace process early on. Spoilers are created *before* a peace agreement is signed. It is therefore imperative to engage with would-be spoilers throughout the negotiation process and not only during the post-agreement phase. Peacemakers need to identify and include the broadest possible range of societal actors so that excluded parties do not emerge as spoilers later down the road. Inclusion makes it more likely that spoilers will become stakeholders of the peace. Including figures of authority and opinion leaders from various societal groups in the peace process ensures that key provisions of the agreement meets their interests. This involves recognizing that criticism of an agreement is legitimate, and finding creative ways in which potential spoilers can see at least some of their grievances addressed.

The Good Friday (Belfast) Agreement signed in April 1998 following two years of multiparty talks between Northern Ireland's Unionists, Nationalists, and Republicans and the Irish and British governments illustrates the importance of inclusion in managing spoilers. Establishing a power sharing government between Northern Ireland's Unionists and Nationalists, the negotiations that led to the Good Friday Agreement were based on the principle that all of the conflicting parties should be part of the peace process and that the major paramilitary groups should become signatories. Thus, once the IRA agreed to a cessation of military operations (albeit without the requirement that it decommission its weapons), Sinn Fein was invited to join the multiparty talks. The inclusion of Sinn Fein increased Republican support for the peace process while reducing the likelihood of Republican spoiler violence.[16] Significantly, the Good Friday Agreement prevented spoiling by ensuring that all actors that had been signatory to the peace accord could present it to their respective communities as legitimate. Via the use of "constructive ambiguity," the terms of the agreement could be read positively by each constituency, thus decreasing the likelihood that spoilers could label the signatories as stooges or sell-outs. As Stacie E. Goddard notes, "The agreement's success did not lie in deception; it was not that each of the coalitions came away from the agreement believing they [sic] were getting something they were not. Rather, the ambiguity of the agreement's language allowed each of the parties to claim the settlement as legitimate, and perhaps more importantly, portray it as legitimate to their relevant constituencies."[17]

In contrast to the Good Friday Agreement, consider the Rwandan Arusha Peace Agreement, which empowered spoilers by marginalizing groups from the political process. Indeed, the Rwandan case highlights how ostracizing key political actors, by creating new institutions that instead of sharing power centralize power in the hands of particular groups, can end up derailing the peace. In August 1993, the Hutu dominated government of Rwandan President Juvenal Habyarimana and the Tutsi-led Rwandan Patriotic Front (RPF) signed an agreement in an internationally sponsored effort to end Rwanda's civil war that began three years earlier. Even before the accord was signed, in 1990 and 1991, Habyarimana had initiated a series of political reforms, and the legislature approved a multiparty constitution with executive power shared between president and prime minister. These changes opened up the political system but had a negative impact on the course of the conflict. Democratization challenged the Hutu grip on power as moderate Hutu parties became the RPF's allies. The ruling elite tried to strengthen its power by appealing to ethnic Hutu solidarity. Thus, a previously bilateral conflict between the government and the RPF was transformed into a multilateral competition, and solidified a conservative political alliance that saw a negotiated outcome as inimical to its political power in the new democratizing context. As Benjamin A. Valentino notes, "The accords all but locked the Hutu extremist parties out of power…The moderate Hutu political parties were prepared to acquiesce to this deal, but the extremists could never have accepted it. Its biased terms simultaneously steeled their resolve to deal with the 'Tutsi problem' by any means necessary and played into the extremists' strategy of polarizing Rwandan politics and society."[18]

By February 1993, as escalating violence threatened to sink the peace process, the RPF broke the ceasefire and launched a large scale offensive against government troops. The failure of the ceasefire was a turning point; it tested the military capabilities of both sides, but also the unity of the multiparty political consensus that had sustained the Arusha negotiations. The military stalemate had propelled the peace process, but so too had the moderate coalition's desire for peace. After the RPF's offensive, the alliance between moderate Hutu opposition parties and the RPF began to fray. Radical factions emerged in the mainstream moderate opposition parties. Extremists could more easily use this fragmentation to raise doubt about the wisdom of ethnic reconciliation. Later, after the military coup in Burundi in October 1993 in which the democratically elected Hutu President, Melchior Ndadaye, was assassinated by the Tutsi military, opponents of Rwanda's Arusha agreement could again discredit it. The events in Burundi were an important trigger to the unraveling of the peace agreement because they undercut the position of the Hutu political party alliance that had been the core of the consensus on pursuing negotiations.[19]

Responding decisively to violent spoiling. Because societies engaged in protracted conflicts do not trust each other, it is vital that central governments engaged in peace negotiations adopt a zero tolerance policy to actors who use violence to derail them. Here too, the collapse of the Israeli-Palestinian peace process in the 1990s is instructive. While many different explanations for the failure of Oslo have been raised and revisited, key among them is that violent spoiling, on both sides, was not nipped in the bud. On the Palestinian side, as has been noted in several studies, terrorism became a means for various political parties to secure public support in a democratizing political space. Indeed, as political rivals (Hamas and Islamic Jihad) began to garner increased public support in the aftermath of successful suicide bombing campaigns, Yasir Arafat's Fatah party also eventually became an internal spoiler by jumping on the terrorism bandwagon. Terrorism was not only meant to scuttle the peace process by generating a harsh Israeli counter-terrorism response and bringing right wing, anti-Oslo Israeli leaders to power. It was also a way to outbid political contenders who had to vie for the vote in a newly democratizing Palestinian territory.[20]

For its part, the Israeli government's response to Jewish Israeli extremism should have been more determined and resolute. Consider the Rabin government's reaction to the Hebron massacre on February 25, 1994 when Baruch Goldstein, an American-born Israeli physician who lived in the Jewish community of Kiryat Arba on the outskirts of Hebron opened fire within the Cave of the Patriarchs' Ibrahmi Mosque, killing 29 worshippers and injuring over one hundred. The extremist political parties Kach and Kahana Chai were immediately outlawed in the aftermath of the Hebron atrocity, but the late Prime Minister Yitzhak Rabin never evacuated Hebron's Jewish enclave. He did not have to; Hebron was not part of the Oslo agreement. Yet responding decisively to an extreme settler's violence would have gone far to mitigate the growing Palestinian mistrust of the peace process. Rabin's lackluster response to the Hebron terror event, which took place within a sacred site revered by Muslims and Jews alike, gave Hamas and other spoilers on the Palestinian side a convenient series of anniversaries on which to time their own acts of terror.[21]

Coping with Spoilers: A Framework for Analysis

The central ingredient of all durable peace agreements is creating an inclusive process that can be sustained by preventing potential would-be spoilers from becoming actual ones, and turning resisters of the peace into its stakeholders. Yet the types of strategies that will prove useful for managing spoilers when authoritarian states engage in peace efforts are not necessarily the same policies that will be effective in democratic settings. When nondemocratic states negotiate, potential spoilers often retain militias and violent dissent is typically the norm. Authoritarian leaders engaged in a peace process with neighboring states or rebel movements can crush dissent through violent suppression, but so too can would-be spoilers employ violence to undermine the agreement and the public's support for it. By contrast, because democratic states have a legitimate monopoly on the use of force, and conflicts between the state and society are meant to occur through peaceful means, the government cannot easily use violence to suppress those societal groups that oppose its negotiation efforts. By their very nature, democracies provide room for debate over public policy, including peacemaking. Thus, leaders who commit to peace negotiations must deal with organized opposition groups and cannot simply stifle or ignore domestic backlashes to peace negotiations. Once committed to negotiations, a democratically-elected government must create a national consensus for peace among the societal majority, but it also cannot stymie the organized mobilization of spoilers (who may espouse a hard line, anti-peace agenda) by running roughshod over democratic principles. Democratic cultures provide opportunities for groups that oppose the peace to mobilize the larger society against these efforts, and to influence the government decision making process by exercising veto power within institutional frameworks. Figure 1 provides a visual depiction of these dynamics that emerge between negotiating central governments and their respective societies.

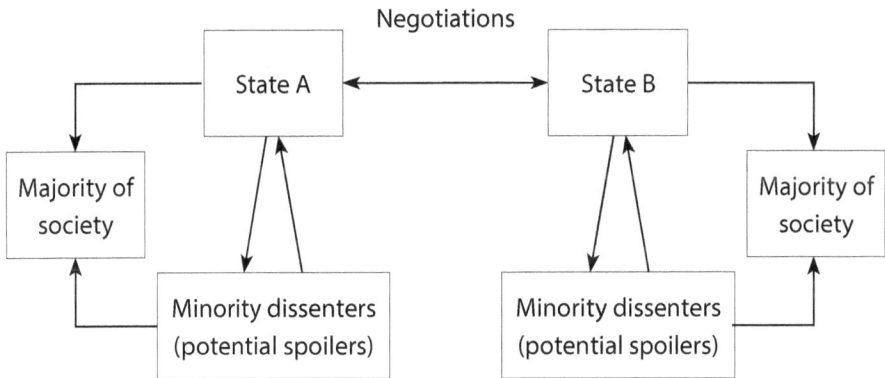

Figure 1. Spoilers of Peace in Democratic Settings: Interactions between States and Societies

Conclusion and Policy Recommendations

In negotiations to resolve longstanding protracted conflicts, spoilers – actors who either reject efforts at peacemaking with the enemy in general, or who disagree with the central contours of the peace agreement in particular – can derail the peace by using either violent or nonviolent measures. In non-democratic settings, spoilers are more likely to resort to violence to both stymie peace efforts and delegitimize the government; in countering them, authoritarian states involved in negotiations are also more likely to employ force to repress and marginalize dissenters. By contrast, in democracies, while they may adopt vigilante tactics that can verge into a violent civil disobedience, for the most part spoilers are far more likely to choose nonviolent strategies to derail the peace. Their tactics will involve working within the democratic rules of the game to thwart peace coalitions and undertaking a public relations campaign to delegitimize the government's peacemaking efforts and convince the larger society that the negotiations and peace settlement undermine the national interest. Democratic governments also cannot resort to violence in order to suppress societal dissent to peacemaking efforts. Managing spoilers requires that the government co-opt potential spoilers, and convince the larger public that negotiations are worth the risk and that peace is worth the cost. Thus, in democratic settings, for both the spoilers of peace and negotiating governments, persuasion is the key to success.

Given the importance of persuasion, stakeholders (central governments, societal actors, including NGOs, and third party mediators) engaged in negotiations whose goal is to resolve protracted conflicts should consider adopting the following policies in order to better cope with spoilers:

a. *Transform would-be spoilers into stakeholders of the peace by including a wide number of societal actors into the peace process early on.* Especially in democratic settings, where potential spoilers are in fact members of the voting public, it is vital to find creative and innovative ways to persuade these actors of the value of peace. Inclusion in the peace process ensures that the interests of potential spoilers will be incorporated into the agreement, thus minimizing the likelihood of post-agreement spoiling.

b. *Frame peace processes as incremental advances, rather than end of conflict agreements.* This is especially important for advancing peace efforts in times of conflict, where ongoing crises can enable spoilers to frame the negotiations as detrimental to the national interest, thus undermining public support for peace. Incremental steps, by creating tangible differences in the lives of peoples involved in protracted conflicts, will increase the likelihood of maintaining a national consensus for peace within the competing societies, and will prevent the capacity for spoilers to dominate the discourse. Since such steps will advance the reality of peace without the fanfare of a high profile summit, named agreement, or an end of conflict peace plan, actors who reject peacemaking will be unable to frame such moves as mere shams. Moreover, by locking in concessions, these moves will signal a credible commitment to conflict resolution.

c. *Consider how the government of the opposing side can affect the public debate regarding the value of peacemaking through concessions that undermine and marginalize the rhetoric of spoiler groups.* Negotiators should realize that concessions that facilitate a national consensus for peace on the opposing side will be a means for ensuring that their counterparts can credibly commit to a just and final deal. Innovative and out of the box thinking is needed to fashion concessions that appeal to the societal majorities of both sides in the conflict, as well as to minority dissenters. Here, third party mediators can assist the interlocutors in appreciating how such concessions can become part of a comprehensive package of confidence building measures.

d. *Respond effectively to spoiler violence early on in the negotiation process.* A failure to respond decisively to spoilers that use violence will have negative repercussions on the peace process as it creates a climate of distrust and makes it more likely that spoilers will be able to discredit ongoing negotiations. Fear of altercations with violent spoilers should not dissuade governments from pursuing peacemaking efforts preferred by the societal majority. Stakeholders should recognize that creative and empathetic attempts to incorporate would-be spoilers into the peace process, however, will often minimize the need to confront violent spoilers down the road.

Notes

1 This paper draws on Miriam Fendius Elman, "Spoilers of Peace and the Dilemmas of Conflict Resolution," in *Spoilers of Peace and the Dilemmas of Conflict Resolution*, eds. N. Goren and M. Fendius Elman (Ramat Gan, Israel and Syracuse, NY: The Israeli Institute for Regional Foreign Policies [MITVIM] and the Program for the Advancement of Research for Conflict and Collaboration [PARCC], 2012).

2   Caroline A. Hartzell, "Settling Civil Wars: Armed Opponents' Fates and the Duration of Peace," *Conflict Management and Peace Science* 26, no. 4 (2009): 347-65.

3   Matthew Hoddie and Caroline A. Hartzell, "Introduction," in *Strengthening Peace in Post-Civil War States: Transforming Spoilers into Stakeholders*, eds. M. Hoddie and C. A. Hartzell (Chicago: University of Chicago Press, 2011), p. 3.

4   For an extended discussion see Kelly M. Greenhill and Solomon Major, "The Perils of Profiling: Civil War Spoilers and the Collapse of Intrastate Peace Accords," *International Security* 31, no. 3 (2006/7): 7-40.

5   Michaela Mattes and Burcu Savun, "Fostering Peace after Civil War: Commitment Problems and Agreement Design," *International Studies Quarterly* 53 (2009): 737-59.

6   Andrew Kydd and Barbara Walter, "Sabotaging the Peace: The Politics of Extremist Violence," *International Organization* 56, no. 2 (2002): 263-96; Wendy Pearlman, "Spoiling Inside and Out: Internal Political Contestation and the Middle East Peace Process," *International Security* 33, no. 3 (2008/9): 79-109; Desiree Nilsson and Mimmi Soderberg Kovacs, "Revisiting an Elusive Concept: A Review of the Debate on Spoilers of Peace Processes," *International Studies Review* 13 (2011): 606-26.

7   Stephen John Stedman, "Spoiler Problems in Peace Processes," *International Security* 22, no. 2 (1997): 5.

8   Miriam Fendius Elman, "Does Democracy Tame the Radicals? Lessons from the Case of Israel's *Shas*," in *Democracy and Conflict Resolution: The Dilemmas of Israel's Peacemaking*, eds. M. Fendius Elman, O. Haklai, and H. Spruyt (New York: Syracuse University Press, 2014), p. 105.

9   Oded Haklai, "Spoiling the Peace: State Structure and the Capacity of Hard-Liners to Foil Peacemaking Efforts," in *Democracy and Conflict Resolution: The Dilemmas of Israel's Peacemaking*, p. 73.

10 Juliette Shedd, "When Peace Agreements Create Spoilers: The Russo-Chechen Agreement of 1996," *Civil Wars* 10, no. 2 (2008): 95.

11 For an extended discussion of spoiling in the Russo-Chechen case see Michael Makara, "Understanding Spoiler Behavior Following the First Russo-Chechen War," *E-PARCC Collaborative Governance Initiative* (Syracuse, NY: Program for the Advancement of Research on Conflict and Collaboration, Maxwell School of Syracuse University, 2010), www.maxwell.syr.edu/parcc.

12 Jeremy Pressman, "The Second Intifada: Background and Causes of the Israeli-Palestinian Conflict," *Journal of Conflict Studies* 23, no. 2 (2003): 12; See also Laura Zittrain Eisenberg and Neil Caplan, *Negotiating Arab-Israeli Peace: Patterns, Problems, Possibilities* (Bloomington: Indiana University Press, 2010), pp. 211-14.

13 Pressman, "The Second Intifada," p. 114.

14 Mia Bloom, "Palestinian Suicide Bombing: Public Support, Market Share, and Outbidding," *Political Science Quarterly* 119, no. 1 (2004): 66-67.

15 Eisenberg and Caplan, *Negotiating Arab-Israeli Peace*, p. 221.

16 Gregory M. Maney, Ibtisam Ibrahim, Gareth I. Higgins, and Hanna Herzog, "The Past's Promise: Lessons from Peace Processes in Northern Ireland and the Middle East," *Journal of Peace Research* 43, no. 2 (2006): 181-200.

17 Stacie E. Goddard, *Indivisible Territory and the Politics of Legitimacy: Jerusalem and Northern Ireland* (New York: Cambridge University Press, 2010), p. 228.

18 Benjamin A. Valentino, "Still Standing By: Why America and the International Community Fail to Prevent Genocide and Mass Killing," *PS: Political Science and Politics* 1, no. 3 (2003): 571. For more on how the Arusha Accords marginalized Hutu power see, for example, Bruce D. Jones, *Peacemaking in Rwanda: The Dynamics of Failure* (Boulder, CO: Lynne Rienner, 2001).

19 Gilbert M. Khadiagala, "Implementing the Arusha Peace Agreement on Rwanda," in *Ending Civil Wars: The Implementation of Peace Agreements*, eds. D. S. Rothschild and S. J. Stedman (Boulder, CO: Lynne Rienner), p. 485.

20 Mia Bloom, "Palestinian Suicide Bombing: Public Support, Market Share, and Outbidding," *Political Science Quarterly* 119, no. 1 (2004): 61-87; and Wendy Pearlman, "Spoiling Inside and Out: Internal Political Contestation and the Middle East Peace Process," *International Security* 33, no. 3 (2008/9): 96-105.

21 For an extended discussion of the consequences of the Hebron massacre for the Oslo peace process see, for example, Ehud Sprinzak, *Brother against Brother: Violence and Extremism in Israeli Politics from Altalena to the Rabin Assassination* (New York: Free Press, 1999), pp. 244-85.

Disarming Militant Groups from Within: Building Support for Peace among Combatants in Northern Ireland

Benedetta Berti, Ariel Heifetz Knobel, and Gary Mason

This study examines the internal process that led Northern Irish combatant groups, mainly the Loyalist camp, to relinquish armed struggle as a viable strategy to accomplish their political goals. Rather than looking at the content of the peace agreement or at the negotiation and reconciliation processes between Loyalists and Republicans, the authors focus on internal dynamics, i.e., intra-group negotiations and consensus building mechanisms that Loyalist militant organizations employed with their own members to switch from violence to nonviolence, and from confrontation to engagement with the enemy. The paper underlines how the consensus building process was multi-faceted and included a combination of carefully structured internal deliberations amongst combatants, together with the crafting and implementation of targeted programs to empower and transform militant organizations and their role within society. The paper also focuses on the specific roles ex-prisoners and key faith leaders played in shaping this monumental transformation. The paper emphasizes the importance of building widespread support for peace and of engaging, rather than alienating, potential opponents. In addition, by examining the policies used to deepen support for nonviolence throughout the past 17 years following the Good Friday Agreement, the paper underscores the importance of continuing peace efforts in the post-agreement phase. Finally, the authors examine the main lessons that can be learned from the consensus building process among Northern Irish Loyalist combatants and discuss its relevance to other intractable conflicts.

The Hidden History of Making Peace: The Importance of Intra-Group Consensus Building

> Following a direct engagement with all the units and departments of our organization, the leadership of the Ulster Volunteer Force and Red Hand Commando today make public the outcome of our three year consultation process…. as of 12 midnight, Thursday 3 May 2007, the Ulster Volunteer Force and Red Hand Commando will assume a non-military, civilianized role…All recruitment has ceased; military training has ceased; targeting has ceased and all intelligence rendered obsolete; all active service units have been de-activated….We encourage our volunteers to embrace the challenges which continue to face their communities and support their continued participation in non-military capacities.[1]

In 2007, the three main Loyalist militant groups in Northern Ireland – the Ulster Volunteer Force (UVF), the Red Hand Commando (RHC), and the Ulster Defense Association (UDA) – announced their transition from military to civilian/political organizations, and all have since handed over the vast majority of their weapons.

The issue of how militant organizations shed their violent ways and adopt a constructive civilian role within their communities is crucial and intimately related to the relatively under-explored topic of conducting internal negotiations within, rather than between, communities.

Indeed, whilst a large part of the negotiation and conflict resolution literature focuses on the content and process of negotiations between "warring parties," less attention has been generally devoted to understanding the process of accommodation and negotiation occurring *within* a given side. Specifically, we know substantially less about how intra-group negotiations and consensus building for peace occur within violent groups.[2] Yet, these internal consultations and consensus building processes are just as vital as the official ones taking place between warring parties.[3]

The lack of solid backing from a leader's constituency in general and in this case, from the combatant community, can jeopardize and ultimately hinder a peace process before, during, and after inter-party negotiations. Sitting at the negotiating table without coordination and support from other allied factions, as well as well as from one's militant constituency, substantially increases the chances of these actors sabotaging the political process. Active opponents can sink ongoing inter-party negotiations as well as trigger an escalation of violence, effectively freezing a peace process.

Second, when militant members are alienated from their leadership, this can result in defection to more radical groups or in the creation of irredentist splinter groups. Such factionalism is extremely dangerous as internal disagreement is not at all synonymous with the decline in the use of violence as a strategy, and – as aptly explained by Martha Crenshaw – "splits and merger are a form of propagation of terrorism."[4]

Third, when a given organization sits at the negotiating table against the wishes of its own constituency, it is more restricted in its capacity to make significant concessions, as the perception of "giving in" would risk igniting additional internal conflict and further weaken the group's cohesion and status.[5] Finally, lack of intra-group consensus complicates efforts to implement any peace agreement, while also making such arrangements more fragile and less likely to endure.

Therefore, for broader inter-party peace negotiations to succeed, it is absolutely vital for the main actors involved, both at the state and non-state level, to look inward and invest in building consensus internally and within the broader communities that support them. Consensus building is by no means a one-time trick; it is instead a relational and dynamic process that requires constant interaction between the leadership and the supporting bases as well as a strategic and long-term approach.

Looking at the Northern Ireland conflict, the post-agreement consensus building process for nonviolence and disarmament was just as crucial (if not more) as the pre-1998 mobilization to support official peace negotiations, as its aim – to embed a permanent nonviolent strategy and to transform the role of combatants within society – was ambitious yet essential to shift from conflict to both engagement and coexistence in a shared society. The process did not end with the definitive decommissioning of weapons on both sides; rather, it evolved from embedding nonviolence to transforming societal and personal relations within Northern Ireland, moving a little farther down the long and winding road to reconciliation.

From Ceasefire to Peace Treaty to Disarming to Re-Integration: Loyalist Militant Groups in Northern Ireland

On Good Friday, April 10, 1998, after 800 years of conflict on the island of Ireland, 80 years of partition, and thirty years of the Northern Irish civil war known as the "Troubles," costing the lives of over 3,600 people and resulting in over 35,000 casualties, with 16,000 charged with terrorist-related offenses, 34,000 shootings, and 14,000 bombings (all this in a relatively small population of 1.7 million people), the official negotiations finally culminated in the Belfast or Good Friday Agreement (GFA).

Since the late 1960s, Northern Ireland had become the stage of a bloody conflict between Republicans and Loyalists. At its core, the conflict saw two separate, non-integrated communities fight over radically different and mutually exclusive political ideals: the reunification of Ireland versus the permanent ratification of the 1921 partition of the island and integration into the United Kingdom. The Nationalist and Republican communities (mostly Catholic) identify as Irish and seek an all-island Republic of Ireland, while the Unionist and Loyalist communities (mostly Protestant) identify as British, loyal to the United Kingdom. In addition, the tensions were fueled by the deeply unequal nature of the political, social, and economic system which de facto placed the Catholic community in a state of structural discrimination, political underrepresentation, and economic marginalization.[6]

Reaching an agreement was no easy task: the process that led to the GFA was long and complex, and was preceded by deep internal changes within both sides, as well as years of back channel talks, two main ceasefires, increased international involvement, and a significant change in the UK's approach towards the conflict. Approved by Northern Ireland's main Nationalist/ Republican (pro-Irish) political parties and most of the Unionist/Loyalist (pro-British) parties, and ratified in a popular referendum held in May 1998, the GFA recognized the right to self-determination for all people in Northern Ireland and established local political institutions on the basis of power sharing principles.

Implementing the GFA has been an accomplishment of monumental proportions, especially given the challenge of keeping opponents such as splinter groups, the Loyalist Volunteer Force (from disaffected UVF members),[7] as well as the Real IRA and Continuity IRA (from the IRA, the Provisional Irish Republican Army) at bay. Nevertheless, all the main militant organizations (IRA, INLA which joined after the referendum, UDA, UVF, and RHC) maintained their commitment to the peace process and, notably, did so while preserving cohesion and preventing mass-scale defections.

The Good Friday Agreement did not solve all of Northern Ireland's problems, and in the decade following the agreement, the main armed groups embarked on a long and difficult process towards disarmament, or "weapons decommissioning" (the phrase accepted by all parties involved). Although violent incidents did not subside completely, they became sporadic, instigated by fringe groups, and condemned by all major factions. In this context, the main task with respect to the combatant communities shifted from preventing spoilers to re-integrating former militants.

In parallel to the decommissioning process, the main political parties also began a complex engagement to learn how to govern through power sharing, while society slowly focused on the long journey of reconciliation.

The Challenge of Selling Peace to Combatants

Keeping the combatant community on board while committing to a ceasefire, peace negotiations, and finally to renunciation of armed struggle is vital to the success of any peace process. While some militants embrace armed struggle through peer pressure and others even come to regret their initial involvement, combatants can often be ideological hard-liners less likely to embrace the logic of moderation and reciprocity. Their experience as fighters has taught them resentment and distrust towards their "enemy"; thus, for them, the psychological leap from conflict to engagement is an especially hard one to make. More substantially, many combatants, especially if extensively involved, have direct incentives to continue fighting, as they may derive economic benefits along with a sense of identity, belonging, and social prestige.

In the case of Northern Ireland, building consensus for the peace process was a continuous, dynamic process that began nearly ten years before the peace agreement, when combatants began challenging their organization's use of force as an effective strategy.

Internal Agents of Change: The Role of Ex-Prisoners

Former Loyalist prisoners played, and continue to play, a key role in this process. Indeed when the first life-sentenced prisoners were released in Northern Ireland in the late 1980s and early 1990s, they brought with them deep questions that challenged the ideology of working class Loyalism and its use of force. Loyalist ex-prisoners re-entered their communities saying, "I served 15 years to preserve the British state, and it was the British state that put me in prison. What does that say about our battle? About our political ideology?"[8] Their status as prisoners gave them enough credibility and legitimacy as loyal patriots "to ask questions and be heard" when they began both to publicly criticize the British government and to reflect upon the personal and community price paid to sustain armed struggle. They were "fed up,"[9] with the toll the conflict had taken on working class Loyalist communities, and this "began to influence change."[10]

In the immediate years preceding the GFA, intra-group discussions within Loyalism focused increasingly on building support for engagement with the enemy, while enforcing a ceasefire and policy of "restraint." On this front, ex-prisoners continued questioning the use of violence *after* the 1994 ceasefires, asking whether it was "really helping to transform Loyalist communities." Whilst becoming "agents of change" by stressing the dire local impact of violence, such discussions gradually eroded "the old-school" ethos of other combatants in the community.[11]

In the decade that followed the agreement, Loyalist militant organizations embarked on a transformative process that led to the relinquishment of armed struggle in favor of an unarmed, nonviolent political strategy, while surrendering their weapons along the way.

All throughout this period, Loyalist leaders employed multiple strategies to gain buy-in from their members. Some of the most prominent ones are reviewed in the remaining sections of the paper.

Tools for Building Support for Ceasefires and Official Peace Negotiations (1992-1998): Explanation, Reframing, and Consultation

Throughout the 1990s, Loyalist leaders were able to convince their members to observe a ceasefire and then to favor peace negotiations with the IRA by first explaining and reframing the enemy's behavior. This was possible due to the increased understanding of the Republicans among senior Loyalists, particularly ex-prisoners, having been exposed to them in prison. Loyalist ex-prisoners were able to think analytically about the IRA and Sinn Fein, whereas most members on the outside viewed them as monolithic.[12] Additionally, in the early and mid-1990s, clergy-facilitated back channels, as well as NGO-facilitated workshops and dialogues, gave senior militants further insight into the internal dynamics of their enemies. Such knowledge convinced leaders to remain committed to the ceasefire and later to the peace talks, despite setbacks. They understood (or felt they understood) how the other side was functioning, using this information to keep their members on board.

For example, in 1993, Sinn Fein leader Gerry Adams, who had been pushing to start peace talks, was photographed at a funeral carrying the coffin of a notorious IRA bomber following a deadly attack. Despite public outcry and raw anger particularly among Unionists and Loyalists, behind closed doors Loyalist leaders knew that if Adams was to lead the IRA away from violence (which he did one year later), such gestures were required.

Five years later, following commencement of official Track I talks, several violent incidents threatened to derail the whole process. However, thanks to back channel conversations (both militant-to-militant and militant-to-government), militant leaders stayed on board and did not allow ongoing tit-for-tat terrorist attacks to spoil the larger process.

Following the 1998 peace agreement, the ability of these leaders to explain and reframe actions and words of the "other side" was essential. For instance, when Loyalists heard Adams' Republican rhetoric flare up in the post-agreement phase, UVF leaders explained that such comments were only meant "to keep their own people on board," stressing that people "shouldn't pay much attention because he probably doesn't mean it literally."[13]

While getting to a more nuanced view of their Republican enemy, Loyalist leaders also began to reframe positive steps taken by Republicans to sell the transition towards peace internally: for example, when the IRA finally declared its "cessation" of armed activities in August 1994, the Loyalist organizations framed it as "surrender" in order to justify their own subsequent ceasefire.[14] The sense of victory served to convince those Loyalists who were more pessimistic about the IRA's intentions, as well as to maintain internal legitimacy.

In the years preceding the 1994 ceasefire, inclusive internal negotiations also helped minimize the chance of Loyalist spoilers. A key tool to get to consensus was to focus on ensuring prisoners' endorsement for steps towards peace. The Combined Loyalist Military Command (representing the UVF, UDA, and RHC) insisted on gaining access to prisons "to persuade and explain" to their inmate counterparts.[15] This meant that security authorities allowed wanted "terrorists" to pass through their doors.

The UVF held a systematic internal "consultation process" that included multiple briefings to its prison population. Similarly, the CLMC stressed that "before any decision would be taken, the UDA leadership insisted that it would first have to consult with its prisoners." With the help of Reverend Roy Magee, Loyalist politicians from the Ulster Democratic Party and Progressive Unionist Party (political proxies of the UDA and UVF, some of whom overlapped as senior decision makers in these militant groups) visited Long Kesh to meet their leaders in prison.[16]

This particular meeting resulted in a UDA letter from prisoners to the outside leadership on Oct. 10, 1994: "We the UDA/UFF LPOW [Loyalist POWs]… feel we must be seen to be giving this fragile peace process every opportunity to succeed and that our permanent cessation of violence should last as long as the republican complete cessation of violence."[17] By the time the CLMC held its final meeting to approve the decision to implement a ceasefire "all segments of Loyalism were present: prisoners, combatants on the outside, wailers in the community, and nobody dissented."[18]

Tools for Building Support for A Permanent Unarmed Strategy (1990s – present): Reframing, Consultation, Political Empowerment, and Community Development

Throughout the peace process, and especially following the GFA, Loyalist (as well as Republican) leaders focused not only on ensuring support for a ceasefire, but also on reframing nonviolence as a continuation of their struggle, a key face-saving mechanism.

The 1994 prisoners' letter mentioned above emphasized the strategic nature of their attempt at peace: "To continue our military campaign under the present circumstances could be counterproductive and in the long term detrimental to our cause."[19] A decade after the peace agreement, this rationale continues, as exemplified in the 2007 endgame statements of the UVF, RHC, and UDA, in which they explained that violence was no longer relevant to their cause, while never denouncing its past role. The UDA stated: "the battle flags of the UFF will be furled in a hope that they may never have to see light of day again, but stand in readiness."[20] For the UVF and RHC, nonviolence was justified because "the mainstream Republican offensive has ended...the Union remains safe."[21] This new framing of violence and its role allowed combatants to preserve the legitimacy of the armed struggle while effectively shelving it in favor of an unarmed strategy.

Finally, the practice of internal strategy discussions and consultation with the wider membership of Loyalist organizations continued well beyond the 1994 ceasefire and the 1997-8 peace process. Nearly a decade later, the UVF conducted 3 years of so-called "roadshows" leading up to disarmament. This systematic approach fanned out leaders across Northern Ireland and Britain to meet with local branches in order to explain the reasoning and importance of decommissioning the organization's weapons and to ensure support for the act. Finally in 2009, the organization handed over the vast majority of its weapons to the satisfaction of the International Commission on Decommissioning.

At the same time, moving towards permanent nonviolence required a deep investment to reintegrate former combatants and empower their own working class Loyalist communities. After the ceasefires, EU peace funding came to Northern Ireland, and ex-prisoners initiatives grew,[22] with ex-combatants setting up non-profits to improve socio-economic conditions and to lobby state institutions. Consensus was reached regarding "accountability of politicians" via lobby groups.[23] Loyalist combatants began coordinated efforts with IRA leaders to prevent violence and to stop unauthorized incidents from escalating.[24] These volunteers, who were members or affiliates of paramilitaries, called themselves "community workers" or "community activists,"[25] an independent role that allowed them to meet with their counterparts from the IRA as well as with government officials and traditional politicians.[26] The impetus to transition to institutional politics, public service, and community activism was described by CLMC leader Plum Smith: "Loyalists saw political empowerment as the only way out."[27]

As more ex-prisoners moved into community development roles, the prospects for socio-economic growth seemed promising, especially with the rise of government economic packages. In turn, this helped strengthen the transition and decommissioning process: as one UVF ex-prisoner recalls: "We were told that the lack of investment in these areas was a result of the conflict, and people thought things would get better: inward investment, job creation, etc."[28] Thus, making peace "was a political process as much as it was an economic process."[29]

An example of the use of community and political development in demobilization of combatants is a program called Action for Community Transformation (ACT), which was founded by UVF and RHC ex-combatants in 2008 following the organizations' endgame declarations, and was intended to be a "model of politicization which supports the reintegration of former combatants in partnership with critical friends and the wider community."[30] It was initially presented in small-scale consultations to senior militants, offering an alternative to the armed struggle and a model of conflict transformation through "positive active citizenship," and "collaboration with all elements of civic society."[31] Throughout six years of internal discussions, ACT achieved endorsement by the entire UVF and RHC leadership, which has "actively directed volunteers to engage in this process."[32]

The ACT program consists of three phases. First, a "transitional" phase sets up learning processes targeting former combatants, with the objective of preparing volunteers to engage their communities more constructively. A 12-week training program takes volunteers on a "journey of exploring their personal and social history and connecting this to their present-day experience and role within the community."[33] They also partake in workshops on a wide range of topics, from adaptive leadership, mediation, and transitional justice to suicide prevention, community safety, media training, and employment preparation and placement.[34] By 2012, 1,647 UVF and RHC members had been "trained, engaged or consulted." ACT's second phase, the "operational" stage, connects UVF and RHC volunteers and their local communities with organizations and networks for community development. The third "political" phase moves volunteers more deeply into civic engagement, encouraging participation in local elections, "residents' groups, forums, cultural and historic societies, or whatever is relevant to their communities."[35]

The impact of ACT is visible, among other things, in the formation of Area Action Groups throughout Northern Ireland of about 1000 people actively organizing at a given time, which address issues that had traditionally been handled outside of the law, such as grievances regarding policing and justice (including unsolved cases), and defending cultural expression and parades. ACT has also increased the level of engagement with the Police Service of Northern Ireland through consultation, training, and liaison roles with hundreds of ex-combatants, including one district in which over 200 ACT graduates became qualified as Parade Marshalls (to help contain the violence around sectarian parades).[36] ACT's impact can also be seen in the 2012-13 "flag protests," in which hundreds of youth (mostly Protestant) were arrested. In the past, these youth "may have been easily recruited" into the militant organizations, but instead, ACT ex-combatants developed outreach workshops to represent their violent pasts "as a deterrent."[37]

External Agents of Change: Key Faith Leaders as Combatants' "Critical Friends"

Most of the 1,200 Protestant and Catholic clergy on the island of Ireland were not directly involved in peacemaking, though many helped to foster better inter-community relations in their local communities. There was only a small core – about a dozen – who greatly aided the peace process, engaging those committed to violence in achieving their goals.[38] Their contributions took the form of transferring messages as intermediaries, facilitating private meetings, and assisting "political groups to evaluate their strategies and goals."[39] These roles continue to this day.

The third function is most closely tied to the process of consensus building within militant groups. Beginning in the early 1990s, a few local Protestant clergy assisted Loyalist organizations' transition to nonviolence by serving as same-side proponents. For example, Reverends Roy Magee and Harold Good "took part in a loyalist commission to support leading peacemaking loyalists in their questioning of the philosophy and morality of loyalist violence."[40]

Methodist Reverend Gary Mason, whom the UVF and RHC call a "critical friend," sits on the board of ACT and is chairperson of Northern Ireland Alternatives, ACT's Restorative Justice program. For 27 years he has worked in the inner city of Belfast and promoted urban, social, and economic development as a way to serve Loyalism by arguing that "we can do it better" (unlike most Protestant clergy who chastised Loyalist combatants and former combatants).[41] Mason listened to combatants and ex-combatants, affirmed their humanity and their pain, and accompanied them in unfamiliar contexts including invitations to share their stories and listen to others. They discussed accountability, forgiveness, and new beginnings, among other issues. Mason facilitated difficult, meaningful engagement both among Loyalists and with their traditional adversaries, such as other combatant groups, politicians, victims groups, and security services.

"Critical friends" like Mason and others often come under scrutiny for "talking to men of violence." As Mason explains: "I am well aware of the risks that one can be seen to be endorsing violence or at least giving violence credibility. But my role is one of engagement, not endorsement. I firmly believe that the person of faith in any religious tradition should be taking risks for peace that politicians simply can't take because of their political support base."

In addition to independence, this role requires humility, understanding that even a reverend or a priest could have taken the path that these men took. It is important for these leaders not to turn their backs on the community that shaped them.

Loyalist communities continue to struggle with internecine feuding and conflict, deindustrialization, cultural unease and ambiguity, and a continuing decline in educational standards. In this fragmented context, the positive contribution of former combatants may go unnoticed. The media's thorough coverage of their participation in violence has left a "tough man" stereotype that does not allow for the kind of journey to peace that many of these men have taken. Moreover, given that what they do may be considered politically covert, their involvement has not been included as part of the official story, which makes the work of critical friendship even more essential for affirming their dramatic journeys to peace.

The Internal Road to Nonviolent Engagement: Lessons Learned

The consensus building process towards embracing disarmament in Northern Irish Loyalist communities was complex and multi-faceted. Tools to build internal support for peace negotiations and subsequent implementation of a political agreement are varied: at the top-down level, leaders invested in direct and indirect communication to their supporting bases to reframe the understanding of both the conflict as well as the advantages of pursuing a political, rather than armed, strategy. In doing so, prominent, trusted and credible figures, especially well-known combatants and ex-prisoners, effectively promoted the strategic shift from violence to nonviolence. In addition, consensus building also focused on internal discussions and consultations to improve the level of grassroots ownership in the process and the commitment to its outcome. Moreover, engaging combatant communities required crafting short and long-term political and ideational alternatives to convince militants to relinquish their weapons.

Looking at the experience of Northern Ireland and its applicability to other intractable conflicts, the consensus building process underlines the following directives:

a. Engage: integrate, rather than alienate, opponents and potential spoilers. The process of dialogue between communities and within communities requires a strategy of engagement with, and acknowledgement of, both opponents and their narratives.

b. Reframe: understand that the enemy may reframe your actions to look victorious. This allows him flexibility to move towards peace. Reframing can also be used as a face-saving tool to convince your own constituency that you are not abandoning your cause. In turn, this may allow both sides to frame the compromise as a "victory" while also shifting strategy without having to denounce the past.

c. Promote grassroots ownership: invest in direct communication and consultation with bases of support; actively seek to prepare people for peace.

d. Rely on internal "agents of change": involve credible trustworthy supporters like community leaders or former prisoners where relevant.

e. Involve external "critical friends" to support militant groups in sustaining their transition to "civilianization" and to facilitate communication with other actors.

f. Develop the community around combatants: offer alternative roles and ways to demonstrate loyalty. Accordingly, the process should focus on creating viable and sustainable re-integration programs that address former combatants' financial needs, political identity, and psychological well-being; as Mason has coined it, "decommission people's minds, not only their weapons" by providing combatants with nonviolent community management approaches.

g. Recognize that consensus building for every step takes time. Consensus building must be seen as continuous and dynamic processes (even 17 years post-agreement), for implementation and beyond. The question should not just be how to reach a deal, but also how to create conditions for negotiations and how to keep that initial consensus for a peace agreement after the peace is signed. Thus, a long-term consensus building strategy is needed.

While each of these points needs to be further developed and put into context, it is clear that Northern Irish Loyalists' transformation to peace represents an important and powerful legacy, as well as cautious tale of hope with respect to managing and potentially resolving long-standing, embedded, and bitter internal conflicts.

Notes

1   "UVF Statement in full," *BBC News,* May 3, 2007, http://news.bbc.co.uk/2/hi/uk_news/northern_ireland/6618365.stm.

2   Kristin M. Bakke, Kathleen Gallagher Cunningham, and Lee J. M. Seymour, "A Plague of Initials: Fragmentation, Cohesion, and Infighting in Civil Wars," *Perspectives on Politics* 10, no. 2 (2012): 266.

3   See Jannie Lilja, "Outbidding and the Decision to Negotiate," in *The Slippery Slope to Genocide: Reducing Identity Conflicts and Preventing Mass Murder,* eds. I. Zartman, M. Anstey, and P. Meerts (Oxford Scholarship Online, DOI: 10.1093/acprof:oso/9780199791743.001.0001, January 2012).

4   Martha Crenshaw, "How Terrorism Declines," in *Terrorism Research and Public Policy,* ed. Clark McCauley (London: Frank Cass, 1991), pp. 80-81.

5   See Gavin Moore, Neophytos Loizides, Nukhet A. Sandal, and Alexandros Lordos, "Winning Peace Frames: Intra-Ethnic Outbidding in Northern Ireland and Cyprus," *West European Politics* 37, no. 1 (2014): 159-81.

6   Benedetta Berti, *Armed Political Organization: From Conflict to Integration* (Washington: Johns Hopkins University Press, 2013), pp. 131-33.

7   David McKittrick and David McVea, *Making Sense of the Troubles* (London: Penguin Books, 2001), p. 331.

8   Debbie Watters, co-founder of Northern Ireland Alternatives and member of Northern Ireland Policing Board, Interview with Ariel Heifetz Knobel, Belfast, Northern Ireland, August 2010.

9   Paul Hoey, former UVF Interlocutor to the International Commission on Decommissioning; Ulster Volunteer Force ex-prisoner, Interview with Ariel Heifetz Knobel, Belfast, Northern Ireland, August 2010.

10 Watters interview with Ariel Heifetz Knobel.

11 Ibid.

12 Ed Moloney, *Voices from the Grave: Two Men's War in Ireland* (New York: PublicAffairs™ Perseus Books Group, 2010), p. 408.

13 Tom Roberts, Director of Ex-Prisoners Interpretative Center; Ulster Volunteer Force ex-prisoner, Interview with Ariel Heifetz Knobel, Belfast, Northern Ireland, August 2010.

14 Jim Wilson, former peace talks negotiator for Progressive Unionist Party; Red Hand Commando ex-prisoner, Interview with Ariel Heifetz Knobel, Belfast, Northern Ireland, August 2010.

15 Brian Rowan, *Behind the Lines: the Story of the IRA and Loyalist Ceasefires* (Belfast: Blackstaff Press, 1995), pp. 134-35.

16 Ibid., pp. 119-20.

17 Ibid., p. 121.

18 Plum Smith, co-founder of Red Hand Commando and ex-prisoner, Remarks made on community panel, *Feile an Phobail*, attended by Ariel Heifetz Knobel, Belfast, Northern Ireland, August 2010.

19 Rowan, *Behind the Lines*, p. 120.

20 Brian Rowan, *How the Peace Was Won* (Dublin: Gill and Macmillan Press, 2008), p. 223.

21 Ulster Volunteer Force / Red Hand Commando Endgame Statement on May 3, 2007, reprinted in Rowan, *How the Peace Was Won,* p. 221.

22 Unnamed Loyalist, Interview with Ariel Heifetz Knobel, Belfast, Northern Ireland, August 2010.

23 Paul Hoey, former UVF Interlocutor to the International Commission on Decommissioning; Ulster Volunteer Force ex-prisoner, Interview with Ariel Heifetz Knobel, Belfast, Northern Ireland, August 2010.

24 Unnamed Loyalist, Interview with Ariel Heifetz Knobel, Belfast, Northern Ireland, August 2010.

25 Gary Mason, Public lectures attended by Ariel Heifetz Knobel, Boston, Massachusetts, November 2011.

26 Clem McCartney, "The Role of Civil Society," *Accord,* Conciliation Resources, 1999, http://www.c-r.org/our-work/accord/northern-ireland/civil-society.php.

27 Smith, Remarks made on community panel, *Feile an Phobail.*

28 Unnamed Loyalist, Interview with Ariel Heifetz Knobel, Belfast, Northern Ireland, August 2010.

29 Mason, Public lectures.

30 "Action for Community Transformation: The ACT Initiative Policy Document," in "Bone of our Bone. Flesh of our Flesh": A Forum for Former UVF/RHC Political Prisoners! http://www.longkeshinsideout.co.uk/?page_id=12.

31 Ibid.

32 "Action for Community Transformation: The Demobilisation and Reintegration of the Ulster Volunteer Force & Red Hand Commando," Position Paper, Belfast, 2015.

33 Ibid.

34 Ibid.

35 Ibid.

36 Ibid.

37 Ibid.

38 Gary Mason, Methodist Reverend of East Belfast Mission and intermediary to Loyalist paramilitaries, Interview with Ariel Heifetz Knobel, Belfast, Northern Ireland, 2010.

39 McCartney, "The Role of Civil Society."

40 Geoffrey Corry, "Overview of Peace Process Concepts from the Perspective of a Practitioner," unpublished paper, 2007, revised with Patrick Hynes, Dublin, 2009, p. 9.

41 Mason interview with Ariel Heifetz Knobel.

When the Diaspora Becomes an Obstacle: The Armenian Diaspora and the Negotiations between Turkey and Armenia, 2009-2010

Gallia Lindenstrauss

The involvement of diasporas in state-of-origin peace processes is usually categorized as either "positive" or "negative." Some scholars, when explaining "negative" involvement, point to the identity-related issues that cause extreme and non-compromising views among diasporic members. This article claims that any major development in the homeland forces the diaspora to reflect on its identity, and that this reflection can cause resentment, and even lead to actions against such developments. This issue can be linked to the concept of "ontological security," that is, the idea that routine in relations with significant others contributes to a consistent sense of identity. The claim is supported by analyzing the case of the Armenian diaspora and the 2009-2010 negotiations between Armenia and Turkey.

Members of the Armenian diaspora are mainly descendants of survivors of the Armenian genocide of 1915, and as such feel they are the custodians of Armenian identity. The protocols signed by Turkey and Armenia on October 10, 2009, that were meant to establish diplomatic relations and open the shared border between the states, were received by most Armenian diasporic organizations with more resentment and protest than in Armenia itself. Two clauses in particular have raised an outcry. The first is the establishment of an intergovernmental subcommittee to examine the historical differences between the countries. This conflicts with Armenia's longstanding insistence on referring to the events of 1915 as genocide. The second clause requires Armenia's recognition of the border between Armenia and Turkey, a demarcation that Armenia, since gaining independence, has refused to recognize officially. This article posits that achieving Turkish recognition of the genocide is a constitutive element of Armenian diasporic identity; thus, the diasporic organizations found it difficult to accept negotiations with Turkey without the precondition of such recognition. Acknowledging this identity-based issue can help to explain why major Armenian diasporic organizations were hostile to the negotiation process.

The negative response of large segments of the Armenian diaspora to the signing of the protocols between Turkey and Armenia highlights the need to address the issue of diaspora involvement in peace negotiations of the state of origin. The main claim in this article is that any major development in the homeland forces the diaspora to reflect on its identity, and that this reflection can lead to resentment in the diaspora, and even to measures to reverse these developments. In such cases, it is essential to consider the views of the diaspora; as Shain emphasizes, state-of-origin governments that are not attentive to the wishes of the diaspora are in danger of de-legitimization by segments of the diaspora. This can result in the failure to implement these actions, and even in the downfall of the leaders instigating them.[1] Interestingly, when diasporas perpetuate the conflict and act as peace-wreckers, they may antagonize not only those in the international community trying to mediate but also their kin in the state of origin.[2]

This article is divided into three sections. First, the evolving literature on diaspora and peacemaking in the state of origin is discussed. In the second section, identity-related issues and the concept of ontological security are examined and linked to the study of diaspora. An emphasis is placed on the influence of ontological security on the existence and prevalence within diasporic communities of extreme and non-compromising views of peace initiatives in the state of origin. The article addresses Steele's observation of the lack of sufficient research on the costs of ignoring threats to ontological security.[3] In the third section, theoretical claims are demonstrated through the case of Armenia and Turkey: more specifically, through an analysis of the Armenian diaspora's reaction to the signing of protocols to establish diplomatic relations between Armenia and Turkey in October 2009.

The signing of these protocols was seen by the international community as a major breakthrough, following decades of strained Turkish-Armenian relations due to Turkish refusal to acknowledge the events of 1915 as genocide and over conflict with regard to Nagorno-Karabakh.[4] However, the process of ratification of the protocols has yet to materialize: Armenia's ruling coalition in parliament in April 2010 decided to freeze ratification of the protocols, a decision that can be linked to the opposition from some Armenian diasporic organizations, and in February 2015 President Serzh Sarkisian decided to recall the protocols from the Armenian parliament.

Diasporas and Peacemaking in the State of Origin

A growing literature addresses the role of the diaspora in the peace processes of its state of origin. Diaspora involvement in such peace processes depends not only on the diaspora's desire and intrinsic qualities, but also on opportunity.[5] In most host states in the West such opportunities seem to abound. In addition, not only are most conflicts open to outside influence, but in fact the opposing sides usually actively seek such intervention.

Most research tends to emphasize the negative impact diasporas can have. However, such valuation of "positive" or "negative" is in the eye of the beholder; for example, the preservation of the status quo may be beneficial to one side of the conflict only.[6] Some scholars address diaspora involvement in the prolongation of conflict, pointing to their ability to transfer weapons and funds to the fighting factions in the homeland. Others stress the role of the diaspora in the domestic politics in the state of origin. Drawing on Robert Putnam's concept of a two-level game, Shain, for example, writes of a three-level game, where leaders address the demands not only of their domestic constituencies and their adversary, but also of the diaspora.[7] This complication is exacerbated by the fact that diasporic members can be the most extreme and hard-lined of constituencies. Thus, members of the diaspora themselves may become spoilers in a peace process, or they may fund local spoilers.[8]

While the negative role of diasporas is frequently mentioned in scholarly work, it should be stressed that the opposite phenomenon exists as well.

As Shain notes, there is a range from staunch support of the peace process (in which diasporic organizations and their members even act as catalysts) to extreme hostility (in which diasporic organizations and their members might act to spoil the process).[9]

On the positive side of the continuum, diasporic communities can export liberal values and norms from their host state that contribute to peaceful resolution of conflicts and stability; they can help in reframing the conflict; they can participate in problem-solving workshops; and they can support moderates in the state of origin.[10] As Bercovitch states, "When it comes to reconciliation, people in the homeland are more accepting and willing to listen to advice from members of the diaspora rather than other foreigners."[11] Diasporas can also play a role in post-conflict reconstruction through funds and remittances, and may contribute to stabilizing and strengthening civil society. Moreover, host states that are interested in promoting peace processes related to conflict in the state of origin can encourage "positive" actions of the diaspora and penalize "negative" actions.[12]

Smith points out that diasporas may act as peacemakers at one stage and as peace-wreckers at a later stage, or vice versa.[13] In spite of the continuum between certain peace-supportive and peace-wrecking actions and motives, the two aspects can, and should, receive individual scholarly attention,[14] as some explanations are more useful in understanding one type of involvement than the other.

One prevalent explanation for diasporic members' tendency to hold extreme views is that the diaspora is not the one to face the consequences of non-compromising attitudes.[15] While this explanation carries some weight, a number of points discredit it: diaspora members are at times most willing to volunteer to fight; they usually have family connections to those involved in conflict; and the diaspora, through funding, does in fact absorb substantial material costs of the conflict in the homeland.[16] Another explanation is that extreme and nationalistic views prevail in diasporic groups that have not successfully integrated economically and socially into their host societies.[17] While such an explanation highlights the importance of developments in the host state as well as the state of origin, it cannot explain the prevalence of these views in an established and integrated diaspora. An additional explication for negative diasporic involvement is that members of the diaspora send funds to the origin state without considering or taking responsibility for their final destination. This explanation has merit mostly with regard to the role of the diaspora in sustaining the fighting. It has less explanatory power in addressing the active role of diasporas in the domestic politics of the state of origin.

Lyons, among other scholars, has stressed the need to address the motives behind migration as a factor in diasporic attitudes toward the conflict at home. Thus, conflict-generated diasporas, or what is termed victim diaspora,[18] tend to be more extreme in their outlook than economically driven migrants. By highlighting identity-related aspects, this explanation complements the one suggested in this article. It should be stressed, though, that the distinction between voluntary/involuntary migration is not always clear: Van Hear notes that the economic hardships behind certain migrations are not always ones that could have been lived with, and hence the term voluntary is somewhat questionable.[19]

Although all the existing explanations of negative involvement of the diaspora have some power of explanation, they need to be further developed and better linked to existing concepts in international relations literature. In particular, issues related to identity dimensions are worthy of such expansion.

Ontological Security and Diasporas

Ontological security refers to the notion that routine in relations with significant others contributes to a consistent sense of identity.[20] As McSweeney states, ontological security concerns "the essential predictability of interaction through which we feel confident in knowing what is going on and that we have the practical skill to go on in this context."[21] Actors who are used to certain practices cannot easily discard them, since they may have become constitutive to their identities. While in its original conception ontological security referred to individuals, scholars have since applied the term to collective actors.

An interesting and important question pertains to the identity of the "other" with regard to the diasporic community.[22] It can be argued that in fact there are three significant others relating to a diaspora. The first are the other groups in the host state. Since one of the defining qualities of a diaspora is resistance to full integration with the host state, its differentiation from other groups is significant. The second "others" are rival groups with which the diaspora (as part of the larger ethnic group) is in conflict. This enmity, which is constitutive to the identity of the ethnic group a whole, will most likely retain its identity-defining qualities in the diaspora. The third "others," although this may prove a contentious point, are the kin in the state of origin. While the diaspora and its originating kin group have much in common, there is a constant debate about the meaning and long-term legitimacy of the diasporic experience.

Although people in the state of origin as well as the diaspora may suffer from ontological insecurity, the assumption of this article is that the diaspora is more susceptible to such problems. The diaspora is more sensitive to fluctuations of ontological security, as their daily encounters with other groups in the host state make it much more aware of identity issues and their importance. Furthermore, the basic contradictions in the diasporic situation – such as the de-territorialized nationalism of such groups[23] – also highlight the significance of identity.

On a more concrete level, the discourse surrounding the issue of ontological security could be analyzed, identifying the utterances one could expect to see when a problem arises. Blunt statements admitting the difficulties of adapting to a changing reality are unlikely, since they mostly portray those voicing such views in a negative light.[24] Rather, one can expect statements that attempt to revalidate and re-affirm the threatened identity; statements that place the current threat in the context of recurring threats that have been successfully dealt with in the past; and statements and actions that rebuff the need for change and de-legitimize the agents of such change.

Ontological Security, Diasporas, and the Transition from Conflict to Peace in the State of Origin

In her 2006 groundbreaking article, Mitzen claims that one of the obstacles to advancing a peace process when trying to solve a protracted conflict is the emergence of an ontological security dilemma, suggesting that even destructive routines can provide continuity and thus ontological security. As a result, some states and societies are willing to sacrifice their physical security to ensure ontological security. What is somewhat puzzling, however, is that if issues of identity arising from the peace process are so influential, one would not expect to see a great divergence of opinions between the homeland constituency and the members of the diaspora regarding this process. However, this is not always the case, and some diasporic communities hold more extreme views on average than the homeland population.

It has been shown that the diaspora tends to hold on to grievances caused by a conflict longer than the kin group in the state of origin.[25] As Bercovitch claims, "Diasporic communities tend to get involved in conflicts that touch on identity, beliefs, values, cultural norms or a way of life. Such conflicts are over issues that are quite intangible, and are often referred to as zero-sum conflicts. Intangible issues tend to make a conflict more violent, less amenable to compromise and resolution, and more prolonged and intractable."[26] Diasporas, especially those that were at one time "stateless diaspora,"[27] often feel they are the guardian of the group's identity and react harshly to any threat to this identity. Diasporic organizations see one of their main aims as passing on the memories of their traumatic experience and displacement to the next generations.[28]

Peace processes, along with other major developments in the state of origin, force the diaspora to reflect on its identity, and thus may undermine ontological security. Major events also tend to highlight the differences between the narratives of the homeland community and the diaspora, whereas normally the distance between the two communities allows each to maintain "its own spin on the national narrative and live out their shared identity in its own way."[29] Thus, this self-reflection and awareness can lead the diaspora to experience resentment – and even to taking measures to reverse such developments. This reaction is especially possible if the actions were taken without sufficient consultation with the diaspora.

The Armenian Diaspora and the Negotiations between Armenia and Turkey

The Armenian Diaspora: Background

There is no consensus on the number of Armenians in the world – estimates range from seven million to ten million. However, more than half of the world-wide population of Armenians is in the diaspora, including the former Soviet Union (excluding Nagorno-Karabakh and the surrounding areas).[30] The majority of the established Armenian diaspora members come from the western regions of the Armenian homeland (those that were part of the Ottoman Empire). In spite of the wave of immigration at the end of the nineteenth century, most members of the established diaspora are descendants of the survivors of the Armenian genocide. The three main parties of the Armenian diaspora – rooted in the Armenian nationalist upsurge at the end of the nineteenth century – are the Dashnaks (ARF), the Hnchaks, and the Ramgavars. Traditionally, the ARF has held the most extreme and nationalistic views among the diasporic parties. The territory of the Republic of Armenia today lies in a relatively remote corner of the ancient Armenian homeland, and some diaspora members, especially those in the ARF, strive for the resurrection of "Greater Armenia."[31]

The largest diasporic communities in the West are in the US and France. In the former, Armenian-American diasporans mainly reside in California (specifically in Los Angeles) and in Massachusetts. Two notable achievements of the Armenian-American diaspora since Armenia regained independence in 1991 are the substantial American humanitarian aid to Armenia (one of the highest per capita allocation of American foreign assistance) and the successful campaign to persuade Congress in 1992 to ban US aid to Azerbaijan through Section 907 of the Freedom Support Act.[32]

The Signing of the 2009 Armenia-Turkey Protocols

The signing of the 2009 protocols was a culmination of a lengthy, mostly secretive, negotiation process between Turkey and Armenia with Swiss mediation. The negotiations led to what has been called "football diplomacy," after Turkish President Abdallah Gul was invited by Armenian President Sarkisian to attend the World Cup 2010 qualifying match in Yerevan between Armenian and Turkish national teams in September 2008. Saskisian later reciprocated with a visit to Istanbul in October 2009 to watch the rematch.

On August 31, 2009, it was reported in the media that Turkey and Armenia were embarking on six weeks of intensive negotiations prior to signing two protocols. One was on the establishment of diplomatic relations and the other on the development of bilateral relations. The signing ceremony on October 10, 2009 in Zurich went as planned; however, no statements of the signing parties were made during the ceremony because the Armenians objected to Turkish reference to the issue of Nagorno-Karabakh.[33] After the signing, the hope was for a swift ratification process in both national parliaments and, later, the opening of the shared border between the states (which had been closed by Turkey in 1993, protesting Armenia's actions regarding the question of Nagorno-Karabakh). However, the ratification process has not advanced in either state, and, as already mentioned, Armenia has halted the process.

In an effort to raise support in the diasporic communities for the protocols with Turkey and to deal with opposition, Sarkisian embarked on an intensive tour of the major Armenian diasporic communities just before the signing. In early October 2009, he visited Paris, New York, Los Angeles, Beirut, and Rostov-on-Don in Southern Russia.[34] Sarkisian was greeted with much protest in the diasporic communities, and his tour failed to garner the support he had hoped for the signing of the protocols.

Some may question treating the diaspora as a unitary actor,[35] pointing out that several diasporic organizations did in fact show support for the signing of the protocols. However, the diaspora on the whole showed a stronger than expected opposition to the protocols, while people in Armenia showed milder than expected resistance.[36] Even those organizations that did support the signing of the protocols did not see this as compromising the basic demand that Turkey recognize the Armenian genocide, and in fact some claimed that the protocols would advance such recognition.[37] Hence, the following is a discussion of the prevailing voice among diasporic organizations; analysis of diverging views is left for later works.

The Sources of Armenian Diaspora Objections to the Protocols

As outlined in the theoretical section, three forms of utterances can indicate that a problem of ontological security has arisen: statements that concern revalidation and re-affirmation of the threatened identity; statements that place the current threat in the context of recurring threats and how they have been dealt with in the past; and statements that rebuff the need for change and that de-legitimize the agents of change.

Revalidation and re-affirmation of the threatened identity. The collective traumatic memory of the Armenian genocide has been the most significant factor in shaping the diasporic identity, in the cohesion of the diaspora, and in the elites' ability to mobilize support.[38] The struggle to achieve Turkish recognition of the genocide has become a constitutive element of Armenian diasporic identity. It has also been one of the main issues around which the diasporic organizations easily unite.[39] Hence, the Armenian diaspora finds it hard to accept an agreement between Turkey and Armenia without the precondition that the Turks acknowledge the events of 1915 as genocide. As Richard Giragosian, director of the Yerevan-based Armenian Center for National and International Studies claims, "The diaspora has a one-issue identity; it's the genocide and nothing more. They see this whole rapprochement with Turkey as a threat to their very identity. They don't see it in the same context that the Armenian government sees it, in terms of a need to open the border and a need for normal relations…The only benefits that could come will be accrued by the Armenian government and the Armenian population. *The diaspora sees nothing but harm and nothing but a threat.*"[40]

The diaspora also raised an outcry over the clause in the protocols concerning the establishment of an intergovernmental subcommittee on the "historical dimension," a clause that clashed with Armenia's longstanding insistent opposition to such deliberations.[41] The Armenians claimed that most Western historians agree that the events of 1915 constitute genocide, and they maintain that any debate over this issue would only contribute to continued Turkish denial.

Related to the question of acknowledging the genocide is the question of reprisal. Over the years, the Turks have feared that their recognition of the genocide would generate Armenian territorial demands in eastern Turkey. Turkey's suspicions were fueled by the fact that Armenia, since gaining independence in 1991, has refused to officially recognize the border between the two states. Part of the protocol process was Armenia's recognition of the demarcation. This clause was also received with anger in the diaspora, since, as mentioned above, most members of the diaspora are descendants of genocide survivors who had originally lived in the eastern parts of today's Turkey. Armenian Youth Federation (AYF) chairman Arek Santikian, in a protest rally on Sarkisian's visit to Los Angeles, stated, "He's here trying to convince the diaspora that these protocols are good for Armenia, whereas our stance is that we want peace and normalization with Turkey, but *we don't want it at the cost of selling our historical rights and rights to our land*, and that's what these protocols are doing."[42] The slogan "We remember, We demand, We refuse" – which protesters in Beirut wrote on placards in a demonstration during Sarkisian visit to Lebanon[43] – sums up the lasting effect of the constitutive element of the memory of the genocide and the struggle for recognition in Armenian diasporic identity.

Placing the current threat in the context of recurring threats. As the Armenians are one of the ancient peoples of the world, it is not difficult for diasporic Armenians to place current threats in the context of recurring threats. However, the diaspora also placed the current threat in the context of threats that it *as a diaspora* has dealt with in the past. For example, Kenneth Hachikian, the chairman of the Armenian National Committee of America (ANCA), in an event marking the 119th anniversary of the foundation of the ARF, placed the current threat from the Armenian-Turkish protocols in the context of past challenges that have been successfully dealt with: "In our unity we will find strength…Just as we have, for so many years, seen the value of unity in our work in defense of Armenia's rights and Nagorno-Karabakh's freedom…We have seen this time and again, our community united behind a common purpose, yet still subject to foreign attacks, typically through proxies, aimed at undermining our unity and playing divide and conquer games at our expense. We saw this in: our defense of Section 907, our attack on the Turkish Armenian Reconciliation Commission, our opposition to the Hoagland nomination,[44] and, once again, today on the Protocols and the Madrid Principles."[45]

Some voices placed the current threat in a more pessimistic light, according to which the Armenians have repeatedly been on the losing side. Georgette Avagian, a member of an organization related to the ARF, spoke about the signing of the protocols between Armenia and Turkey: "Now April 24 and October 10 become days of mourning for us because today we have lost our historical lands, and the issue of the recognition of the Armenian Genocide has turned to dust."[46] In a similar vein, ANCA stated, "The success of Turkey in pressuring Armenia into accepting these humiliating one-sided protocols proves, sadly, that genocide pays."[47]

Rebuffing the need for change and de-legitimizing agents of change. Armenians advocating the importance of the protocols for Armenia and of opening the shared border with Turkey stressed that the blockade by Azerbaijan and Turkey has had devastating effects on the Armenian economy and has caused a massive exodus of Armenians from Armenia. However, diasporans remained suspicious of explanations touting the economic benefits for Armenia of signing the protocols, claiming that only very few Armenians – mostly businessmen – would in fact benefit (these "businessmen" were, moreover, linked to corruption in Armenia).[48]

President Sarkisian was also personally attacked in an attempt to de-legitimize his actions. Hachikian, chairman of ANCA, claimed that his actions were "naive" "reckless," and "simply irresponsible."[49] In this respect, it was claimed that the Turks cheated Sarkisian into providing an excuse for U.S. President Barack Obama to renege on his presidential election campaign pledge to call the 1915 massacres genocide.[50] The U.S. was also accused of pressuring Armenia to sign the protocols against its interest. ANCA, just before the signing of the protocols, stated, "The U.S. arm-twisting of the government in Yerevan to accept an agreement that would call this very crime against humanity into question both squanders America's moral capital in the cause of genocide prevention and sets back the cause of genuine Armenian-Turkish dialogue by many years."[51]

In its commentary on the protocols, ANCA stressed that "the Armenian Diaspora is a core stakeholder in the rights, interests, and future of the Armenian nation. The Armenian Government represents the 3 million citizens of Armenia, but cannot rightfully or legitimately speak in the name of the more than 8 million Armenians living around the world."[52] Harut Sassounian, publisher of the *California Courier*, the oldest independent English-language Armenian newspaper in the U.S., also criticized the absence of diasporic representatives in the negotiations: "The Armenian government made no attempt during the lengthy negotiations with Turkey to consult with Diaspora Armenians, despite the fact that the Protocols addressed vital pan-Armenian issues. Months ago, when organizations and individuals expressed serious concerns regarding the preliminary text of the Protocols, they were simply ignored by the Armenian authorities. Attempts to hold discussions at the eleventh hour are futile, since the Armenian Foreign Minister has declared that the Protocols cannot be amended."[53] Thus, part of the resentment in the diaspora arose because the Armenian state's actions – which would have serious repercussions on the Armenian diaspora – were taken without sufficient consultation with the diaspora. This lack of dialogue exacerbated the ontological security concerns.

Conclusions

This article asks why the diaspora in general takes a more extreme and non-compromising stance than the state of origin when it comes to settling prolonged conflicts of the origin state, and demonstrates that part of the answer lies in perceived threats to the ontological security of diasporas. In the Armenian case, the article asserts that the objections of the diaspora to the signing of the protocols without Turkish recognition of the genocide can be explained by the constitutive element in the diasporic identity of achieving such acknowledgement.

The logical question that follows is what can be done to encourage more positive involvement of the diaspora? One possibility is to actively inform diaspora leaders in real time about major policy shifts of the state of origin in order to make the transition from conflict to peace more gradual. Moreover, it might be important to involve, if possible, diasporic leaders themselves in the peace negotiations.[54] Østergaard-Nielsen suggests that dialogue should be conducted not only with the diaspora but between opposing factions within the diaspora.[55] This can be done also in Track II initiatives, although until now Armenia-based civil society organizations showed reluctance to involve diaspora members in normalization projects, because they thought their presence might block any advances. Another obstacle has been the fear of diaspora members that they might be used for public relations purposes by the Turkish government, and this fear should be alleviated in order to proceed.[56] While it may seem at first that these new venues would only further complicate matters, they may contribute in the long run to more stable peace. Helping the diaspora to create a "new identity" and new roles in the post-conflict period would also ease the tensions related to the fear that the "old identity" will no longer be relevant. The diaspora is also potentially an actor that has a long-term approach that many times is needed for post-conflict reconstruction and reconciliation.[57]

Notes

The author would like to thank the Leonard Davis Institute for International Relations at the Hebrew University for its generous support for conducting this research.

1   Yossi Shain, *Kinship and Diasporas in International Affairs* (Ann Arbor: University of Michigan Press, 2007), p. 101.

2   Hazel Smith, "Diasporas in International Conflict," in *Diasporas in Conflict: Peace-Makers or Peace-Wreckers*, eds. H. Smith and P. Stares (Tokyo: United Nations University Press, 2007), p. 15.

3   Brent J. Steele, *Ontological Security in International Relations: Self-Identity and the IR State* (London: Routledge, 2008), p. 3.

4   Nagorno-Karabakh is a source of tension in the bilateral relations between Turkey and Armenia since the Turks support Azerbaijan's positions regarding the conflict and because Armenians view Azerbaijanis as "Turk."

5   Khatharya Um, "Political Remittance: Cambodian Diasporas in Conflict and Post Conflict," in *Diasporas in Conflict: Peace-Makers or Peace-Wreckers,* p. 255.

6   Camila Orjuela, "War, Peace and the Sri Lankan Diaspora: Complications and Implications for Policy," in *Diasporas, Armed Conflicts and Peacebuilding in their Homelands*, ed. A. Swain, Uppsala Report No. 79, 2007, pp. 62-63.

7   Shain, *Kinship and Diasporas in International Affairs,* pp. 101-2.

8   Yossi Shain and Ravinatha P. Aryasinha, "Spoilers or Catalysts? The Role of Diasporas in Peace Processes," in *Challenges to Peacebuilding: Managing Spoilers during Conflict Resolution*, eds. E. Newman and O. Richmond (Tokyo: United Nations University Press, 2006).

9   Shain, *Kinship and Diasporas in International Affairs*, p. 114.

10 Gabriel Sheffer, *Diaspora Politics: At Home Abroad* (Cambridge: Cambridge University Press, 2003), p. 216; Jacob Bercovitch, "A Neglected Relationship: Diasporas and Conflict Resolution," in *Diaspora in Conflict: Peace-Makers or Peace-Wreckers*, pp. 26, 30, 33-34.

11 Bercovitch, "A Neglected Relationship: Diasporas and Conflict Resolution," p. 35.

12 Smith, "Diasporas in International Conflict," p. 13.

13 Ibid., p. 10.

14 There is in fact currently a bias toward studying the "peace-wreckers" rather than the "peace-makers" phenomenon. See Jonathan Hall, Roland Kostic, and Ashok Swain, "Diasporas and Peace Building: A Multifaceted Association," in *Diasporas, Armed Conflicts and Peacebuilding in their Homelands*, p. 10.

15 Stephen M. Saideman and Erin K. Jenne, "The International Relations of Ethnic Conflict," in *Handbook of War Studies III: The Intrastate Dimension,* ed. M. I. Midlarsky (Ann Arbor: University of Michigan Press, 2009), p. 266.

16 Jolle Demmers, "Diaspora and Conflict: Locality, Long Distance Nationalism, and Delocalisation of Conflict Dynamics," *The Public* 9, no. 1 (2002): 95.

17 Hall, Kostic, and Swain, "Diasporas and Peace Building," p. 14.

18 Robin Cohen, *Global Diasporas: An Introduction* (London: UCL Press, 1997).

19 Nicholas Van Hear, *New Diasporas: The Mass Exodus, Dispersal and Regrouping of Migrant Communities* (Seattle: University of Washington Press, 1998), p. 42.

20 Jennifer Mitzen, "Ontological Security and World Politics: State Identity and the Security Dilemma," *European Journal of International Relations* 12, no. 3 (2006): 342. See also Ayse Zarakol, "Ontological (In)Security and State Denial of Historical Crimes: Turkey and Japan," *International Relations* 24, no. 1 (2010): 3.

21 Bill McSweeney, *Security, Identity and Interests: A Sociology of International Relations* (Cambridge: Cambridge University Press, 1999), p. 155.

22 In this respect, see Jolanta A. Drzewiecka, "Reinventing and Contesting Identities in Constitutive Discourses: Between Diaspora and Its Others," *Communication Quarterly* 50, no. 1 (2002): 2-3.

23 Fiona B. Adamson and Madeleine Demetriou, "Remapping the Boundaries of 'State' and 'National Identity': Incorporating Diasporas into IR Theorizing," *European Journal of International Relations* 13, no. 4 (2007): 492.

24 An exception might be a more legitimate nostalgic yearning, but this is more likely to occur in much later stages.

25 Paul Collier, V. L. Elliot, Havard Hegre, Anke Hoeffler, Marta Reynal-Querol, and Nicholas Sambanis, *Breaking the Conflict Trap: Civil War and Development Policy* (Washington: World Bank and Oxford University Press, 2003), p. 86; Shain, *Kinship and Diasporas in International Affairs,* p. 115; Terrence Lyons, "Diaspora and Homeland Conflict," in *Territoriality and Conflict in an Era of Globalization*, eds. M. Kahler and B. F. Walter (Cambridge: Cambridge University Press, 2006), p. 111.

26 Bercovitch, "A Neglected Relationship: Diasporas and Conflict Resolution," p. 24.

27 On the importance of the differentiation between state-linked diasporas (such as the Koreans and the Cubans) and stateless diasporas (such as the Kurds and the Palestinians) see also Cohen, *Global Diasporas*, p. 193.

28 Lyons, "Diaspora and Homeland Conflict," p. 114.

29 Shain, *Kinship and Diasporas in International Affairs*, pp. 103-4.

30 The low estimate of the number of Armenians appears in Susan P. Pattie, "Longing and Belonging: Issues of Homeland in the Armenian Diaspora," *Working Paper, Transnational Communities Programme-99-11* 1999, www.transcomm.ox.ac.uk/working%20papers/pattie.pdf, p. 4. A high estimate can be found in "Armenian Population of the World," http://www.armeniadiaspora.com/population.html.

31 Pattie, "Longing and Belonging," pp. 3-4.

32 The U.S. Freedom Support Act passed by the Congress in 1992 aimed to facilitate economic and humanitarian aid to the former republics of the Soviet Union. Due to pressures from Armenian lobby groups, in section 907 of the act, Azerbaijan was excluded from direct assistance until it lifted the blockade on Armenia, which was set up in response to the conflict over Nagorno-Karabakh.

33 "Turkey's Proposal Clears Last-Minute Snag in Zurich," *Today's Zaman*, October 12, 2009.

34 Sara Khojoyan, "Around the World in Seven Days: Sargsyan on Diaspora Tour amid Simmering Protest against his Turkey Deal," *Armenianow.com,* October 2, 2009, http://www.armenianow.com/news/10566/around_the_world_in_seven_days_sar.

35 In this respect, see Fiona B. Adamson, "Mechanisms of Diaspora Mobilization and the Transnationalization of Civil War," in *Transnational Dynamics of Civil War*, ed. J.T. Checkel (Cambridge: Cambridge University Press, 2013), p. 66.

36 Policy Forum Armenia, "Armenia-Diaspora Relations: Twenty Years since Independence," Policy Forum Armenia website, August 2010, p.19, http://www.pf-armenia.org/sites/default/files/documents/files/PFA%20Diaspora%20 Report.pdf. See also David L. Phillips, *Diplomatic History: The Turkey-Armenia Protocols* (New York: Columbia University Institute for the Study of Human Rights and Harvard Kennedy School Future of Diplomacy Project, March 2012), p. 78.

37 See for example "AGBU President Berge Setrakian Addresses Questions on the Protocols for the Process of Normalization of Relations Between Armenia and Turkey," Armenian General Benevolent Union website, October 23, 2009, http://www.agbu.org/pressoffice/article.asp?id-640 [accessed January 21, 2010].

38 Rachel Anderson Paul, "Grassroots Mobilization and Diaspora Politics: Armenian Interest Groups and the Role of Collective Memory," *Nationalism and Ethnic Politics* 6, no. 1 (2000): 28.

39 Gerard J. Libaridian, *The Challenge of Statehood: Armenian Political Thinking since Independence* (Cambridge, MA: Blue Crane Books, 1999), p. 128.

40 "At Home and Abroad: Turkey Deal a Tough Sell for Armenian President," *EuroNest*, October 9, 2009, http://euronest.blogspot.com/2009/10/at-home-and-abroad-turkey-deal-tough.html, emphasis added.

41 Vicken Cheterian, "The Armenia-Turkey Protocols: A Year On," *OpenDemocracy* October 20, 2010.

42 Liana Aghajanian, "Thousands in Los Angeles Protest Armenia-Turkey Protocols," *Ianyan*, October 4, 2009, http://www.ianyanmag.com/?p=1313, emphasis added.

43 "Lebanon Armenians Protest Sarkisian by the Thousands," *StopTheProtocols.com,* October 6, 2009, http://www.stoptheprotocols.com/2009/10/06/lebanon-armenians-up-in-arms-over-planned-turkey-deal/.

44 Armenian-Americans strongly opposed the appointment of Richard E. Hoagland as U.S. ambassador to Armenia in 2006. Hoagland was supposed to replace John Evans, who was recalled after he had named the events of 1915 a genocide, contrary to U.S. formal position.

45 "Hachikian Stresses Imperative for Unity against Protocols at ARF Day Celebration," *Asbarez.com*, December 11, 2009, http://www.asbarez.com/74765/hachikian-stresses-imparitive-for-unity-against-protocols-at-arf-day-celebration/.

46 "Armenian Diaspora Threatens to Stop Financing Armenia after Turkey Deal," *Turkish Daily Mail*, October 13, 2009.

47 Ibid.

48 See for example responses on the StopTheProtocols website: "Responses to Reading between the Lines," September 22, 2009, http://www.stoptheprotocols.com/2009/09/22/reading-between-the-lines/.

49 "Message to Armenian Assembly Members, Supporters, Activists and Friends," Armenian Assembly of America website, October 8, 2009, http://www.aaainc.org/fileadmin/aaainc/pdf_1/Protocols/2009__Oct_8__AAA__Msg_to_Members.pdf.

50 Marc Champion, "Armenia Scraps a Border Deal with Turkey," *Wall Street Journal*, April 23, 2010.

51 Umit Enginsoy, "Radical US Armenians Protest Ankara-Yerevan Protocol," *Hurriyet Daily News & Economic Review*, October 9, 2009.

52 "The Turkey-Armenia Protocols explained," ANCA website, September 14, 2009, http://www.anca.org/assets/pdf/misc/protocols_explained.pdf.

53 Harut Sassounian, "10 Major Concerns Regarding Armenia-Turkey Protocols," *California Courier*, September 24, 2009, http://www.armeniapedia.org/index.php?title=10_Major_Concerns_Regarding_Armenia-Turkey_Protocols.

54 Gallia Lindenstrauss, "Diaspora Involvement in Peace Processes," in *In the Spirit of Einstein: Germans and Israelis on Ethics and International Order*, ed. A.M. Kacowicz (Jerusalem: Einstein Center and Leonard Davis Institute, June 2009), p. 102.

55 Eva Østergaard-Nielsen, "The Kurds in the EU and the Conflict in Turkey," in *Diasporas, Armed Conflicts and Peacebuilding in their Homelands*, p. 59.

56 Esra Çuhadar and Burcu Gültekin Punsmann, *Reflecting on the Two Decades of Bridging the Divide: Taking Stock of Turkish-Armenian Civil Society Activities* (Ankara: Tepav, 2012), pp. 66-71.

57 Alexandra Cosima Budabin, "Diasporas as Development Partners for Peace? The Alliance between the Darfuri Diaspora and the Save Darfur Coalition," *Third World Quarterly* 35, no. 1 (2014): 167.

A Conflict within a Conflict: The Fatah-Hamas Strife and the Israeli-Palestinian Political Process

Anat Kurz

Never monolithic, the Palestinian national movement has always comprised a large array of competing organizations and factions. During the second intifada, the rivalry between the two most prominent Palestinian movements, which began in the early days of the first intifada, culminated in a full-fledged split. The mainstream, secular-oriented Fatah, which reached the helm of the Palestine Liberation Organization (PLO) in the late 1960s and has led the Palestinian Authority (PA) since its formation in 1994 under the Oslo Accord, has been pitted against Hamas, which in the late 1980s grew out of the Palestinian branch of the Muslim Brotherhood. This rivalry evolved into a division of the Palestinian political arena into two authorities: the Fatah-led PA that rules in the West Bank, and Hamas that controls the Gaza Strip. It has also meant the evolution of the Israeli-Palestinian dispute into a three-party conflict.

The split in the Palestinian arena has significantly undermined the already limited Israeli confidence in the possibility of formulating and implementing understandings designed to promote conflict resolution. It has also curtailed the freedom of decision making enjoyed by the PLO/PA. Clearly, it was not the intra-Palestinian rivalry that generated the protracted periods of deadlock in the political process. Rather, it was the political stagnation that encouraged the ongoing search in the Palestinian arena for ideological and strategic alternatives to disappointing negotiations and to the leadership that has failed to fulfill national aspirations. In other words, the political impasse reinforced Hamas, which in accordance with its fundamentalist Islamic orientation, rejects the idea of a negotiated end to the conflict. Inevitably, this development came at the expense of the Fatah-led camp that is committed to such a resolution.

A structural analysis of the association between the intra-Palestinian split and the peace process shows how the inter-party power struggle and the absence of an authoritative Palestinian interlocutor joined the complex array of factors that has forestalled the achievement of a final status agreement. Based on the premise that a unified Palestinian representation is a vital Israeli interest, it is suggested that Israel temper its objection to Fatah-Hamas accommodation and even make an active effort to enhance – though not unconditionally – inter-party institutional cooperation.

The Road to the Intra-Palestinian Institutional Split

Somewhat ironically, the Fatah-Hamas rivalry was accelerated by international and Israeli demands that were designed to enable the resumption of negotiations, specifically, a halt to Palestinian violence and institutional reform in the PA. This dynamic was especially evident during the second intifada, which broke out following the failed talks held in 2000 under American auspices on a comprehensive solution to the conflict.[1] In addition, the Israeli withdrawal from the Gaza Strip in 2005 drew a clear line between the territorial strongholds of the two rival parties.

Setting the stage for Hamas. Israel's insistence on complete security calm before any dialogue could resume actually defined for Hamas and other militant Palestinian factions the nature of activity that would prevent the political process from getting back on track. The escalation of violence by Hamas – terrorist assaults and rocket fire from the Gaza Strip – triggered military responses and rounds of confrontation that prevented efforts to restore mutual Israeli-Palestinian trust and bring the Israeli and Palestinian teams back to the negotiating table. For their part, Fatah's forces sought to preserve their supremacy by leading a violent campaign of their own. However, this strategy, which in essence was crafted to address domestic institutional needs, entailed a high price. Israel held the PA responsible for the escalating violence, no matter who was the perpetrating faction, and reacted against its security agencies and institutions.[2] The resulting anarchy in the territories enabled Hamas to consolidate its military infrastructure, and in any event, Hamas was largely perceived to be less corrupt and more trustworthy than Fatah. Hence, support grew for the party as a promising substitute to the Fatah-led PA.

Institutional reform in the PA as a prerequisite for dialogue. Disappointment with Fatah's political, security, and administrative conduct was the basis for the call for institutional reform in the PA, advocated by the United States administration and the Roadmap for Peace in the Middle East, issued by the Quartet (the international forum for advancing peace in the Middle East, comprising the United States, the European Union, Russia, and the United Nations).[3] Israel joined a demand for reform stipulated in the Roadmap, despite reservations about the U.S. call for general elections in the PA that was motivated both by the general support for democratization and by the hope that democratization in the greater Middle East would curb the regional drift towards fundamentalist Islam.

Like Israel, the PA was not enthusiastic about holding elections, out of concern that results would reflect the widening influence of Hamas. Nonetheless, it acceded to the U.S. demand and prepared for the elections that were held in January 2006. Recognition of the inability to hold elections during a violent confrontation with Israel drove Fatah to try and coordinate the campaign with Hamas. The Hamas leadership assented to the call and agreed to suspend the inter-party struggle and the fight against Israel during preparations for the elections. In reality, the inter-movement coordination was intended by the respective parties to promote antithetical interests. The PA hoped that the election results would reinforce its international status, and this in turn would strengthen its standing at home. The Hamas leadership, on the other hand, sought public support that would allow it to continue to undermine Fatah's status and foil moves toward a political settlement.

The two sides attained their objective, though Hamas' achievement was more concrete. The PA was again recognized as a partner for negotiations because of its readiness to hold general elections. However, Hamas' victory in the elections in the Palestinian territories in January 2006, which were marked by widespread criticism of the PA due to its poor administrative/governmental performance more than genuine sympathy for Hamas, brought in its wake a period of political paralysis. The Israel-Hamas mutual non-recognition dramatically reduced prospects for continuing the Israeli-Palestinian political process.

Leaving Gaza. Against the backdrop of the political deadlock, Israel initiated a comprehensive unilateral withdrawal from the Gaza Strip. Underlying the move was the desire to free itself from the burden of combatting the Palestinian violent struggle in and from the Strip; the drive to reduce direct friction with Palestinians; and the desire to gain international legitimacy for military responses to violent provocations. In August 2005 Israel disengaged from the Gaza Strip.

The subsequent period saw a dramatic intensification of the inter-party tension over control of the area. In November 2006, in response to calls in the Palestinian arena and the Arab world for restraint, Hamas and Fatah agreed on a lull in the struggle between them and against Israel, as well as on principles for a national unity government.[4] A unity government was subsequently established on the basis of understandings that were formulated in February 2007 by representatives of the two parties in Mecca, Saudi Arabia, but its platform did not include revival of the negotiations with Israel.[5] In any case, it was short-lived. Fatah's refusal to transfer control of the PA's security forces to the interior ministry headed by Hamas (as required by the Authority's basic law) prevented effective power sharing. In June 2007, fierce hostilities broke out in the Gaza Strip between the two camps. Hamas forces defeated and expelled Fatah operatives, and assumed control of the Strip.

Hamas entrenched itself in the Gaza Strip under the Israeli and Egyptian-imposed strict limitations on movement of people and goods in and out of the area. It was boycotted diplomatically and economically by Israel, the United States, and the European Union (with the exception of consumer goods defined as essential). For its part, having lost control over the Strip, the Fatah-led PA focused on preserving its hold on the West Bank, while enjoying increased economic and military support from external sources – primarily the US, the EU, Jordan, and Israel. This aid to the PA's intensive institutional and security reforms as well as economic buildup was provided with the goal of preventing the West Bank from falling into Hamas hands, and on the basis of the PA's declared adherence to the political process.[6]

Particularly the security reform did much to enhance normalization of life in the West Bank. However, given that the reform was sponsored by the United States and EU member states and coordinated with Israel, and given that the forces were almost exclusively composed of Fatah-affiliated personnel, the status of the PA itself was further undermined.

The Three-Party Gordian Knot

Renewal of the Israeli-Palestinian dialogue – the Annapolis track. Although demonstrating the weakness of Fatah, the Hamas takeover of the Strip inspired hope for the renewal of the Israeli-Palestinian dialogue since it appeared to draw a clear dividing line between the camp officially committed to the goal of a negotiated comprehensive settlement and the camp rejecting this resolution.[7] This distinction, bolstered by the drive to undercut Hamas' influence, underlay the renewed interest, shared by Israel, the Palestinian Authority, and international actors relevant to the political process, to revive the dialogue. Talks were launched in November 2007 in Annapolis in an international conference under American aegis.[8]

A spoiler in action. Hamas, which was not present at the negotiating table, nevertheless remained a key player in molding the Israeli-Palestinian arena, and in late 2008 effected an end to the Annapolis talks. A war broke out in the Gaza Strip, after Hamas failed to regard explicit Israeli warnings that a military offensive loomed if it did not stop the escalating rocket fire from the Strip into Israeli territory. The end of the war, which caused many Palestinian civilian casualties and massive damage, left Hamas in control of an incapacitated area. Iranian aid helped Hamas restore and further augment its military infrastructure, although civilian rehabilitation was delayed by Israeli-imposed sanctions and the distribution of resources by Hamas itself, which favored military entrenchment. Hamas became a target of public criticism for provoking the Israeli offensive, but the erosion in its domestic prestige did not help Fatah restore its own control of the Strip. Yet another outcome of the war was the impact on Israeli public opinion. Sentiments inspired by the confrontation were reflected in the results of the general elections held in February 2009: the public supported parties that advocated a hard line toward both Hamas and the political process. Specifically, the war reinforced concerns over redeployment in the West Bank, let alone withdrawal from the area.

The political process remained frozen for about four years. Differences on opening conditions for talks, and indeed, on the very purpose of the talks, magnified the fundamental obstacles that time and again have prevented the peace process from moving forward. As a condition for returning to negotiations, the PA demanded a complete freeze on Israeli construction in the West Bank. It also demanded that discussions begin with the question of borders. For its part, the government of Israel called for resumption of dialogue without preconditions. However, it also demanded that security arrangements be placed at the top of the agenda and conditioned the conclusion of an agreement on Palestinian recognition of the State of Israel as the home of the Jewish people – demands that were continually rejected by the PA.[9]

Renewed attempts at Palestinian reconciliation – the Cairo Agreement. In an effort to circumvent the blocked bilateral path, the PA launched an international campaign to enlist support for a vote in the UN General Assembly on recognition of a Palestinian state within the 1967 borders. The announcement that the United States would veto a Security Council resolution to recognize Palestinian statehood upset the original plan, and instead, in November 2012 the PA turned to the General Assembly with a request to upgrade its observer status. The approval by the GA of the petition to recognize Palestine within the 1967 borders as a UN non-member observer reinforced the PA's international status. However, since there was no concrete progress toward Palestinian independence, the PA could not translate its diplomatic achievement into a change of the balance of power with Hamas.

The PA's drive to broaden its popular base and reinforce its democratic image, as part of the preparations for applying for international recognition of a Palestinian state, led it to renew a plan to hold general elections. Yet holding elections without Hamas threatened to deny the results any legitimacy and hence the PA revived its efforts to reach an agreement with Hamas, at least on the elections process. Hamas, which viewed the inter-party coordination as an opportunity to breach the boundaries of its geographical and political isolation, conditioned its participation in the elections on institutional coordination, that is, power sharing with the PA.

The leaderships of both Fatah and Hamas were driven by a widespread popular call for unity to embrace – at least rhetorically – the campaign for inter-party reconciliation. Demonstrations that were held under the banner of unity were presumably inspired by the concurrently growing assertiveness of the masses throughout the Middle East and the Arab Spring protests that were sweeping the region. Concern over a spillover of the riots to the Palestinian territories was yet another factor that played a role in laying the groundwork for the reconciliation effort. For its part, Hamas at that time was also losing its stronghold in Damascus, with the civil war in Syria.

Therefore, in May 2011 in Cairo, and under the auspices of the Temporary Supreme Military Council that had replaced Mubarak's toppled regime, Fatah and Hamas signed an agreement of principles for institutional coordination. The agreement focused on an intention to prepare jointly for presidential and legislative council elections and to revise the structure of the PLO in order to enable Hamas integration into its ranks.[10] However, the agreement did not refer to Hamas' massive military infrastructure – the PA chose to postpone dealing with the sensitive matter of the monopoly of weapons until after elections and the official delineation of the power relations between Hamas and Fatah based on the election results.

The move toward inter-party reconciliation encountered severe criticism from Israel. Israel responded by blocking the transfer of funds to the PA, although it revoked the sanction under international, particularly European pressure. The reaction of the United States administration, on the other hand, was quite restrained and demonstrated an evolving change in the approach to the inter-party rift.[11] A State Department spokesman expressed hope that the Cairo agreement would improve chances for renewing the peace process, should Hamas meet the demands posed by the Quartet as prerequisites for dialogue: recognition of Israel, a halt to violence, and recognition of agreements signed between Israel and the PLO. However, the parties did not manage to overcome the hostility between them and move beyond their contentious ideological and political directives to even draft election procedures.

A renewed round of violence. Further confirmation of Hamas' control over the strip was registered following a renewed round of hostilities that broke out in the Gaza sphere in November 2012. As in the previous round of confrontation, in early 2009, the large scale fighting had a major effect on the Palestinian inter-party balance of power. Hamas' military infrastructure was severely damaged, while yet again, the confrontation also highlighted its popularity, necessarily at the expense of the Fatah-led Palestinian Authority, and ended with ceasefire agreements that attested to and confirmed Hamas' control over the Gaza Strip. The political backing that was given this time to Hamas by the Muslim Brotherhood-led government of Egypt, as well as the United States support of the indirect dialogue between Israel and Hamas on terms for a ceasefire, constituted a diplomatic achievement for Hamas. It also earned credit in the Palestinian arena due to its standing up to the military might of Israel. Yet another accomplishment was the conclusion drawn by the Israeli opposition to further redeployment in the West Bank: the war exacerbated the concern over security risks emanating from the entrenchment of Hamas in any territory evacuated by Israel.

Resumption and suspension of the Israeli-Palestinian dialogue. A new round of Israeli-Palestinian talks was launched under American auspices in July 2013. Both Israel and the PLO/PA were driven to the negotiating table by the wish to avoid paying the price of refusing an American request. Under pressure applied by U.S. Secretary of State John Kerry, they agreed to discuss all the core issues of the conflict. However, mutual mistrust and shared skepticism as to prospects for generating a breakthrough kept the talks confined to procedural matters. In fact, from the very initiation of the talks the two sides sought to place the responsibility for their expected failure on each other. This attitude proved to be a self-fulfilling prophecy. In April 2014, toward the end of the assigned negotiating period, the U.S. administration acknowledged its failure to have the two sides even discuss a framework of principles for continuation of the talks. An end to the negotiations was announced officially and President Obama expressed the commonly-shared conviction that a time out in the political process was in order.[12]

Just prior to this, the PA revived two initiatives intended to pressure Israel to soften its positions or, alternatively, to advance toward Palestinian statehood not necessarily within the context of bilateral talks. The PA applied for signature on 15 UN treaties so as to join their respective organizations. Concurrently, the Fatah-Hamas talks on institutional accommodation culminated in yet another agreement in principle on establishing a unity government of technocrats during preparations for the long overdue elections in the territories. Once again, Hamas, invited by Fatah, moved closer to the center of the Palestinian and hence the Israeli-Palestinian political stage. President Mahmoud Abbas stressed that the inter-party agreement should not contradict the underlying logic of the political process.[13] As far as Israel was concerned, the very attempt to regulate intra-Palestinian relations was an immediate catalyst for suspending the negotiations and announcing tenders for new housing units in settlements in the West Bank. This was also the backdrop for renewed thought regarding the potential benefit of unilateral steps toward separation from the Palestinians.

Fatah-Hamas rapprochement – a recurrent dynamic. The Fatah-Hamas interim unity government was announced in early June 2014. Despite Israel's criticism and insistence on non-recognition of Hamas as a political partner as long as it did not recognize Israel's right to exist, the U.S. administration expressed readiness to cooperate with the unity government.[14] Similar reactions were registered world-wide, including recognition of the unity cabinet by all other Quartet members.

To be sure, from the outset prospects of establishing solid and lasting institutional cooperation between Fatah and Hamas seemed quite slim. Fatah's leadership was unlikely to concede to Hamas' persistent demand for a structural reform of the PLO, which would facilitate Hamas' road to prevalence in the Palestinian national movement.[15] As for Hamas, its spokesmen declared that even within the context of a unity deal, the party would not recognize Israel and accept the PA's weapons monopoly in the Palestinian territories, particularly in the Gaza Strip.[16] Thus, this move toward reconciliation appeared to face the same problematic dynamic that thwarted previous attempts to reunite the Palestinian political sphere. Moreover, the inter-party reconciliation was not Hamas' ultimate ambition, but rather a step within the framework of undermining the national prevalence of the Fatah-led PLO and hindering efforts to formulate strategic understandings with Israel. Thus, Israel's reaction to the establishment of the unity government provided Hamas with an interim, tactical gain.

Indeed, the unity cabinet lost effective meaning against the backdrop of a series of violent events that culminated in the eruption in July 2014 of yet another war between Israel and Hamas. However, the issue of a Palestinian unity government rose again to the surface in the context of intensive talks that were held at a regional and international level concerning reestablishing security quiet in the Gaza sphere and rehabilitation of the area following the massive damage that was caused in the course of the war. Egypt insisted that the PA take part in managing the rehabilitation enterprise. Actually, Egypt hoped this to be a stage toward the return of the PA to the Strip. From the early days of the war, President Abbas took part in Cairo's efforts to articulate terms for a ceasefire between Israel and Hamas and principles for the future relations among Hamas, Egypt itself, the PA, and Israel. Israel, for its part, encouraged this policy, acknowledging the inevitability of coordination between Hamas and Fatah, if efforts to rehabilitate the Strip were to succeed.

At the same time, two developments that were clear both during the war and as the fighting drew to a halt threatened to jeopardize prospects for establishing genuine, practical cooperation between the two rival parties: Hamas' control over the Strip was regionally and internationally confirmed, and public opinion polls indicated a dramatic increase in Hamas' popularity among the Gaza Strip and West Bank populations.

Understandings that were articulated in order to reach a ceasefire were testimony to the fact that Israel, the United States, Egypt, and other regional actors view Hamas as the ruler of the Strip. This affirmation of a given situation also confirmed the bifurcation of the Palestinian political sphere into two authorities. This recognition of Hamas' rule over the Strip compensates Hamas partially for the resentment and harsh criticism of its conduct – in particular, provoking the Israeli counter attack on the Strip – on the part of Arab states.[17]

The rise in the popularity of Hamas was directly associated with its proven ability to stand up to Israeli military power for over seven weeks.[18] It also compensated Hamas for public criticism accusing it of rendering the Strip into a crisis zone, for the sake of organizational survival and preservation of its control over the Strip.

What follows is that it does not really matter what official role will be assigned to the PA in the areas of security, administration, and rehabilitation in the Strip. Rather, the scope and quality of coordination established between Fatah and Hamas and the balance of power between the two rival camps will eventually determine the ability of the PA to rehabilitate its own position and status in the Strip, and hence in the Palestinian arena as a whole.[19]

Untying the Gordian Knot

The circular connection between the political stalemate in the Israeli-Palestinian sphere of conflict and the internal rift in the Palestinian arena might possibly be broken by the establishment of a Palestinian coalition government. Progress in this direction can be expected to coincide with reduced strength of the Palestinian opposition and encourage a softening of rejectionist stances within the diverse Palestinian forces, first and foremost, Hamas. Thus far, repeated Fatah-Hamas reconciliation attempts have failed, but their recurrence reflects the persistence of their underlying motivation. Both Fatah and Hamas share an interest in institutionalizing the balance of power between them created over the years and the awareness of the need to formulate new rules of the game, whereby they will continue to conduct their political struggle. Moreover, this appears to be the only way to establish an authority in the Palestinian arena that will enjoy the legitimacy essential for concluding a settlement with Israel, let alone guarantee its implementation.

Hence, a unified and broadly-based Palestinian leadership should be considered a focal Israeli interest. In order to facilitate its evolution and consolidation, Israel should not only abandon the paradigm of driving wedges between Fatah and Hamas – by resisting rapprochement between the two parties and conditioning negotiations with the PLO on the marginalization of Hamas – but even endorse active encouragement of reconciliation and cooperation between the various Palestinian parties.

From a purely structural perspective, it should not really matter what parties join a Palestinian coalition government, as long as Israel and other international actors relevant to the political process have a clear address on the Palestinian side. However, ideological determinants cannot be totally ignored. They matter, since a nationally-unified Palestinian representation would challenge progress toward viable peace if established while Hamas still adheres to its rigid ideological directives. Therefore it is essential for Israel that demands that were presented to Hamas as preconditions for dialogue, which essentially imply endorsement of the two-state final status agreement, remain on the international agenda.

At the same time, in order to disentangle itself from the trap of the three-party conflict and also leave an opening for an eventual acceptance by Hamas of Israel's existence, it will be enough for Israel, at least during negotiating terms for a comprehensive agreement, to settle for the existing, de facto mutual recognition with Hamas. This would mean accepting the results of elections in the territories – if indeed they take place. The Palestinian national leadership should reflect the voice of the Palestinian people. Boycott of a coalition Palestinian government by Israel will not change the people's choice but rather further reduce the already shrinking chance of putting concrete negotiations toward an end-state solution back on track.

There is no way to ensure that establishing a Palestinian coalition leadership and moving the political process forward will transform the atmosphere in the Palestinian territories and diminish militant inclinations among radical factions. At the same time, it is also possible that a concrete political process, along with progress toward unification of the Palestinian political arena, will challenge the resolution to the hardships and grievances of the Palestinian people formulated in Hamas' platform. Perhaps this is the only path toward normalization of Israeli-Palestinian relations.

Notes

1   Rallying public support for territorial and political concessions is a challenge that faces the Israeli government as well. Presumably, however, accomplishing this goal will be much more complicated in the Palestinian arena.

2   The criticism leveled at Israel at that time for attacking the PA's agencies and infrastructure was offset by the U.S. understanding of Israel's struggle against Palestinian violence, particularly after the attacks of September 11, 2001.

3   The Roadmap detailed three stages, starting with a cessation of violence and reforms in the PA and a freeze on Israeli construction in the West Bank, followed by general elections in the territories and the establishment of a Palestinian state within provisional borders, and the establishment of a permanent settlement in the course of 2005. See "A Performance Based Roadmap to a Permanent, Two-State Solution to the Israeli-Palestinian Conflict," http://2001-2009.state.gov/r/pa/prs/ps/2003/20062.htm.

4   Egypt, Jordan, and Saudi Arabia, concerned over the Iranian penetration of the Gaza Strip through support for Hamas and by the deadlock in the political process, mediated principals for the formulation of a national unity government.

5   *Towards Palestinian National Reconciliation* (Ramallah and Geneva: Geneva Centre for the Democratic Control of Armed Forces (DCAFF)), pp. 46-56; Anat Kurz, "The Riyadh Summit, the Mecca Agreement, and What Lies Between them," *INSS Insight* No. 15, April 22, 2007.

6   *Building the Palestinian State: Sustaining Growth, Institutions and Service Delivery,* Economic Monitoring Report to the Ad Hoc Liaison Committee, The World Bank, April 13, 2011. On Israel's policy on economic development in the Palestinian arena, see *Measures Taken by Israel in Support of Developing the Palestinian Economy and Socio-Economic Structure*, Report of the Government of Israel to the Ad Hoc Liaison Committee, Brussels, April 13, 2011.

7   There is a debate within Hamas over two conflicting approaches: one holds that the time has not come to articulate terms for a permanent settlement; the other holds that pragmatic policies should be considered that will not necessarily focus on the maximal aspirations of the Palestinian people. This has been at the backdrop of expressions of readiness in principal to accept a settlement with Israel, should one be attained by President Mahmoud Abbas, without a requirement that Hamas recognize Israel and commit to an end-state agreement. See, for example, "Hamas will Accept any Agreement that has a Majority [among the Palestinian Public]," *Ynet*, October 21, 2010; Nathan J. Brown, "Is Hamas Mellowing?" Carnegie Endowment, January 17, 2012, http://carnegieendowment.org/2012/01/17/is-hamas-mellowing; Anat Kurz, Benedetta Berti, and Marcel Konrad, "The Institutional Transformation of Hamas and Hizbollah," *Strategic Assessment* 15, no. 3 (2012): 87-98.

8   Roni Sofer, "Olmert: Annapolis Strength Lies in Absence of Hamas," *Ynetnews*, November 26, 2007.

9   This demand was presented as prerequisite for the very initiation of talks. See, for example, Amos Harel, Avi Issacharoff, News agencies, and Akiva Eldar, "Netanyahu Demands Palestinians Recognize 'Jewish State,'" *Haaretz*, April 16, 2009, http://www.haaretz.com/news/netanyahu-demands-palestinians-recognize-jewish-state-1.274207; "Netanyahu: If the Palestinians Recognize the Jewish State, We will Agree to Another Freeze [on construction in the West Bank]," *Haaretz*, October 22, 2010; "Netanyahu: For Peace, Palestinians Must Recognize Jewish Homeland," *Jerusalem Post*, October 6, 2013. The Palestinians remained adamant in their refusal to recognize Israel as a Jewish state, even during the round of talks that was initiated in July 2013. See, for example, Khaled Abu Toameh, "Abbas Reaffirms Refusal to Recognize Israel as a Jewish State," *Jerusalem Post*, November 1, 2013, http://www.jpost.com/Diplomacy-and-Politics/Abbas-reaffirms-refusal-to-recognize-Israel-as-a-Jewish-state-337854.

10 For the reconciliation agreement, see "Fatah-Hamas Reconciliation Agreement," http://middleeast.about.com/od/palestinepalestinians/qt/Fatah-Hamas-Reconciliation-Agreement.htm.

11 "US to Palestinians: Unity Deal Must Advance Prospects of Peace with Israel," *Haaretz,* May 4, 2011; See also Quartet Statement on preconditions for dialogue with Hamas, January 30, 2006, http://www.un.org/news/dh/infocus/middle_east/quartet-30jan2006.htm.

12 Matt Spetalnick, "'Pause' Perhaps Needed in Israeli-Palestinian Talks; Obama," *Reuters*, April 25, 2014, http://www.reuters.com/article/2014/04/25/us-palestinian-israel-obama-idUSBREA3O0RW20140425.

13 Abbas: "Any government formed would comply with our national agreements... to recognize the State of Israel and renounce terror," in Ruth Eglash, "Palestinians Signal Willingness to Continue Peace Talks," *Washington Post*, April 26, 2014.

14 Barak Ravid and Jack Khoury, "Despite Israel's Stance, U.S. Likely to Cooperate with Palestinian Unity Government," *Haaretz,* May 19, 2014, http://www.haaretz.com/news/diplomacy-defense/.premium-1.591607; Julian Pecquet, "Congress to Obama: Cut Aid to Palestinians," June 2, 2014, *al-Monitor*, http://www.al-monitor.com/pulse/ru/originals/2014/06/congress-cut-aid-palestine-reconciliation-hamas.html#; Barak Ravid, "Netanyahu's Diplomatic Meltdown on Palestinian Unity," *haaretz.com*, June 5, 2014, http://www.haaretz.com/news/diplomacy-defense/.premium-1.597060.

15 Tamara Cofman Wittes, "What Matters, and What Doesn't, About Palestinian Unity," *Brookings UpFront*, April 25, 2014, http://www.brookings.edu/blogs/up-front/posts/2014/04/25-palestinian-reconciliation-israel-wittes.

16 "Zahar: Palestinian Unity Deal will not Make Hamas Recognize Israel's Right to Exist," *Jerusalem Post*, April 29, 2014.

17 Kareem Fahim, "Palestinians Find Show of Support Lacking from Arab Leaders Amid Offensive," *New York Times*, July 19, 2014, http://www.nytimes.com/2014/07/20/world/middleeast/palestinians-find-show-of-support-lacking-from-arab-nations-amid-offensive.html?_r=0; Khaled Abu Toameh, "Palestinians: The Arabs Betrayed Us – Again," Gatestone Institute, July 21, 2014, http://www.gatestoneinstitute.org/4463/paletinians-arabs-betrayed-us.

18 "Special Gaza War Poll," Palestinian Center for Policy and Survey Research (PSR), September 2, 2014, www.pcpsr.org/en/node/489.

19 Elie Hanna, "Meshaal: Full Partnership in the Palestinian Authority and a Palestinian State within pre-1967 Borders," *al-Akhbar English*, September 6, 2014, http://english.al-akhbar.com/node/21414.

Religious Dialogue as a Contribution to Political Negotiations: A Practitioner's Report

Trond Bakkevig

Religion has increasingly become a factor in international as well as internal conflicts. Religious leaders have gained prominence by contributing to intensification of conflicts, but also as peacemakers. Dialogue between religions and between religious leaders is in some instances seen as constructive contributions in a process toward sustainable peace. The purpose of this article is to explore how dialogue among religious leaders can assist political negotiations and contribute to lasting peace. Such dialogues are not about religious ideas; they are about religious issues which are relevant to political negotiations, and about political issues which have religious implications. Such dialogues can happen as part of political processes, or in the absence of political negotiations. The usefulness of such dialogues should be measured by their political effect. However, since politicians and diplomats often are caught up in their own, limited circles, the usefulness of religious dialogues should also be evaluated by civil society and independent observers.

Religion and Identity

In many political conflicts, religion plays a crucial role when it is linked to ethnic or national identity. Religious categories can be tagged on to groups, or they can be used by the groups themselves. Examples are Catholics and Protestants in Northern Ireland, Shias and Sunnis in Iraq, Muslims in the Qingui province in China, or Christians and Muslims in Lebanon. The conflict in the Holy Land is a conflict between Israelis and Palestinians, but Judaism, Christianity, and Islam are involved as well. Samuel Huntington tried to link his idea of "a clash of civilizations"[1] to presumed and deep-seated religious identities of civilizations. His idea has, however, shown itself to be far too simplistic. "Civilization" is not an easily defined construct, as different "civilizations" may incorporate similar religions. In addition, most conflicts are within civilizations, not between.

National, ethnic, and personal identities are composed of many elements. History, buildings, places, and politics play a role in the mixture. Religion is often one of the key elements, intertwined with all the others. In this world, religion is not a standalone concept. Every religion is also part of a human, national, and ethnic culture and context. They are intertwined in such ways that it is impossible to sort out that which possibly could be of a pure, religious nature; religious identity is always part of a larger identity.

Identities are usually linked to historical narratives which are continuously memorized, reproduced, and celebrated in the lives of nations, peoples, and individuals. They often recount origins, which may include what an outsider might consider to be mythological elements. Whether or not they are historically factual, they are of a constitutional nature in the history of a people.

Religious identities are also present when people define themselves in relation to outsiders. Identities are linked to narratives and places. Political conflicts often involve control and sovereignty over sites whose national and religious significance cannot be separated. Consequently, religion cannot be separated from political negotiations over these sites.

Religion, Governance, and the Public Sphere

Politicians relate to sentiments that are prevalent in civil society. Such sentiments, especially in situations of conflict, are often expressed through religion or with use of religious language. Western politicians, journalists, and scholars often seem surprised by the fact that "religious fundamentalism and religious difference have emerged as crucial factors in international conflict, national security and foreign policy."[2] It is as if they did not notice what Jose Casanova wrote in 1994, "Despite all the structural forces, the legitimate pressures, and the many valid reasons pushing religion in the modern secular world into the private sphere, religion continues to have and will likely continue to have a public dimension."[3] Religion has always been part of reality in the public sphere; as Hurd writes about the West, "the return of religion is not 'a special atavistic anomaly' but is integral to modern politics itself."[4]

The fact that religion is integral to the public sphere, does not, however, mean that it is easy to map the exact relationship between religion and politics, between governance and religion.

> Religion and politics are not well-defined and stable categories of a broader set of fixed binary divisions between public and private with their origin in the European Enlightenment. Secularist divisions between religion and politics are neither stable nor universal. They are fundamentally contested categories.[5]

Europe has seen a "transformation of the church from a state-oriented to a society-oriented institution,"[6] while the separation of church and state in the United States transformed religion into a "society-oriented institution," though it does exert influence on government. In the Middle East, religion is perceived as "society-oriented," though one must wonder whether religion is "state-oriented," or the state is "religion-oriented," or both. For instance, in several Arab states religious courts deal with issues which in the West would be considered tasks of the state, or a public court system, including marriage, divorce, inheritance, etc. In Israel, the religious judicial system is parallel to the civil one, but has a much more limited role.

Relations between religion, politics, and governance vary; in the United States, religion is not organizationally linked to governing structures, but it has an important role in the public sphere. Religion in West European societies is becoming increasingly detached from governing political structures, though it is the focus of deliberations such as in discussions regarding the fate of refugees and asylum seekers, in shaping the public opinion against the American-led invasion in Iraq, in the debate about development aid, etc.

In Eastern Europe, mainly in countries whose majority belongs to the Orthodox Church, state and church have been drawing closer. One example is the relationship between Russian President Vladimir Putin and the Russian Orthodox Church. Consistently wearing a cross around his neck, Putin is often photographed in churches and with high clergy. The Russian Orthodox Church, on its side, has started redeveloping and recirculating old ideas about links between church, state, nation, and soil.

In the Middle East, a common denominator between Israel and its neighboring countries is that they all have family laws which give religion and religious courts a strong influence in society. The Islamic states appoint the Sharia judges, and the Israeli government appoints the two Chief Rabbis. The influence of religion and clergy on general government policies varies from country to country, but again, the common denominator is that there are strong groups of religious extremists with considerable political influence.

Pertinent issues that must be addressed when discussing conflicts include the role of religious elements in the narratives of the relevant societies, the significance of holy sites, and the formal and informal relationships between religion and governing bodies.

The Role of Religious Actors Goes beyond Clergy

Religion is an organized enterprise, while religious faith and religious participation are a private matter. Opportunities for participation in religious activities and the transfer of the content of faith from generation to generation are always organized. To secure continuity, institutionalization of religion is inevitable.

The desire and need for religious dialogue and cooperation usually stem from crises, since crises tend to lead to increased religious activity. When people and society experience outside threats, feel insecure, or sense a need for strengthening group identities, there is always an increase in religious activity. It is as if people feel the need for protection by a higher power. This is also why religious leaders have special responsibilities in such situations; religion can be used to exacerbate and deepen conflicts. Therefore, religious leaders must show that religion is not only a refuge, but can also be a source of strength which is needed to take believers on the path to peace. Religious dialogue and cooperation between religious communities are useful instruments in such cases.

Peace negotiation-oriented dialogue does not take place on the individual level. Communities can open up to other communities, and individual members can contribute by establishing friendship, visiting other communities, and creating groups where encounters can take place. Clergy is important in such cases because of the leadership roles in the faith community. Religious scholars are important because contentious issues need to be dealt with on the basis of knowledge, insight, and professional judgment.

However, the author believes it is necessary to approach religious dialogue with a wider perspective. When religious dialogues seek to be relevant for peace negotiations, ties between political establishments and religious representatives must be strong, and include clergy, scholars, and lay people.

Religious Leaders' Tasks

If religious leaders want a role in efforts to create peace, they must rise above their own beliefs, history, or national politics.

a. Religious leaders must be able to recognize, respect, and appreciate the religious faith of followers of another religion. They are expected to bear witness to what they believe is the truth of their own religion, but they must be capable of listening to the other, even if they regard it as heresy or a false religion. The willingness to listen establishes faith itself as the common ground.

b. Religious leaders must have a perspective beyond their own faith and religion, showing an appreciation to how religion is intertwined with the identity of their people, their tribe, their nation, or their state. By doing so, they acknowledge that both their own religion and the religion of the other can be connected to culture, nationality, or ethnicity. This opens a field where dialogue can facilitate understanding of both oneself and the other.

c. Religious leaders should refrain from claims to superior access to God or the mind of God. An Iranian ayatollah once said that if we were to trust anyone's claims to speak on behalf of God, we would have many gods, since many make such claims. In a religiously charged environment like Iran, that was a political statement. It had, however, profound relevance for situations elsewhere, especially in the Holy Land. Such insight should lead to humility in both the face of God and other believers.

d. Holy Scriptures are dear to believers, and religious leaders are guides in interpreting them. The faithful can find in Holy Scriptures arguments for war, conflict, and no room for other faiths, but the same Scriptures also teach respect, peace, forgiveness, and reconciliation. Interpretation of Holy Scriptures means making choices. Religious leaders need to clarify what principles and what clues are needed to read Holy Scriptures in support of peace and justice.

e. In Western Europe, the Americas, and Africa, we are used to separation between religion and state. Religious leaders and scholars have their independence from the state. If and when the state is not dictatorial, this opens a space where religious leaders can act independently and freely speak their mind. But, according to Hurd, "secularist divisions between religion and politics are neither stable nor universal. They are fundamentally contested categories."[7] Different types of divisions and the seeming absence of such do not necessarily imply that there is no freedom of religion, or that political leaders direct the actions of religious leaders. Primarily, it means that the relationship between religion, politics, and civil society is organized differently, formally and/or informally. In many predominantly Muslim countries, religious leaders are closely linked to the political establishment and vice versa. In Judaism, the situation differs; between the Roman occupation and 1948, there was no Jewish state. In the modern state of Israel, the Chief Rabbinate is the Jewish authority and part of the government. The scope of the Chief Rabbis' involvement in politics differs; some speak critically of the government, others are linked to it and hesitate to criticize.

f. Religious leaders can intensify or escalate conflicts by stressing religious elements, claiming partial or exclusive ownership over places, words, symbols, narratives, and history. Particularly in instances where two or three religions have different narratives linked to the same place, one party cannot demand that others accept their account. Nevertheless, they can demand respect for their particular narrative. Competing narratives can be mutually enriching. Instead of delegitimizing the religious attachments of others, it is possible to seek a common vision for issues, places or symbols. Examples of delegitimizing behavior are when a Chief Rabbi asks why Muslims need Jerusalem as a holy city when they already have two others, Mecca and Medina. Or, a Supreme Judge of Sharia Courts says that Jews have no cultural or historical connections to Jerusalem.

They both reveal lack of respect for the other and perpetuate destructive divisions.

g. Religious leaders have a special responsibility for identifying religiously charged elements of a conflict. They should provide theological reasoning as to why and how these elements are charged, and their possible solution. Theology is about the relationship of the divine and the earthly. It must be instrumental in solving problems in respect of the shared belief that all humans are created by the same God and are supposed to live and survive in this world.

h. When religious leaders enter dialogue, internal discipline within the group is important. The following is an example of a pledge which was signed by all participants in the Council of Religious Institutions of the Holy Land;[8]

> *We declare that* (1) the meetings we have held, and wish to hold in the future, of leaders and representatives of the Religious Institutions and Establishments in the Holy Land are of urgent and utmost importance for a better future for our communities, locally and regionally, in order to achieve just peace and coexistence among the peoples of the region; (2) our private meetings have helped us find a formula for mutual dialogue; (3) statements published by us should be objective in order to improve the atmosphere of the dialogue.
>
> *Accordingly each one of us declares* (1) my statements emphasize the value of our collective effort and the fact that we are working to improve the atmosphere of dialogue between one another; (2) we shall avoid any public statement that could endanger our ability to work together; (3) collectively, we shall discuss the details of those matters upon which we most deeply disagree in our private meetings and not in public; (4) we shall emphasize the importance of our dialog and the good will between us despite our differences.
>
> *Each one of us will exercise the right to* acknowledge that there are issues upon which we disagree, but at the same time assert that we are discussing these issues with mutual respect

in an effort to reduce disagreement and promote dialogue towards comprehensive, just peace in the region and not declaring disagreement publicly so that we can achieve the aim of the dialogue.

We confirm that each one of us is committed to our endeavor to meet regularly in order to establish agreement and a shared agenda for discussion and action in the forthcoming months.

This code helped the Council overcome some serious difficulties at the time it was signed, and later made it possible to say that cooperation with some of the participants was no longer possible.

Facilitating Religious Dialogue

Religious dialogue is influenced by governments, bureaucrats, and public opinion, as much as it is directed by religious leaders.

The ability to listen must be transformed into a capacity to interpret what goes on in the dialogue itself. In a dialogue there are always significant differences between participants; some are well trained in theology, used to religious discourse, and have a good command of the language used. Others have scarce theological training, no experience in dialogue, little knowledge of other religions, and are in need of translation. Such differences in skill and training easily create tensions which can make mutual understanding difficult, and are detrimental to progress.

For instance, when one part wishes to freeze talks, the facilitator needs to listen in such a way that he or she can make the concerns of the one party understandable to the other. A freeze is not necessarily a negative development; it might be a necessary break providing the next meeting a good start.

Participation in religious dialogues may arouse a variety of emotions, including humiliation, superiority, anger, and a deep desire for being seen and heard. Some have a sense of humor, some do not. Some need to share a meal to speak, but a common meal is not always easy in interreligious dialogue. Religious sensitivities around food, cutlery, plates, and drinks can all be factors which may ease dialogue or strengthen tensions.

Knowledge of and curiosity about relevant religions are necessary qualifications for a good facilitator. Knowledge is necessary in order to foresee which issues are relevant for, and can be brought up in relation to an actual peace process. Curiosity is important because it demonstrates the personal involvement and engagement of the facilitator. A facilitator is always there as a person, relating to everybody, though he or she is not a religiously neutral person. In fact, no one is. Human beings always belong to or have a background in a religious tradition, whether or not they are believers.

The role of the facilitator must begin with deep respect for partners and their faith. A facilitator will be respected in his or her identity, but will be expected to rise above religious adherence. The same holds true for a facilitator's political viewpoints. What is most important is that a facilitator must be able to value and respect all positions and concerns. That must supersede any religious conviction or personal or political opinion a facilitator might otherwise possess.

Theories of religious dialogue often present roadmaps for how a dialogue can proceed. In real life, such maps are mostly irrelevant. Dialogues in conflict situations seldom proceed according to previously determined schemes. Too many unknown actors and factors are involved. Progress can be agreed, planned, but in the end is unpredictable. A facilitator will usually be tempted to move fast because he or she is an outsider who may have come to the conflict with clear goals in mind. To listen in and see what movements are possible and what may be counterproductive, is the special task of a facilitator. Patience is a virtue.

Closely linked to this, is the fundamental requirement that a facilitator must always be able to voice the concern of the other. When speaking with or to one of the parties, the other parties must be able to trust the facilitator to present their opinions and sentiments.

Someone once commented that a good facilitator must have "a passion for anonymity." While that might not be the final role of a facilitator or the role during dialogue, it is still a valid requirement in terms of general attitude. A facilitator must keep in mind that the participants own the process; a facilitator must be able to take, justly or unjustly, blame for failure, while success is attributed to the actors. Finally, a facilitator should strive to be unneeded, and should leave the scene once both sides are able to view and convey their counterpart's situation and conditions.

Relevant Issues for Religious Dialogues

When religious dialogue is part of wider efforts for peace, the key issues are not the concept of God, prayer, or redemption. Participants in this kind of religious dialogue are also part of a political conflict. Relevant issues for religious dialogue in conflict situations include the following:

Land. Many religions make connections between the land, the people or the nation, and faith. Connections can be made with reference to history – often with a mythological beginning – or by just stating that the land is given to them by God. The situation in the Holy Land is illustrative of this; both Jews and Muslims maintain that the land was given to them by God. Some Jews maintain that this awards them ownership of the land, the right to govern it, and to determine for others their rights and their place. Other Jews consider the land as given to them, but add that land should be governed by justice and with equal rights for all. Some Muslims claim that since the land was once controlled by Islam, it remains Islamic. Others want equal rights for all.

Holy sites. A site can be holy to one religion but not to another. In other cases, it can be holy to one religion, but is then taken over by another and made into a holy site. Former synagogues and mosques were transformed to churches in Spain; Hagia Sophia in Istanbul was built as a church, and then became a mosque. Now it is a museum. Then there are holy sites which are significant to more than one religion. The religious significance can be similar or different. The most contentious site in the conflict between Jews and Muslims in the Holy Land is the Haram al-Sharif/Temple Mount. Other examples are the Ibrahimi Mosque/Abraham's Tomb in Hebron, and Rachel's Tomb in Bethlehem.

Access to holy places. This issue is of course linked to the former, but is also related to religious liberty. Illustrative of this are examples from the Holy Land, where some sites are inaccessible because they are on the wrong side of the security fence/wall, as is the case with Rachel's Tomb in Bethlehem. Some are only partly accessible because security considerations are used to refuse entry, as is the case when access is limited or denied to the Church of the Holy Sepulchre in Jerusalem, the Church of the Nativity in Bethlehem, or the al-Aqsa Mosque in Jerusalem.

Concept of the other. Some religions have Holy Scriptures with descriptions of the other, like the Christian Bible and its description of Jews, or the Quran with its descriptions of Jews and Christians. Schoolbooks, newspapers, and other media may contain derogatory descriptions of the other. Religious dialogue has a special responsibility to see to it that their own educational materials treat other religions and believers with respect and dignity. Religious leaders have a special responsibility not to incite, but to speak well of each other and educate their congregation in doing likewise.

Acting together. The urge to action is a common human orientation which demonstrates the seriousness of our words and, in this case, the religious dialogue. Examples of such actions are (1) joint statements or calls to action which demonstrate agreement, but are also bold enough to mention those issues where there is disagreement and where the partners promise to discuss and hopefully deal with them; (2) study projects about schoolbooks, media, or theology. Relevant issues here are the concept of the other and derogatory statements, but also themes like justice and peace; (3) promoting contact between the faithful in the different communities; (4) discussing statements, sermons etc., which are issued by one of the parties and which may be heard or understood to be harmful by other parties in a dialogue; and (5) creating an office that can serve as a secretariat for the dialogue, but also as an informal meetings space for participants.

An established dialogue among religious leaders should seek encounters with those responsible for political negotiations for peace. That will enrich and introduce new elements both to the religious dialogue and to the political negotiations. Ideally this should make both of them more relevant to a process toward a sustainable peace.

Conclusion

Religious dialogue can present religion as a community of believers, who are all created by God; establish a theological foundation of the common humanity, a foundation which is created by God and therefore beyond human tensions; invite partners to identify religious elements which are of relevance to a political conflict, and thereby makes it possible to discuss and deal with them; open one's own religion to questions from other believers, thereby making it possible to discover new resources for peace in their own religion; deny space for religious incitement, and create space for constructive solutions where the integrity of all, religious or non-religious, can be respected.

In short, religious dialogue can clear the way for political decisions.

Notes

1   Samuel Huntington, *The Clash of Civilizations and the Remaking of World Order* (New York: Simon & Schuster, 1996).

2   Elisabeth Shakman Hurd, *The Politics of Secularism in International Relations* (Princeton and Oxford: Princeton University Press, 2008), p. 1.

3   Jose Casanova, *Public Religions in the Modern World* (Chicago: University of Chicago Press, 1994), p. 66.

4   Hurd, *The Politics of Secularism,* p. 145.

5   Ibid., p. 146.

6   Casanova, p. 220.

7   Hurd, *The Politics of Secularism.*

8   Council of Religious Institutions of the Holy Land, "Pledge," http://crihl.org/sites/default/files/2007%2001%20CRIHL-%20Pledge_0.pdf.

"Level II" Negotiation Strategies: Advance Your Interests by Helping to Solve Their Internal Problems

James K. Sebenius

Many negotiators have constituencies that must formally or informally approve an agreement. Traditionally, it is the responsibility of each negotiator to manage the internal conflicts and constituencies on his or her own side. Far less familiar are the many valuable ways that one side can meet its own interests by helping the other side with its "internal," "behind the table," or "Level II" constituency challenges. Moving from theory to practice and from simple to complex, the present paper builds on a moderately theoretical treatment of this challenge previously proposed. It illustrates several classes of practical measures that negotiators can use to advance their own interests by focusing on the other side's Level II negotiations. Beyond tailoring the terms of the deal for this purpose (e.g., with "compensation provisions"), one side can help the other, and vice versa, via a number of devices, alone or in concert. These include: a) shaping the form of the agreement (e.g. tacit vs. explicit, process vs. substance); b) tailoring the form of the negotiating process itself (to send a useful signal to constituencies); c) avoiding (or making) statements that inflame (or mollify) the other side's internal opponents; d) helping the other side attractively frame the deal for Level II acceptability; e) providing the ingredients for the other side to make an acceptance or even "victory speech" about why saying "yes" to the deal you want is smart and in the other side's interests; f) constructive actions at the bargaining table informed by knowledge of the other side's internal conflicts (e.g., not escalating when the other side mainly speaks for domestic purposes); g) having the first side work with the other side to tacitly coordinate outside pressure on the other side's Level II constituents to accept the deal that the first side prefers; and h) in extraordinary cases, by directly negotiating with one's counterparts to design measures that thwart its Level II opponents.

You are more likely to say "yes" to my proposal if it meets your interests. Frequently, your interests entail satisfying – or at least not alienating – less prominent constituencies, which might include a boss, spouse, client, union membership, community group, NGO, political party, or the U.S. Senate that must ratify the treaty you negotiate on behalf of the President. A potent barrier to success in negotiation is often the prospect of constituency rejection of the deal. Given this threat, if I am your counterpart in negotiation, one way to advance my interests can be for me to help you solve your internal constituency problems – in a manner consistent with my interests.

Of course, the reverse holds true as well: you may be able to help me with my constituencies at low cost to your interests. It turns out that sophisticated negotiators have been amazingly inventive in coming up with practical and highly valuable approaches to this often-unexplored challenge. This paper develops and illustrates several such approaches.

The challenge is hardly new. A number of analysts have explored how negotiators can productively synchronize "external," "at the table," or "Level I" negotiations with "internal," "behind the table," or "Level II" negotiations.[1] The useful terms, "Level I" and "Level II," come from Robert Putnam, who developed the concept of "two-level games" in the context of diplomacy and domestic politics.[2] In the simplest version of Putnam's conception, the Level I game focuses on traditional "at the table" diplomatic agreements, while the Level II game focuses on the formal or informal domestic ratification of such agreements "behind the table." Following this usage, but venturing well beyond its diplomatic origins, this paper uses Level I to refer to international/external/at the table negotiations. Level II refers to domestic/internal/behind the table negotiations. Of course, even where Level II parties do not have formal ratification power, they can often facilitate the implementation of agreements that they like and effectively block those that they do not.

In an example cited by Robert Mnookin and Ehud Eiran from Israeli-Palestinian negotiations, the Level II "behind the table" challenges may be even greater than the Level I "across the table" ones. The settlement population and their political advocates on the Israeli side as well as militant factions and diaspora Palestinians may, for separate reasons, make generally desirable deals impossible to reach or even publicly propose, when leaders estimate that they would not be able to gain sufficient public support to make – and to overcome the opposition to – the necessary compromises.[3]

Often implicit in much of this two-level negotiation work is the view that, if a (Level I) deal is reached across the table, each side's leadership is best positioned to manage its *own* internal (Level II) conflicts. Traditionally, a negotiator does this by 1) pressing for deal terms that will attract sufficient internal support and meet internal objections, and 2) effectively "selling" the agreement to key constituencies. Far less familiar are the many ways that one side can meet its own interests by helping the other side with the other's "behind the table" or Level II challenges (and vice versa). A moderately theoretical treatment of this challenge has been previously proposed.[4] Moving from theory to practice, from simple to complex, and from straightforward to creative, the present paper draws heavily and builds on that work. It illustrates several classes of practical measures that negotiators can use to advance their own interests by focusing on the other side's Level II negotiations. It concludes with a brief case study that describes the elegant Level II strategies of former U.S. Secretary of State James Baker and George H. W. Bush in dealing with the then-Soviet Union over German reunification within NATO.

Shape the terms of the deal to respond to their constituency concerns.
In its most familiar form, the deal itself can directly address constituency concerns. Terms can be crafted to meet the interests or overcome objections of enough internal players to permit a deal to be reached and, ideally, implemented and sustained. For example, free trade agreement provisions may be designed to compensate the domestic "losers" (harmed by trade liberalization) who might otherwise block the broader agreement. Or, at least on paper, the deal may be structured to make one or both negotiators "look good" to their bosses or constituents.

In an inventive example early in his career, former NYPD detective and hostage negotiator Dominick Misino faced a potentially explosive situation.

On a sweltering summer night in Spanish Harlem, 300 to 400 people stood outside a crowded tenement in which a young man with a loaded shotgun had barricaded himself. During the tense negotiations with Misino, the young man, a parole violator but not a murderer, told Misino that he wanted to surrender but couldn't because he would look weak. According to Misino,

> I told him that . . . if he let me cuff him, I would make it look as if I had to use force. He put down his gun and behaved like a perfect gentleman until we got to the street, where he started screaming like crazy and raising hell, as we had agreed.... The crowd was chanting "José! José!" in wild approval, and we threw him into the back of the car, jumped on the gas, and sped off. Two blocks later, José sat up, broke into a huge grin, and said to me, "Hey man, thank you." He recognized that I had given him a way out that didn't involve killing people and being killed in turn.[5]

At one level, this is a simple lesson by a savvy negotiator helping his counterpart save face with an important constituency in a potentially lethal situation. In settings from labor relations to high diplomacy, however, many negotiations display more complex versions of this same underlying structure: you (in this example: Misino) negotiate "externally" with your counterpart (here: José) who must somehow deal effectively with his or her "internal" constituencies (here: the crowd, José's community) in order for you to be successful (here: to avoid a shootout, bloodshed, and wider risks to the police, crowd, and neighborhood).

Important constituencies on one side often place high value on a principle whose full practical implementation would be unacceptable to the other side. In such cases, the principle may be enshrined in agreement, but its practical effect drastically reduced. For example, in Israeli-Palestinian negotiations, some "right of return" of Palestinian refugees may be agreed, but limited in practice to a token number of refugees who may actually settle within Israel proper with the majority to settle in the borders of a new Palestinian state.

Shape the form of the deal – from explicit to tacit or from substance to process – to avoid constituency problems. Level II costs may sometimes be reduced by changing the form of the deal. For example, making an agreement tacit rather than explicit may avoid constituency problems. Former U.S. Secretary of State George Shultz remarked about common diplomatic situations in which one of the parties effectively says, "I can live with that as long as I don't have to agree to it, but if you make me agree with it, I won't be able to live with it."[6]

Similarly, the presidents of two neighboring countries with a longstanding, emotional border dispute may privately concur that resolution would be valuable and may well agree on acceptable terms of a border deal. Yet to overtly negotiate and be seen to "concede" anything, for either or both sides, may be too costly in terms of the internal opposition it would arouse. However, submitting the dispute to an international arbitration process, appropriately constituted, may be an acceptable "willingness to go along with international law," with an arbitrator's award outside the will of the two presidents. By this device, the two presidents may reduce constituency costs. Strictly speaking, this approach also changes the content of the deal, from direct resolution of the issue to agreement on a process for resolving it, but its object is reducing Level II costs.

Change the negotiation process itself to enhance Level II acceptability. A closely related approach involves agreement on a negotiation process that sends a valuable signal to Level II players. A prominent labor negotiator once described a simple, if cynical, measure of this kind aimed at swaying union constituents. In this instance, given economic realities, both union and management negotiators clearly understood the feasible deal terms from the outset. However, too quick and easy an agreement would have raised union members' suspicions that their interests had not been vigorously advocated.

As such, the two negotiators tacitly agreed to make a show of locking themselves into a room from mid-afternoon until the wee hours of the morning. Those outside the room would often hear angry shouts and tables being pounded. Inside, the reality was congenial: with nice meals ordered in, plenty of alcohol, friendly reminiscences, and knowing chuckles as the two sides would periodically manufacture loud theatrical sounds to dramatize the negotiating "battle" being "fought" – all for the benefit of outside constituencies. Finally emerging, haggard, in predawn hours, the two sides' "hard won" agreement had a far greater chance of acceptance among union members, given a process that mollified their suspicions of a sellout, without altering the terms of the negotiated contract itself.

Agree to avoid making statements that cause problems among the other's constituents. In an example of inadvertent negative handling of Level II issues, consider the Geneva Accord, a prominent, unofficial effort to craft an Israeli-Palestinian peace deal. After an important negotiating session, a key Israeli participant sought to indicate progress to key Israeli constituents. He was quoted to the effect that the "Palestinians had given up the right of return." This claim echoed negatively among Palestinian publics, generated nearly instant denials, and damaged prospects for wider support of this initiative.[7]

More broadly, leaders on each side may make statements in Arabic or Hebrew about peace talks or agreements that are intended for "domestic consumption." Inevitably, however, such statements rapidly find their way to the other side, generating suspicion and undermining what may be genuine progress at the table. In a media and internet-intensive age, hoped-for "acoustic separation" – separately conveying contradictory messages to different publics – often proves futile.

As such, Level I negotiators may explicitly work together not only on the terms of the deal itself but on what each side will or will not say about it to Level II parties. For example, President Reagan made human rights a top priority in his negotiations with the Soviets. In a glaring illustration of this issue, some sixty Pentecostals were holed up in the U.S. embassy in Moscow seeking sanctuary. In dealing with the Soviet Ambassador Anatoly Dobrynin on this issue, Reagan said, "Let them emigrate. You won't hear any crowing from me." With this assurance, U.S. Secretary of State George Shultz and Dobrynin negotiated, eventually agreeing on the release of the Pentecostals to Israel. As Shultz reported, "Despite the great political temptation to do so, [Reagan] never boasted about the success of this deal, so the Soviets learned that he could be trusted."[8]

In predictably rancorous negotiations with the Soviets over withdrawal from Afghanistan following the invasion of 1979, George Shultz reported that Foreign Minister Eduard Shevardnadze pulled him aside privately. Shevardnadze told Shultz, "We are going to go through familiar arguments out there but I want you to know that we have decided to leave Afghanistan. There will be no immediate announcement, but we've made the decision;

it's behind us. We want to get out by the end of 1988. How the United States acts will make a difference because the quicker we're out, the less blood will be shed." Though it was controversial within the U.S. administration, Shultz reported that the U.S. government was "able to maneuver in such a way that the Soviets left Afghanistan sooner than anyone had expected and much bloodshed was avoided as a result."[9]

Help the other side attractively frame the deal for Level II acceptability; provide the ingredients for the other side to make an acceptance or even "victory speech" about why saying "yes" to the deal you want is smart and in the other side's interests. William Ury observes that "your counterpart's constituents may attack the proposed agreement as unsatisfactory. So think about how your counterpart can present it to them in the most positive light, perhaps even as a victory."[10] Ury offers the following example from the Cuban missile crisis, above and beyond Kennedy's tacit agreement to remove arguably obsolete U.S. missiles from Turkey:

> Kennedy and his advisers...searched for a way to make it easier for Soviet Premier Nikita Khrushchev to withdraw Soviet missiles from Cuba. Kennedy decided to offer Khrushchev his personal pledge that the United States would not invade Cuba. Since Kennedy had no intention of invading anyway, the promise was easy to make. But it allowed Khrushchev to announce to his constituents in the Communist world that he had successfully safeguarded the Cuban revolution from American attack. He was able to justify his decision to withdraw the missiles on the grounds that they had served their purpose.[11]

Ury later counsels Side A to think about helping to equip Side B to write B's "acceptance speech," in a manner that meets A's interests, directed toward B's constituencies. As a tool to help craft the other side's acceptance speech, Ury also suggests making a chart listing several key factors, embellished from the original:

a. Precisely who B's constituencies are along with their likely interests and perceptions of the negotiation.

b. Key themes and framing of the "acceptance speech" or even "victory speech" that will make it persuasive.

c. Most likely criticisms and questions such as, "what exactly did you give up and why"; "you never should have made that concession, which gives away our vital interests"; "that makes us look weak and sets a terrible precedent"; and "you should push back hard rather than giving in!"

d. Best anticipatory and subsequent responses to the most important such criticisms.[12]

In fact, if A has probed and understood B's interests, perspectives, and constituencies in enough depth to help craft a credible acceptance speech for B, the range of actually feasible deals should be much clearer to A. And obviously, the easier a time B foresees having with his or her constituencies, the more likely B is to make a deal with A. This approach should, paraphrasing the words of Italian diplomat Daniel Vare, permit "B to have A's way."

Going beyond mere framing and suggested spin; have the first side actually work with the other side to tacitly coordinate outside pressure on the other side's Level II constituents to accept the deal that the first side prefers. It is possible to go well beyond the statements each side can make, or refrain from making, about how a deal can be framed for domestic consumption, or how one side can help the other write its victory speech. Indeed, Side A can sometimes arrange with Side B to bring outside pressure to bear on Side A's own Level II constituents to change their views in line with Side B's preferences.

For example, U.S. Ambassador Stuart Eizenstat negotiated with Germany in the mid-1990s over Holocaust-era assets and slave labor used by the Nazis and German firms. Key issues in this tense, emotional process included compensation amounts to surviving victims as well as "legal peace," or an end to further claims against German companies after any agreement. Eizenstat and his German counterpart, Count Otto Lambsdorff, had known each other for many years and cultivated a relationship that meant, in Eizenstat's words, that "we were able to share confidences with each other. We were able to share with each other what our constituencies were pressing us to do." Eizenstat elaborated how Lambsdorff helped to orchestrate Presidential pressure on the German Chancellor to be more forthcoming in negotiation:

> And so I had a very good idea from Lambsdorff of the fact that his companies were being recalcitrant on legal peace, [and

why they were] not coming up with enough money. He gave me advice as to how to deal with that, in the same way I gave him advice as to how to deal with my domestic constituents. He suggested that I get President Clinton to send [Chancellor] Schroeder a letter. It was not my suggestion. And that [letter] helped unlock a lot of money that otherwise wouldn't have been forthcoming. So the fact that we had known each other literally for 25 years, had kept in contact with each other, and had complete and utter trust in each other helped us understand each other's constituencies and where the red lines were and where there was room for give.[13]

In a more elaborate example, during the preparations for the 1978 Bonn economic summit, there was significant internal U.S. opposition to oil price decontrol, a policy strongly favored by America's key economic partners as part of a package involving German and Japanese stimulus, policies themselves opposed by powerful German and Japanese factions. In a conventional interpretation, ultimate international agreement on these decontrol and stimulus measures, which were actually implemented in each country, simply resulted from mutually beneficial tradeoffs in a package deal.[14] A closer look, however, reveals actions by each side to help others with their Level II domestic challenges. For example, to overcome potent U.S. domestic opposition to oil price decontrol, Putnam reports that "American negotiators occasionally invited their foreign counterparts to put more pressure on the Americans [at home] to reduce oil imports." Ultimately, such interventions aimed at influencing (Level II) U.S. opponents proved successful.[15]

Similarly, to internal advocates of economic stimulus in Germany and Japan, external pressure for such actions – in some cases orchestrated by these advocates and willingly supplied by foreign counterparts – overcame opposition and tipped the internal balance. As Putnam describes it, "Within Germany, a political process catalyzed by foreign pressures was surreptitiously orchestrated by expansionists inside the Schmidt government... Publicly, Helmut Schmidt posed as reluctant to the end. Only his closest advisors suspected the truth: that the chancellor 'let himself be pushed' into a policy that he privately favored." And in Japan, "Without the external pressure, it is even more unlikely that the expansionists could have overridden the powerful MOF [Ministry of Finance]." "Seventy percent foreign pressure, 30 percent internal politics," was the disgruntled judgment of one MOF insider. "Fifty-fifty," guessed an official from MITI [Ministry of Trade and Industry].[16]

These examples begin to flesh out the means by which a Level I negotiator can help with the other side's Level II challenges. Yet as we will see via the extended example in the next section, these methods hardly exhaust the remarkable repertoire of such devices that can be used singly or in appropriate combination.

Case study: Using multiple Level II strategies in negotiations over German reunification within NATO.[17] A more elaborate episode involved the delicate U.S. diplomacy with the then-Soviet Union over German reunification within NATO after the fall of the Berlin Wall.[18] Soviet President Mikhail Gorbachev faced powerful internal opponents to his policies of perestroika in general as well as his increasing willingness to go along with American advocacy of German unification, especially within NATO. The KGB, the Politburo, and conservative politicians, as well much of the military felt Gorbachev was conceding far too much to the West. With almost 400,000 Soviet troops in East Germany and potent Four Power legal rights earned at the conclusion of World War II, the Soviets had several potent methods at their disposal to block German reunification within NATO.

Wanting perestroika to succeed and Germany to be reunified within NATO, then-President George H. W. Bush and his Secretary of State, James Baker, proved themselves to be extremely skilled Level II negotiators in at least four ways: 1) consciously avoiding actions that would cause domestic problems for their reformist Soviet counterparts, 2) helping the Soviets craft a convincing domestic explanation of the direction that negotiations over Germany were taking, 3) choosing not to escalate around inflammatory negotiating statements made by the Soviets for domestic consumption, and 4) directly working with their Soviet at the table counterparts to help the Soviet reformers overcome their powerful domestic opponents. Their actions in this important, even singular, case carry broader implications.

First, as the Berlin Wall fell, Bush and Baker realized that the American response could exacerbate already huge domestic problems for Gorbachev and Foreign Minister Shevardnadze. Echoing Reagan's agreement not to "crow" about his human rights deal, Robert Zoellick, counselor to Baker and himself a key American negotiator during the reunification talks, cited the value to the process of "Gorbachev's [correct] belief that [President] Bush would not exult . . . or convey any sense of triumphalism." Baker observed that

> [President Bush] got a lot of grief at the time the Wall fell for not gloating and pounding the chest and being more emotional about the fact that finally, after 40 years, the West, led by the United States, had won the Cold War. And I remember we'd sit in these meetings and he'd say . . . I don't want to hear anybody gloating about this, because we've got a lot of business to do still with Gorbachev and [Soviet Foreign Minister Eduard] Shevardnadze. [Bush adopted] that position in the face of a lot of domestic criticism. I never will forget a huge press conference . . . and we had a ton of press there, and they were beating up on him, asking "why can't you be a little more emotional?" He finally looked up at them and he said, look, we've got some business still to do. *We're not going to dance on the ruins of the Wall* [emphasis added].[19]

Baker later reports an encounter between Bush and Gorbachev at which Bush noted the stinging public criticism in the U.S. that Bush had taken for seeming to lack "the vision thing" in the context of German reunification. Bush stated, "I hope you've noticed that as change has accelerated in Eastern Europe recently, we haven't responded with flamboyance or arrogance so as to make your situation difficult. They say, 'Bush is too timid, too cautious'...I've tried to conduct myself in a way so as not to complicate your difficulties'....Gorbachev said that he'd noticed that and appreciated it."[20]

Second, as Robert Zoellick emphasized, "We even helped our Soviet counterparts to develop a public explanation of how the outcome took account of Soviet interests and sensitivities."[21] Baker elaborates how this was done, in part with reference to deliberate Western actions on security, political, and economic issues: "We had already planned to take all these steps individually, but by wrapping them in a package and calling them the 'nine assurances,' we greatly enhanced their political effect and assured the Kremlin that it would see their full impact. The package was designed so that . . . the Soviets would not be handed an abject defeat. Above all, it was an effort on our part to stand in Gorbachev's shoes and help frame the issue so that he would have a domestic explanation."[22]

Third, understanding the other side's political situation may lead to progress via restraint at the bargaining table in the face of apparent provocation and backsliding. As the internal tug-of-war between the Soviet reformers Gorbachev and Shevardnadze and their conservative opponents heated up, at the table progress was the victim. For example, the crucial (positive) turning point in the reunification negotiations occurred at a White House meeting during which Gorbachev agreed to respect German sovereignty after reunification and to permit Germany to choose its alliance. As a practical matter, this meant NATO. Weeks later, however, in Berlin talks, Shevardnadze made a lengthy, confrontational statement in which he harshly repudiated these core concessions. Baker suspected that there had been a reversal in Moscow against the reformers. Choosing to respond firmly, but not to escalate and force the issue, which could have led to a damaging standoff, he sent his top staffer, Dennis Ross, Director of the State Department's Policy Planning Staff, to find out what happened. Ross privately confronted his counterpart, Sergei Tarasenko, with whom he had established a close back channel relationship. "This is a total reversal," Ross said, "you guys just screwed us. What the hell is going on?"[23]

Ross learned that Shevardnadze had been forced to present a Politburo-prepared document, which could not be reversed (was "frozen") at least until the end of the upcoming Party Congress. It soon became apparent to Baker "that [Shevardnadze] was posturing for the benefit of his military, and that what he was saying really wasn't what he believed."[24] At this point, however, in Baker's eyes, Shevardnadze was "as beleaguered as I'd ever seen him," "the domestic situation was clearly overwhelming him," and he "couldn't predict" whether Gorbachev would be able to maintain his status as Party General Secretary.[25]

Fourth, in light of this perilous situation, Bush and Baker took extraordinary negotiating measures. They worked directly with Shevardnadze to equip him and Gorbachev with ammunition to meet their upcoming Party Congress challengers. In part for this purpose, President Bush and Secretary Baker negotiated internal U.S. government agreement on strong, specific measures – arms control and nuclear strategic doctrine – that would increasingly transform NATO more toward a political than a military alliance. As Baker stated, "I told Shevardnadze that we were proposing the adoption of a declaration at the London NATO Summit that would highlight the alliance's adaptation to a new, radically different world."[26] Baker described the unorthodox process and objective of this action:

> [The Declaration] was just twenty-two paragraphs long – exactly the kind of succinct political statement that would play well in Moscow. But first we had to gain agreement from the other fifteen members of NATO. Breaking with tradition, we decided to hold the text closely, and have the President send it to fellow heads of state just days before the summit, and to allow it to be negotiated only by foreign ministers and leaders at the summit itself. NATO, like any institution, has its own bureaucracy, and we couldn't afford to allow bureaucrats to water down what was a critical political document. Moreover, we didn't want any leaks. We wanted the maximum political impact in Moscow when the declaration would finally be released, and that meant following this unusual, and somewhat high-risk strategy.[27]

Not only did Baker lead the negotiations for NATO members to adopt this document in London; he coordinated the process closely with his Soviet counterparts: "To help Shevardnadze, I sent him a draft of the declaration, hoping to put the reformers a step ahead of the reactionaries as the Party Congress heated up."[28] Robert Zoellick later elaborated: This was "extremely helpful, Shevardnadze went on to say, because it would enable him to pre-empt opponents like Marshall Akhromeyev... And that is precisely what he did. We had progressed to the point where the American and Soviet foreign ministers could plan secretly how to use tentative NATO language to persuade the Soviet Union to accept a unified Germany within NATO."[29] Confirming the effects of these Level II actions after the Party Congress, Shevardnadze told Baker, "without the [London NATO] declaration, it would have been a very difficult thing for us to take our decisions on Germany.... If you compare what we're saying to you and to Kohl now with our Berlin document [the basis of Shevardnadze's apparent hardline reversal], it's like day and night. Really, it's like heaven and earth."[30]

Of course, the American negotiating strategy was not limited to helping Soviet reformers with their behind the table challenges, though that is the focus of the present paper. As Dennis Ross emphasizes, a complementary series of American actions was intended to "leave no doubt that it would be futile and counterproductive [for the Soviets] to try to prevent reunification."[31] And it would be the height of misinterpretation to imagine that Bush and Baker were motivated by altruism or primary concern for the other side. Rather, these Level II actions and understandings were aimed at accomplishing a central goal of American foreign policy at the Level I table. As Baker stressed at a particularly contentious moment in negotiating NATO acceptance of its extraordinary declaration:

> "Gentlemen," I was forced to say at one point, "we should keep our eye on the ball. The reason we are here, the reason we are working on this declaration, is to get Germany unified. We do not need to water down this document. It would be a mistake. We have one shot at this. These are different times. This is not business as usual."[32]

Synthesis: Helping the Other Side with Its Level II Barriers

To help the other side with its behind the table challenges requires first and foremost that one understand the other side and the barriers it faces. As James Baker stressed in his remarks upon receiving Harvard's 2012 Great Negotiator Award, "If there was a single key to whatever success I've enjoyed in business and diplomacy, it has been my ability to crawl into the other guy's shoes. When you understand your opponent, you have a better chance of reaching a successful conclusion with him or her. That means paying attention to how he or she views issues and appreciating the constraints they face." Beyond German reunification, Baker elaborated: "This approach helped us build the Gulf War coalition that ejected Saddam Hussein from Kuwait in 1991. Effective U.S. leadership depended on our ability to persuade others to join with us. That required us to appreciate what objectives, arguments, and trade-offs were important to our would-be partners."[33]

In part, this meant direct understanding via high level personal diplomacy, backed by expert staff work drawing on regional experts. Yet carefully cultivating close back channel relationships, such as the one between Dennis Ross and Shevardnadze's chief assistant and confidant Sergei Tarasenko, also proved vital. Similar back channel relationships were consciously developed between Americans and Germans: Robert Blackwill at the National Security Council with Horst Teltschik, Kohl's national security advisor, and Robert Zoellick with Frank Elbe, right hand man to Hans-Dietrich Genscher, Germany's Foreign Minister.[34]

The admonition to understand the other side is, of course, standard negotiation advice. Yet the most common objective of mutual understanding lies in figuring out a creative deal design that meets each side's interests. The actions of Baker and his team with respect to German reunification, however, highlight another rationale for developing such an understanding: helping the other side overcome its constituency barriers. As Ross put it, "I would coordinate with Tarasenko before the meetings to avoid surprises or to find out where there were problems that would have to be managed.... [These] made it possible to understand a Soviet move and how U.S. or German responses might affect the maneuverings in Moscow... It also permitted us to design the words and actions that each of us could use to help the other."[35]

To successfully craft actions for this purpose, one side cannot limit its knowledge of the other to the interests of at-the-table negotiators. Rather, one side must deeply understand the context in which its counterpart is enmeshed: the web of favorable and opposing constituencies as well as their relationships, perceptions, sensitivities, and interests. Recall the value for this purpose of direct, trusting relationships such as that nurtured by Stuart Eizenstat with his German counterpart, Otto Lambsdorff, in negotiations over Holocaust-era assets and slave labor.

Armed with this understanding, it becomes possible for one side to help the other side with its Level II challenges. Beyond tailoring the terms of the Level I deal for this purpose (e.g., with "compensation provisions"), one side can help the other, and vice versa, via a number of devices, alone or in combination:

a. by the form of the agreement (e.g. tacit vs explicit, process vs. substance);
b. by the form of the negotiating process itself (to send a useful signal to constituencies);
c. by avoiding (or making) statements that inflame (or mollify) the other side's internal opponents;
d. by helping the other side attractively frame the deal for Level II acceptability;
e. by providing the ingredients for the other side to make an acceptance or even "victory speech" about why saying "yes" to the deal you want is smart and in the other side's interests;
f. by constructive actions at the bargaining table informed by knowledge of the other side's internal conflicts (e.g., not escalating when the other side mainly speaks for domestic purposes);
g. by the first side's working with the other side to tacitly coordinate outside pressure on the other side's Level II constituents to accept the deal that the first side prefers; and
h. in extraordinary cases, by directly negotiating with one's Level I counterparts to design measures that thwart its Level II opponents.

A negotiator's primary (Level I) task, of course, is to work out a great deal with his or her counterparts. And each negotiator bears a substantial responsibility to successfully manage his or her internal (Level II) constituency challenges. These familiar subjects have attracted large literatures. Yet another potentially valuable tool in the sophisticated negotiator's toolkit involves each side helping the other with the other's Level II, behind the table constituency conflicts and challenges. While under-researched and under-appreciated, this rich Level II dynamic deserves far more attention from researchers and negotiators than it has thus far received.

Notes

I appreciate useful input from and most helpful conversations with Max Bazerman, Nancy Buck, Shai Feldman, Alex Green, David Lax, Paul Levy, Robert Mnookin, William Ury, Michael Wheeler, and participants in the Harvard Negotiation Roundtable. This paper draws directly and heavily on James K. Sebenius, "Level Two Negotiations: Helping the Other Side Meet Its 'Behind-the-Table' Challenges," *Negotiation Journal* 29, no. 1 (2013): 7-21.

1   See, for example, Richard Walton and Robert McKersie, *A Behavioral Theory of Labor Negotiations* (New York: McGraw-Hill, 1965); David A. Lax and James K.

Sebenius, *The Manager as Negotiator* (New York: Free Press, 1986), chapter 17; Robert D. Putnam, "Diplomacy and Domestic Politics: The Logic of Two-Level Games," *International Organization* 42, no. 3 (1988): 427-60.

2   Putnam's "Diplomacy and Domestic Politics" builds on a long tradition of "internal-external" negotiation analysis, starting with Walton and McKersie in the field of labor relations, as well as Howard Raiffa, *The Art and Science of Negotiation* (Cambridge, MA: Harvard University Press, Belknap Press, 1982); and Lax and Sebenius that extensively analyzed games with multilevel structures. Robert H. Mnookin and Ehud Eiran, in "Discord 'Behind the Table': The Internal Conflict among Israeli Jews Concerning the Future of Settlements in the West Bank and Gaza," *Journal of Dispute Resolution* 1 (2005): 11-44, has more recently developed this theme in the context of Israeli settlements.

3   See note 2.

4   Sebenius, "Level Two Negotiations."

5   Dominick Misino, "Negotiating Without a Net: A Conversation with the NYPD's Dominick Misino," *Harvard Business Review* (October 2002): 49-54. Bill Ury directed me to this example.

6   George P. Shultz, *Ideas & Action: Featuring the 10 Commandments of Negotiation* (Erie, PA: Free to Choose Press, 2010).

7   I learned about this incident from Shai Feldman.

8   Shultz, *Ideas & Action*, p. 95.

9   Ibid., p. 75.

10   William Ury, *Getting Past No* (New York: Bantam, 1991), p. 122.

11   Ibid., p. 123.

12   William Ury, *The Power of a Positive No* (New York: Bantam-Dell, 2007).

13   Stuart E. Eizenstat, transcript (electronic, without page numbers), Great Negotiator Awards Program, Program on Negotiation, Cambridge, Mass: Fletcher School of Law and Diplomacy at Tufts University and Harvard, 2003.

14   Putnam, "Diplomacy and Domestic Politics." See also R. Putnam and N. Bayne, *Hanging Together: Cooperation and Conflict in the Seven-Power Summits* (Cambridge, MA: Harvard University Press, 1987).

15   Ibid., p. 429.

16   Ibid., pp. 428-29.

17   This section draws directly from Sebenius, "Level Two Negotiations."

18   This pivotal episode has generated a vast literature. Among the best accounts are Philip Zelikow and Condoleezza Rice, *Germany Unified and Europe Transformed: A Study in Statecraft* (Cambridge, MA: Harvard University Press, 1995); and Frank Elbe and Richard Kiessler, *A Round Table with Sharp Corners: The Diplomatic Path to German Unity* (Baden-Baden: Nomos, 1996). The following discussion

relies heavily on these sources plus, especially, James A. Baker, *The Politics of Diplomacy: Revolution, War and Peace, 1989-1992* (New York: Putnam, 1995); James A. Baker, transcript (electronic, without page numbers), Great Negotiator Awards Program, Program on Negotiation, Cambridge, Mass: Harvard University, 2012; Dennis Ross, *Statecraft* (New York: Farrar, Straus and Giroux, 2007); and Robert B. Zoellick, "Two Plus Four: The Lessons of German Unification," *National Interest* (fall 2000): 17-28.

19 Baker, transcript.

20 Baker, *The Politics of Diplomacy*, p. 170.

21 Zoellick, "Two Plus Four," p. 19.

22 Baker, *The Politics of Diplomacy*, p. 251.

23 Ibid., p. 256.

24 Baker, transcript.

25 Baker, *The Politics of Diplomacy*, p. 257.

26 Ibid.

27 Ibid., p. 258.

28 Ibid., p. 259.

29 See Zoellick, "Two Plus Four," pp. 19, 25.

30 Baker, *The Politics of Diplomacy*, p. 259.

31 Ross, *Statecraft*, p .41.

32 Baker *The Politics of Diplomacy*, pp. 259-60.

33 Baker, transcript.

34 Ross, *Statecraft*, p. 45.

35 Ibid.

Constructive Negotiations in Contentious Contexts

Louis Kriesberg

Negotiations are often conducted in the context of ongoing contentious behavior by members of the adversarial sides. In some cases such behavior prevents the adversaries from reaching or implementing a negotiated agreement. In other cases, some behavior beyond the negotiations table hastens reaching an agreement or improves its qualities. This article focuses on large scale conflicts and examines the coercion-related conduct of the leaders and the negotiating teams of the opposing sides, of various factions within the opposing sides, and of parties not directly engaged as partisans in the conflict. It then considers how those sets of people can behave more constructively and reduce the destructive coercion of other stakeholders in the conflict. It concludes with six policy recommendations.

Negotiations are affected not only by negotiators and their superiors who direct them. Some members of one or more adversarial collectives may also influence the negotiating positions of their side to be tougher or more conciliatory. In addition, they may also act directly toward the opponents in order to change the conduct of the other side in the negotiations. Moreover, the beginning of negotiations between contending adversaries does not necessarily mean the end of coercive or even violent actions between them.[1] The coercive actions may continue at the behest of the leaders on both sides, or they may be perpetrated against the wishes of those leaders, being intended to stop or shape the negotiations.

Coercion is generally seen as harmful to negotiating mutually beneficial agreements. This is particularly evident in the Israeli-Palestinian negotiation attempts. During the negotiations that began in July 2013, mediated by Secretary of State John Kerry, leaders on each side viewed actions by the other as coercive and as sabotaging the negotiations. At the same time, however, coercion can be useful and its ill effects lessened.

Multiple Stakeholders Affecting Coercion in Negotiations

Any side negotiating in a contentious relationship is never entirely unified. Some factions or elements of one or more sides may strive for outcomes that are harsher or more conciliatory than what the negotiators believe to be correct. How much unity there is among one side may be unclear, certainly to the other side. Police or military personnel may engage in actions that are more punitive than their civilian superiors would want, or conversely, they may be unwilling to act as punitively as their civilian commanders might wish. In any case, negotiators do not act in isolation either from others on the respective sides or from outsiders who try to influence the negotiations.

Three sets of people can affect negotiations in various coercive ways. First are the leaders directing or engaged directly in the negotiations that at times employ coercion. Two other sets of people, not directly engaged in the negotiations, may believe that their concerns are inadequately represented and thus may resort to coercion in an attempt to advance them. One set comprises people internal to one side in the talks, and includes people publicly protesting and opposition party leaders recommending different bargaining strategies. Some of them may act coercively against their own side's policies or the policies of the other side. Such people may be called spoilers, quitters, traitors, patriots, or many other names, depending upon how their actions are judged by those conducting the negotiations or by observers.[2] Finally, some engaged stakeholders are outsiders who intervene in the conflict, whether to aid one of the negotiating parties or to gain benefits for themselves. Their stake in the conflict may be to prevent it from spreading further, to help protect or advance values that are important to them, or to enhance their own interests.

Negotiators who Coerce

Negotiation leaders often undertake coercive actions openly or covertly in order to improve their bargaining position, impose a settlement, or demonstrate resolve and toughness to their constituents. Clearly, some kinds of coercion are more compatible with negotiations than are others. In President Obama's administration, the mobilization of multilateral sanctions, combined with the offer of serious dialogue, produced an opening for substantive negotiations with Iran.[3] In June 2013, Hassan Rouhani ran as a moderate and won the presidential elections in Iran. In November 2013, Iran and the P5+1 (the permanent members of the Security Council and Germany) announced that they had negotiated an interim agreement. Iran agreed to stop and reduce several elements of its nuclear program and permit a more rigorous inspection system (even though other elements of the deal allowed Iran to move forward in R&D in more advanced generation centrifuges, and these elements offset the restraints mandated by the deal). In exchange, the P5+1 agreed to lift about $7 billion worth of sanctions.

Generally, coercion during negotiations indicates that the terms of an agreement are not viewed as readily attainable and mutually acceptable. It also indicates considerable mutual mistrust. In some such circumstances, carefully crafted mutual confidence building measures may be taken, for example, an exchange of prisoners.[4] Another possibility is to conduct secret negotiations, as was done between National Security Advisor Henry Kissinger and North Vietnamese representative Le Duc Tho during the Vietnam War.[5] These are some operational alternatives or complements to coercion.

Insiders Influencing One's Own Side

Persons and groups trying to influence their own side's negotiating stance may press for either a harder approach or a more conciliatory approach than the one chosen by the negotiators for their own side. In some cases, the official line is attacked from both directions.

Hard Line Approach

The intentions of engaged stakeholders are often to score more for their own side or their specific faction. For a party in a weaker power position, popular agitation often serves to reduce the conflict's asymmetry and gain a hearing and an outcome that is more equitable. Thus, during the civil rights struggle in the American South, Dr. Martin Luther King, Jr. and other leaders of mainstream civil rights organizations conducted nonviolent boycotts and demonstrations in order to achieve specific outcomes. As the civil rights movement grew, some new organizations emerged that used more radical rhetoric and more militant tactics, as exemplified by the Black Power movement and the Black Panthers. This had contradictory implications for the more mainstream negotiators. On the one hand they could use those developments as a warning to their negotiating counterparts that if their demands were not met, more dire demands and acts would be taken by others on their side. On the other hand, the militancy of some on their side could and did raise fears and increase resistance from many whites.[6]

In many circumstances, negotiators believe that actions by hard line advocates in their camp undermine their negotiations, reducing the trust in them by the negotiators on the other side. For example, in 2014, during the initial interim agreement between Iran and the P5+1, many members of the U.S. Congress supported a resolution that would intensify the sanctions against Iran. The Obama administration held firm, contending that such a resolution would undermine the interim agreement, which was the basis for negotiating a comprehensive agreement. The resolution stalled and negotiations continued.

At times small groups may attempt to defame the country's official leaders as overly conciliatory toward an adversary, as happened in the attacks on Israeli Prime Minister Yitzhak Rabin. Many Jewish Israeli critics of the Oslo peace process vilified Rabin, condemning him as a traitor to the Jewish people. The attacks intensified until a Jewish religious extremist assassinated him in November 1995. His successor, Prime Minister Shimon Peres, led the government in implementing the interim agreement that had been signed shortly before Rabin was killed.[7] At the same time, Peres too believed it was important to demonstrate firmness against Palestinian militancy, a stance that in turn was met by suicide bombings against Israeli civilians. The Likud party, led by Benjamin Netanyahu, subsequently won the next elections and negotiations stalled.

In South Africa, violence escalated when the transition toward non-racial democracy began in 1990. From mid-1990, when negotiations for the transition began, until April 1994, when democratic elections were held, about 14,000 South Africans died in politically related incidents.[8] Some deaths were caused by security forces using lethal force in policing public disorder, but much of the violence was among black groups, particularly between two ethnicities, the Xhosa and the Zulu, and two political organizations, the African National Congress (ANC) and the Inkatha Freedom Party (IFP), associated with the Zulu seeking a larger role in the emerging new system. In addition, a "third force," consisting of right wing whites linked to the government security forces, supported violence perpetrated by some of the IFP, in hopes of breaking up the negotiations. According to the Truth and Reconciliation Commission Report, the government initially was allied with the IFP, but abandoned it by June 1992.

Conciliatory Approach

Often elements within one side or another seek to have the negotiators for their side adopt a more conciliatory approach in order to reach a peace agreement. For example, during a few episodes of U.S.-Soviet arms control negotiations during the Cold War, there were spikes in peace movement mobilizations conducting major public campaigns supporting more conciliatory U.S. positions. Such was the case in the mid-1960s, with opposition to nuclear weapons testing in the atmosphere.[9]

The resistance to U.S. engagement in the war in Vietnam during the Johnson and Nixon administrations took several, largely nonviolent, forms. Many different demands were made, including simple withdrawal, but also negotiating a withdrawal on terms acceptable to the North Vietnam government. The widespread resistance to the war included leading political figures, and influenced the entry into negotiations and conclusion of the agreement on the U.S. military's departure from Vietnam.[10] Some of the opposition's tactics and subsequent U.S. defeat, however, offended more traditionally-thinking Americans and contributed to a subsequent legacy of hardliners striving to overcome the Vietnam syndrome.

President Ronald Reagan's aggressive rhetoric and actions were popular with the segment of the American public dismayed by what they viewed as earlier signs of US international weakness. The militancy of the U.S. policies in the early 1980s in turn reawakened vigorous resistance, with implications for arms control negotiations with the USSR. For example, support for a freeze on nuclear weapons spread rapidly across America through local government resolutions and large scale demonstrations.[11] Resistance was also strong and influential against U.S. intervention in Central American countries supporting right wing governments and right wing militia groups challenging left wing governments.[12]

In Israel, following the momentous visit to Jerusalem by Egyptian President Anwar al-Sadat in November 1977, negotiations mediated by President Jimmy Carter reached framework agreements for future treaties. However, negotiations for a peace treaty between Israel and Egypt stagnated. The Israeli Peace Now movement was established in 1978, when Israeli reserve army officers and combat soldiers joined together to urge their government to conclude a peace treaty with Egypt. Peace Now continued to work for a negotiated peace agreement between Israel and the Palestinians, and came to be known for its ability to mobilize mass demonstrations and conduct comprehensive monitoring of Israeli settlement activity in the West Bank.

Outsider Interventions

Persons and groups who are not directly engaged as adversaries in a conflict can act in many ways that affect the course and outcome of negotiations between adversaries in a conflict. This may include their own use of coercion to influence the adversaries' reliance on violence. There are many different kinds of coercion that affect the conditions for negotiation, supporting harder or more conciliatory negotiation goals.

Hard Line Approach

Often outsiders exert their efforts to bolster one side, usually to toughen the position in question. During the Cold War, conflicts in many countries were sustained by U.S. and Soviet government ties to opposing sides. Negotiations, if undertaken in those civil or international conflicts, were prolonged and in many cases fruitless, as the leaders of the opposing sides could hold out for victory with outside help. The end of the Cold War enabled peace agreements to be reached in some of these cases, for example in Central America and Africa. In the struggle of the ANC to end apartheid in South Africa, sanctions by external actors helped reduce the asymmetry in the relationship between the ANC and the South African government. This ANC-encouraged pressure contributed to the South African government's decision to enter into serious negotiations with the ANC.

In recent years, non-state actors such as al-Qaeda have become the source of militant external intervention in civil and international wars. The flow of young Salafist fighters from one place to another is sometimes aided by governments, and the engagement of these militants in conflicts in Afghanistan, Iraq, and Syria affect the course of negotiations in those countries. The ramifications of such intervention vary, but generally they impede the conclusion of mutually acceptable agreements, since they tend to support uncompromising, extremist positions.

Outside interveners, including national governments and international governmental and nongovernmental organizations, increasingly affect the course of negotiations conducted by opposing parties. They may attempt to strengthen one side in the negotiations, enhancing or reducing asymmetries. Whatever the good intentions of the engaged stakeholders, their efforts may have counterproductive and destructive consequences. Awareness of such dangers can help those stakeholders on the sidelines and those undertaking negotiations to foster constructive negotiations, that is, to help achieve mutually acceptable and sustainable agreements that are more equitable than the prior conditions. Neither harder-line nor more conciliatory actions are necessarily conducive to constructive negotiations.

Constructive Forethought and Responses

Negotiation leaders, additional inside stakeholders, and outside interveners may add to the coercive conduct in a conflict while negotiations are underway. They themselves may engage in contentious behavior, as well as aggravate it. The consequences of such conduct, however, are highly variable. Such actions may undermine and delay, even terminate negotiations. Sometimes, however, coercive actions may speed negotiations or increase the equity and sustainability of the resulting agreements; much depends on the nature of the coercive actions and their context. There are examples of various policies that leaders of the negotiations, inside stakeholders, and outside interveners may pursue that foster good negotiations with mutually acceptable and sustained outcomes.[13] A few such strategies are discussed regarding dealing with events that threaten to spoil the negotiations, and in turn creating conditions that reduce the chance of violence and nonviolent coercion hampering the negotiation of generally beneficial agreements.

Strategies for Negotiation Leaders

Negotiation leaders need strategies to overcome disruptive actions by other stakeholders. They also need strategies to mitigate and overcome the possible disruptive effects of their own coercive conduct or that of their adversaries.

Cooperation between leaders on each side to overcome spoiler disruptions can be effective in containing and overcoming disruptive actions. An excellent example of such cooperation occurred during the transformation ending apartheid in South Africa. In April 1993, Chris Hani, a popular ANC leader, was assassinated by an immigrant from Poland, a member of the right wing Afrikaner Weerstandsbeweging. The assassin was seized after an Afrikaner woman provided his license plate number. Nelson Mandela and Frederik Willem de Klerk acted together quickly to isolate the event and move the transformation forward. Mandela spoke that evening on national television to prevent the derailment of the negotiations underway, calling "for all South Africans to stand together against those who, from whatever quarter, wish to destroy what Chris Hani gave his life for – the freedom of all of us."[14] The ANC organized protest demonstrations to allow for nonviolent expressions of anger and resentment, and for its part, the government arrested a member of the Conservative Party in connection with the murder. The negotiations were strengthened by these responses and continued to a successful conclusion.

It is possible to imagine a response to the assassination of Rabin that might have limited the disaster that followed. Political leaders across the political spectrum, including Peres and Netanyahu, might have joined in condemning the political atmosphere that demonized a duly elected Prime Minister. In addition, immediately after the assassination actions might have been undertaken to fully implement elements of the peace agreements that had already been reached.

Officials may also establish procedures and institutions that help avoid disruptive crises. Thus leading officials in opposing sides may institute confidence building measures which minimize fearful surprises. This was done during the Cold War, when the opposing sides notified each other about plans for military exercises or weapons testing and had procedures for validating compliance to agreements. In addition officials from opposing sides may conduct general conversations through informal back channels or through unofficial Track II channels to overcome dangerous misunderstandings. They may also agree upon rules of acceptable conduct, agreeing in advance to counter and try to block inflammatory language or violation of universal human rights.

Non-Leader Insider Strategies

Non-official stakeholders may also act to counter violence that undermines peace negotiations. They may form multi-level civil organizations to delineate rules of conduct, as was done, for example, in South Africa.[15] The extensive violence, noted earlier, had threatened the democratic transformation of South Africa and its social stability. Appeals to stop the violence by Mandela and other ANC leaders and by Mangosuthu Buthelezi and other IFP leaders were ineffective. No single person or organization could stop the violence. Only the South African Council of Churches and the Consultative Business Movement, acting jointly, were capable of calling a broadly representative conference, the National Peace Convention (NPC). A facilitating committee invited representatives from all the major groups to a closed meeting on June 22, 1991. Five working groups were established and tasked to write reports for the NPC meeting on September 14, 1991. The reports were discussed at the convention and the result was the National Peace Accord. Twenty-seven government, political, and trade union leaders signed the NPA. The NPA presented a vision of democracy and stability for South Africa; moreover, it established a network of structures to attain those goals. These structures provided settings for persons from opposing sides to get to know each other and work together at the national, regional, and local levels.

Even without such institutionalization of boundary-setting rules of conduct, conventional understandings of legitimate conduct can set limits to violence between adversaries pursuing negotiations. Thus, mass violence by challengers to the state or the recourse by state officials to gross suppressive violence sometimes offends significant portions of the population, resulting in the loss of widespread support and eventual defeat.

Insiders who are not part of the leadership may follow a variety of strategies that undermine militant leader strategies to impose settlements, even when in the guise of undertaking negotiations. In war time this may include avoiding service in the armed forces. In other circumstances policies of government officials in relation to adversaries may be countered and resisted by a variety of actions, such as was done with the sanctuary movement to demonstrate against Reagan's policies of intervention in Central America.

Another set of strategies involves people drawn from more than one side in the conflict being negotiated. They may act jointly in various ways trying to influence the progress of the negotiations, the conclusion of agreements, and the implementation of agreements. For example, they may engage in Track II diplomacy and exchange information and ideas that they communicate to the official negotiators of both sides.[16] Groups from opposing sides may also engage in mutual exchanges that enhance understandings that contribute to formulation, acceptance, and execution of peacemaking agreements.

One such channel is the Pugwash Conferences on Science and World Affairs, begun in 1957 when persons engaged in the development of nuclear weapons and discussions about their management initiated meetings to exchange ideas about reducing the chances of nuclear warfare.[17] The participants were well positioned to develop transnational connections and to influence government officials on issues related to nuclear weapons. Discussions at Pugwash meetings over many years contributed to negotiating several international treaties, including the Partial Test-Ban Treaty, the Nonproliferation Treaty, the Biological Weapons Convention, and the Anti-Ballistic Missile Treaty.[18]

Outside Interveners

Intervention by people not belonging to any of the primary parties involved in the negotiations can alleviate the destructive consequences of coercive actions between the negotiating parties. External governments and international organizations may try to prevent delivery of weapons. Also, they may impose sanctions against parties inflicting gross human rights violations. The very possibility of international punishment of human rights transgressors may help check extreme reliance on violent suppression.

Outsiders may be able to arrange meetings between high level persons from opposing sides for informal discussions, even when hostile talk and actions are underway. For example, in 2008, then-Pugwash Secretary General Professor Paolo Cotta-Ramusino brought together current and former U.S. officials with representatives of the ruling conservative factions of Iran.[19] Their intensive talks dealt with nuclear issues and other substantive issues and how mistrust between the two sides could be overcome. Some progress was made in understanding each other's positions and underlying interests and establishing personal relations between persons who would become officially engaged in subsequent negotiations. It helped bring about changes in opposing governments that reduced coercive rhetoric and sanctions and the initiation of direct official negotiations discussed earlier.

Certainly, mediators are often an effective way to pursue negotiations, even under the duress of violence. For example, Giandomenico Picco, assistant secretary-general to UN Secretary-General Javier Perez de Cuellar, conducted intensive mediation, shuttling from one country to another in the Middle East negotiating the release of hostages from several countries seized in Lebanon.[20] Pico met with representatives of parties who would not communicate directly with each other and who had profound mistrust of each other. The release of the hostages was part of a complex set of actions by the UN Secretary General, along with the Iranian, Syrian, Lebanese, Israeli, American, British, and German authorities, Hizbollah, and the groups holding the hostages

In addition to mediation by UN officials, representatives of national governments often mediate conflicts, sometimes in conjunction with coercive inducements. A case of mediation accompanied by violence occurred in regard to Kosovo, many of whose inhabitants strove for independence from Serbia after the breakup of Yugoslavia. To settle the status of Kosovo and halt fighting there, the Contact Group (United States, United Kingdom, France, Italy, Germany, and Russia) organized a peace conference, held at Rambouillet, near Paris, in February 1999. The U.S. mediators threatened to bomb Serbia if it rejected an agreement the U.S. deemed acceptable. Serbian negotiators accepted most of the proposed agreement, including regional autonomy for Kosovo and the end of repression there. On February 23, 1999, the Contact mediators delivered the text of the proposed agreement, but with a Military Annex that accorded NATO personnel unrestricted access throughout the Federal Republic of Yugoslavia.[21] Not surprisingly that was rejected by Serbia. Apparently the U.S. government was eager for a Serbian rejection so that NATO military action could ensue, which would demonstrate NAT0's value.[22]

On March 24, 1999, NATO aircraft (70 percent were U.S. planes) began bombing Serbia and Kosovo. Justified as a response to a humanitarian emergency, it resulted in a humanitarian calamity. Serbian repression and ethnic cleansing of ethnic Albanians in Kosovo was unleashed. Escalating bombing continued until June 10, 1999, when a new settlement was accepted that did not authorize NATO movement throughout Serbia. The terms of the settlement were hardly different than those Serbia was ready to accept at the earlier conference in Rambouillet.

In 2005, Palestinian civil society called for a campaign of boycotts, divestment, and sanctions (BDS) against Israel until it complied with international law and Palestinian rights. Several churches and other non-governmental organizations in the United States and other countries undertook various BDS actions. These coercive acts of solidarity were intended to reduce the asymmetry of the Israeli-Palestinian conflict and induce the Israeli government to negotiate in a more conciliatory manner. In many cases, the groups waging BDS campaigns targeted products and corporations associated directly with the Israeli occupation of the West Bank. Such targeting could be presented as not challenging the existence of the State of Israel, thereby lessening the possible counterproductive effects of such campaigns.

In short, coercive actions in conjunction with negotiations may help reach mutually acceptable agreements that are enduring and equitable. However, often coercive and especially highly violent actions interfere with reaching an agreement or with reaching an equitable outcome. It is important to understand how and when coercion, and even violence, can be conducted and not be counterproductive toward attainment of a mutually acceptable agreement. In general, coercion that is humiliating and conveys threats to collective survival will provoke resistance, not compliance.

Conclusions and Policy Recommendations

The policy recommendations that follow are intended particularly for the negotiators and their leaders, although they have relevance for all stakeholders. The recommendations also depend upon what values and interests are to be advanced, and these recommendations reflect the conviction that the outcomes are likely to be broadly beneficial if the interests and concerns of all parties are kept in mind. This is one of the basic ideas of the constructive conflict approach.

a. Negotiation leaders should engage a wide range of stakeholders, even including those who might spoil success. This helps involve many levels of each side's constituency, which aids implementation. Engaging potential spoilers can prevent them from acting to disrupt the negotiations, but must be done carefully so as not to invite spoiler behavior.

b. Excessive asymmetry between adversaries can interfere with reaching an equitable agreement. Asymmetry, particularly when largely relying on violent force, hampers negotiations. Each side in a conflict likes to negotiate from strength, not weakness, which obviously poses problems for negotiations. Negotiation leaders recognizing some value in a rough symmetry can contribute to beginning negotiations and to reaching mutually acceptable agreements.

c. Negotiation leaders should discover and attend to the concerns of the other side in negotiations. Dismissing the positions of the other side as irrational or evil yields no insight. Knowing how the other side views its own conduct can provide clues to mutually acceptable agreements. Evidence of seeking such knowledge by itself can help build trust and respect from the other side.

d. In many circumstances, mediation can bypass and avoid contentious coercion. There are a wide variety of direct and indirect mediation possibilities that can be utilized to explore possible options that are mutually acceptable.

e. Leaders of negotiations from different sides can help each other sustain constituency support for the emerging agreement. They can help each other in performing this important task.

f. When coercion is deemed to be necessary it should be precise and constrained. Nonviolent forms are preferable to violent coercion that raises the stakes for the opponent and therefore is often counterproductive. Nonviolent coercion can be more inclusive and more readily pursued in the context of desiring ultimately a negotiated settlement of some mutual benefits.

In short, coercion and even violence often occur in conflicts, even as adversaries enter into negotiations to settle their conflict. This analysis should make it clear that insiders and outsiders, leaders, and other society members often can find ways that contentious behavior can be employed, but not obstruct the chances of negotiating equitable and enduring agreements. Indeed, it is possible that some kinds of coercion will contribute to more constructive and sustainable agreements, if they are undertaken thoughtfully, taking into account broad considerations.

Notes

1   Beth Roy, John Burdick, and Louis Kriesberg, "A Conversation between Conflict Resolution and Social Movement Scholars," *Conflict Resolution Quarterly* 27, no. 4 (2010): 347-68.

2   Nimrod Goren and Miriam Fendius Elman, *Spoilers of Peace and the Dilemmas of Conflict Resolution* (Ramat Gan, Israel and Syracuse, NY: The Israeli Institute for Regional Foreign Policies [MITVIM] and the Program for the Advancement of Research for Conflict and Collaboration [PARCC], 2012), pp. 1-23; Kelly M. Greenhill and Solomon Major, "The Perils of Profiling: Civil War Spoilers and the Collapse of Intrastate Peace Accords," *International Security* 31, no. 3 (2006/7): 7-40.

3   Jessica T. Mathews, "Iran: A Good Deal Now in Danger," *New York Review of Books*, February 20, 2014.

4   Shai Feldman, *Confidence Building and Verification: Prospects in the Middle East* (Jerusalem and Boulder, CO: Jerusalem Post and Westview, 1994).

5   David Kraslow and Stuart H. Loory, *The Secret Search for Peace in Vietnam* (New York: Random House, 1968).

6   For example, the Federal Bureau of Investigation (FBI), led by J. Edgar Hoover, conducted wide ranging harassment of Dr. Marin Luther King, Jr. and violence against the Black Panther organization.

7   The withdrawal of Israeli occupation forces from Hebron, however, was delayed and remained as a matter of contention when the Likud came to power in 1996, under the leadership of Netanyahu. See Louis Kriesberg, "Negotiating the Partition of Palestine and Evolving Israeli-Palestinian Relations," *Brown Journal of World Affairs* 7 (winter/spring 2000): 63-80.

8   See *Report of Truth and Reconciliation Commission*, Vol. 2, chapter 7.

9   Lawrence S. Wittner, *Rebels Against War: The American Peace Movement, 1941-1960* (New York and London: Columbia University Press, 1969).

10 Charles DeBenedetti and Charles Chatfield, *An American Ordeal: The Antiwar Movement of the Vietnam Era* (Syracuse: Syracuse University Press, 1990).

11 David S. Meyer, *A Winter of Discontent: The Nuclear Freeze and American Politics* (New York: Praeger, 1990).

12 Christian Smith, *Resisting Reagan: The U.S. Central America Peace Movement* (Chicago and London: University of Chicago Press, 1996). The Iran-Contra scandal was an outgrowth of the administration's attempt to bypass Congressional restrictions on aiding the Contra militia in Nicaragua.

13 Louis Kriesberg and Bruce W. Dayton, *Constructive Conflicts: From Escalation to Resolution*, 4th ed. (Lanham, MD: Rowman & Littlefield, 2012).

14 Nelson Mandela, *Long Walk to Freedom* (Boston: Little, Brown,1994), p. 530.

15 Peter Gastrow, *Bargaining for Peace* (Washington, DC: United States Institute of Peace, 1995).

16 Joseph V. Montville, "Transnationalism and the Role of Track-Two Diplomacy," in *Approaches to Peace: An Intellectual Map*, eds. W. S. Thompson and K. M. Jensen (Washington, DC: United States Institute of Peace, 1991), pp. 253-69.

17 Matthew Evangelista, *Unarmed Forces: The Transnational Movement to End the Cold War* (Ithaca and London: Cornell University Press, 1999).

18 David Cortright, *Peace Works: The Citizen's Role in Ending the Cold War* (Boulder, CO: Westview Press, 1993).

19 Trita Parsi, *A Single Roll of the Dice: Obama's Diplomacy with Iran* (New Haven and London: Yale University Press, 2012), pp. 31-42.

20 Giandomenico Picco, *Man Without a Gun* (New York: Times Books, 1999).

21 David N. Gibbs, *First Do No Harm: Humanitarian Intervention and the Destruction of Yugoslavia* (Nashville: Vanderbilt University Press, 2009), pp. 200-1; Oskar Lafontaine, *The Heart Beats on the Left* (Malden, MA: Blackwell, 2000), p. 162.

22 Andrew J. Bacevich, and Eliot A. Cohen., eds., *War over Kosovo: Politics and Strategy in a Global Age* (New York: Columbia University Press, 2001).

Negotiations and Power Sharing Arrangements in Burundi's Peace Process: Achievements and Challenges

Patrick Hajayandi

In October 1993 Burundi's newly elected President Melchior Ndadaye was assassinated in a military coup attempt. This action led to upheaval and mass killings around the country, and ultimately to the eruption of a civil war. The conflict pitted the two major ethnic groups: the disadvantaged Hutu majority representing 85 percent of the population, and the dominating Tutsi minority representing 14 percent. The smallest ethnic group, the Twa, which represents 1 percent, was not involved in the conflict. In order to halt the spiral of violence, the involvement of the regional leadership and the international community became necessary. Following this involvement of external actors, peace negotiations were initiated. In August 2000 a peace and reconciliation agreement was signed between the warring parties despite the reluctance of some political actors who expressed multiple reserves. This paper analyzes three main factors that played a key role in breaking the deadlock of the negotiation process: war fatigue, the regional and broad international pressure, and the charisma of the chief mediator. The paper concludes by showing that monitoring how an agreement is implemented is crucial for peace sustainability.

The civil war that erupted after a military coup in October 1993 against Ndadaye Melchior, the first Hutu President and the first to be democratically elected, plunged Burundi into chaos and violence for more than a decade. It is estimated that around 300,000 people lost their lives in the conflict, while 800,000 people were displaced. In efforts to help Burundians achieve lasting peace, initiatives at regional and international levels took place, shaping the negotiation process. Within Burundi some peace initiatives were launched shortly after the coup by the UN envoy Ould Abdallah in 1994. At the regional level Uganda and Tanzania took the lead with fewer successes to stop violence during the fragile rule of President Sylvester Ntibantunganya in 1995 and 1996. The initial rounds of negotiations lasted more than two years, from 1997-1998 when the first unofficial meeting was held in Rome, Italy under the auspices of the San Egidio Community. This meeting was held between the government under President Buyoya's leadership and the CNDD rebel group when it was still headed by Nyangoma, the former Home Affairs Minister within Ndadaye's government.

The road to peace through negotiations has been long, as many challenges delayed the signing of the peace agreement. This was related in part to a high number of actors involved in the negotiation process. Among the actors were those struggling for power in Burundi, like Front pour la Democratie au Burundi (FRODEBU) and Union pour le Progres National (UPRONA), the Burundi Armed Forces (Forces Armees Burundaises – FAB) and the armed groups, mainly Conseil National pour la Defense de la Democratie-Forces pour la Defense de la Democratie (CNDD-FDD) and Forces Nationales pour la Liberation-Parti pour la Liberation du Peuple Hutu (FNL-PALIPEHUTU). The actors' interests at the regional and international level should not be forgotten in analyzing this case. Three factors played an important role in avoiding the deadlock as the peace process moved on. These factors included war fatigue, regional and international pressure on Burundi's political forces, and the charisma of the chief mediator, Nelson Mandela.

The negotiation process officially launched in 1998 in Arusha, Tanzania, was aimed at resolving Burundi's political crisis. The civil war that followed the President's death threatened to put Burundi on the path of ethnic cleansing. The civil war itself stemmed from conflict over political participation and resource scarcity, compounded by regional imbalances and the society's militarization.[1]

The military coup against Ndadaye was interpreted as a refusal by the army (a monoethnic army dominated by the Tutsi) and the Tutsi minority to the democratic change brought about by the new electoral system adopted in the 1992 Burundi Constitution.[2] Since the Hutu represented a majority (85 percent of the population), the Tutsi thought that the new electoral system would no longer allow them access to power. Another concern referred to reforms that the new government of Ndadaye planned to implement after it was sworn in. The reforms were seen as threatening to the interests of the Tutsi establishment which had been in power since 1966.

The impact of the Burundian crisis in 1993 was evident outside the country as well. Its shockwaves rocked neighboring countries as an influx of refugees entered their territory and rebel groups were formed, sometimes using refugee camps as bases. The crisis had strong ramifications across the region. This is why the regional leaders could not afford to turn a blind eye to the unfolding situation. In addition, the initiative aimed at resolving the crisis in Burundi was in line with the newly emerging policy of the Organization of African Unity (now African Union) calling for "African solutions to African problems" (in terms of self-reliance, ownership, and responsibility) with an eye to preventing spillover effects.

From a historical perspective, the outburst of violence in 1993 between Hutu and Tutsi was just one in a series of ethnic clashes in Burundi. The conflict was not a result of historical hatred between the two main ethnic groups as some analysts tend to suggest.[3] It was in fact linked to the struggle for power between Burundi's political elite. The ethnic dimension of the conflict was a result of political manipulation by this elite, whether Hutu or Tutsi.

The Parties to the Conflict

During the process of filling the power vacuum left by Ndadaye's assassination shortly after the 1993 military coup, a political conflict erupted between FRODEBU and UPRONA. These parties were in fact the main players on the political arena. Attempts to bring together Burundi's conflicting parties began in November 1993. The FRODEBU was dominated by the Hutu majority ethnic group, and the UPRONA was considered as the Tutsi minority party. Contrary to FRODEBU, UPRONA was backed by the Burundi army, which was also under the Tutsi control. The mediation attempt during this period was around discussions on restoring democratic rule and re-establishing the elected institutions. It was initiated by United Nations special envoy Ahmedou Ould Abdallah, who came to Burundi in the early days of the crisis between 1993-1994.

In 1994 the United Nations-mediated process led to a power sharing agreement between FRODEBU and UPRONA parties called the "Kigobe and Kajaga Convention of Government." It enabled UPRONA's members and the Tutsi establishment to reclaim power despite their loss in the 1993 elections.

The crisis was handled in a manner that largely favored the Tutsi. This angered FRODEBU members, as they had won the elections with more than 80 percent in the National Assembly and their presidential candidate winning 65 percent of the votes. Consequently, the new government created in the aftermath of the Kigobe and Kajaga Convention was unable to perform its duties. It suffered from divisions along ethnic lines and was thus inefficient to a certain extent. The inefficiency, failure and weakness of the government led to increased violence and chaos in the country, including killing, looting, and ultimately the formation of armed groups.

In 1996 then-President Ntibantunganya Sylvestre was accused of not being able to stop the chaos in the country and was ousted in a bloodless military coup headed by Major Pierre Buyoya, following which the crisis deepened and new actors entered the political arena, gaining more influence. These included the pro-Tutsi Burundi army (FAB) and pro-Hutu armed groups, the CNDD-FDD and FNL-Palipehutu.

From 1993 to 1998, there were initiatives aimed at bringing all the key actors to the table in order to negotiate a solution for the Burundi crisis. However, the parties were reluctant to sit together. Finally, in June 1998 the conflicting parties agreed to engage in negotiations. Other than FRODEBU and UPRONA, key players joined the process, including the CNDD-FDD which had an armed wing, the Party for National Recovery (PARENA) which drew power from its youth militia, the Buyoya led government, and the National Assembly which was mainly composed by Frodebu Members of Parliament (MP).[4]

The positive point is that from the very start of the negotiation process, the facilitators decided to be as inclusive as possible. The peace talks had to address all the issues in relation to the conflict. During the negotiations, numerous political groups were formed and invited to join the peace talks. The first group constituted political parties and pro-Hutu movements. This group was known as the G7 because it comprised seven consistent political parties. The second group was formed by ten pro-Tutsi political parties. It was clear that the negotiations were going to revolve around the grievances and fears of one or the other ethnic group. Each side presented itself as protecting the interests of its respective ethnic group.

The Peace Process

The fear of a new bloodbath in the Great Lakes Region urged the International community to get involved in the Burundi peace process. It was clear that, after the genocide in neighboring Rwanda, this region was not ready for further genocide or mass killings (which were indeed looming over Burundi). In this perspective, the United Nations, with the Security Council and the Organization of African Union (OAU) were called to play a supporting role while the regional actors took the lead in the search for solutions concerning the Burundi conflict.

Most actors agreed that the conflict in Burundi was a political one with important ethnic dimensions. The peace process took into account both the political and military aspects. According to Ambassador Ayebare, the political track dealt with political players and was aimed at reshaping the political environment in a way that allowed inclusiveness with regard to the different political actors. The military track was directed at establishing protection for political institutions, as well as all political leaders who would return to Burundi after the negotiation process.[5]

From the onset, the objective of the peace process was twofold: on the one hand it was aimed at finding a lasting solution to the enduring conflict and on the other hand it was trying to lay the foundation for a transitional government that would incorporate the representative of the principal parties and factions.[6]

Former Tanzanian President Julius Nyerere was appointed as the chief mediator in Burundi in March 1996. His main task was to help the conflicting parties negotiate an inclusive power sharing arrangement. The initial phase of negotiation under Nyerere auspices was accompanied by Western and

UN preventive diplomacy. This first phase lasted from 1996 to 1998 but it was not successful because of conflicting interests among the parties.

Nyerere's major success was to bring together 19 Burundian delegates representing diverse political parties for talks in the northern Tanzanian town of Arusha in 1998. The negotiators were selected from the parties represented in the National Assembly, and they included members of both the Tutsi and Hutu ethnic groups. It took the mediator three years of wide consultations both within and outside Burundi to determine the representation in the talks. President Nyerere adopted the strategy used by the United Nations that recognized the formal political parties which had participated in the 1993 elections as the major protagonists who should be included in the negotiations, which would eventually lead to power sharing arrangements.[7]

The Role of Regional Leadership

The impact of the Burundi crisis on the Great Lakes Region cannot be underestimated. In order to address the problem, regional leaders needed to combine their efforts. The collaboration between the regional leadership and the Carter Foundation played a key role in fostering the negotiation process. It also made it possible for the stakeholders to coordinate their initiatives aimed at resolving the Burundi crisis. The regional leaders took ownership of the negotiation process with the support of the international community.

The leaders and the mediator himself applied significant pressure on the conflicting parties, calling them to look for alternatives to violence. This position gave an impetus to the negotiation process and obliged the warring parties to limit the use of genocidal rhetoric. The position of the regional leadership was also displayed after President Buyoya came back to power in July 1996 through a military coup. The regional initiative decided to impose sanctions on the Burundi government with a clear message that the use of power to destabilize the region would not be tolerated.

The Role and Support of the International Community

The inter-ethnic massacres observed in the aftermath of Ndadaye's assassination pushed then-UN Secretary General Boutros Boutros-Ghali to propose an international military intervention force for Burundi. The mission for such a force was to prevent ethnic annihilation and restore constitutional order and stability.

Back in 1994, the UN played a leading role in trying to resolve the Burundi conflict in a power sharing process. This process was mainly brokered by the UN Special Envoy to Burundi, Ahmedou Ould Abdallah. The agreement on power sharing involved, to a great extent, members of the FRODEBU party and those of UPRONA. This power sharing agreement was signed in September 1994. Despite the fact that it was not an effective solution to the crisis in the long run, the agreement managed to temporarily restore calm in the country.

The role of the OAU was also important in the search for a sustainable solution for Burundi. As noted by Ambassador Ayebare, "The United Nations' approach to the Burundi conflict did not differ from the strategy pursued by the OAU/AU and other regional peacemakers. Each of these actors perceived the conflict as political, with ethnic connotations. This consensus on the definition of the causes of the conflict was crucial for devising a common mediation strategy."

The OAU was called to react in the case of Burundi as soon as the crisis erupted. Already in October 1993, regional leaders (Rwanda, Tanzania, Uganda, and Zaire) asked for an OAU-led intervention force. The OAU proposed a Mission for Protection and Restoration of Trust in Burundi. The mission consisted of a military force (180 soldiers) and a group of civilian staff. The idea of an intervention force was met with strong opposition from the Burundi army. Consequently, the OAU succeeded only in deploying a team of observers. The extent to which this team was effective is still to be evaluated, but one can affirm that this action did play a deterring role with regard to the Burundi army's actions.

Breaking the Arusha Negotiations Deadlock

From 1999 the warring parties found themselves in stalemate. There was no clear winner or loser. The negotiations were in a deadlock. The combination of the following factors was necessary in order to break this deadlock.

War Fatigue

The signs of war fatigue were evident as early as 1999. After the rebel attack in the north of the capital Bujumbura, it became apparent that the Burundi army was no longer as effective as it used to be. It did not counter attack, as many expected, and there were voices, especially among Tutsi, expressing distrust in the army. This was a significant change in mentality. For over 30 years, the Burundi army was considered a rampart force for the Tutsi minority. One of the best solutions for the apparent ineffectiveness was clearly a negotiated settlement of the conflict, maintaining the minorities' ability to protect their interests.

The apparent war fatigue was connected to several factors. The commanding structure of the army had been dominated by a group of officers from the southern province of Bururi. This was already fueling some tensions and limiting communications and made it difficult for the army to anticipate rebel action.

Despite the substantial increase in resource allocation for the army (around 50 percent of the whole budget), on the battlefield the enemy was difficult to defeat. In the absence of a quick victory, the soldiers were becoming increasingly demotivated. As time passed, some officers became unwilling to risk the lives of their soldiers. On the battlefield, soldiers and rebels noticed that they were living in the same conditions and this brought a kind of solidarity among the two groups. They began to respect each other and occasionally shared food, drinks, and even spoils. The war fatigue the soldiers on both sides were experiencing became a new source of pressure on those involved in the negotiations.

International and Regional Pressure on Burundi's Political Echelon

After Buyoya came to power in 1996, an embargo was imposed on Burundi. The aim of these economic sanctions was to oblige the new government to restore power into civilian hands. Due to ongoing violence, the international community also decided to suspend development aid.

In December 1999, as Nelson Mandela was appointed chief mediator for Burundi, the regional heads of state made it clear to the Burundi conflicting parties that there was no alternative to a negotiated solution. At the same time, they insisted on concluding an agreement as soon as possible. Since

Burundi security, politics, and economy are tightly connected to the region, the main actors had no choice but to seriously analyze the proposed solution. Much pressure was placed particularly on the Buyoya government and the army, because they had more to lose than gain. When Mandela entered the mediating arena, he made it clear that he did not want the negotiation process to go on endlessly.

Mandela's Charisma and Approaches to the Negotiation Process

One of Mandela's important achievements in the negotiations' process was to increase their visibility by internationalizing them. As a consequence, the moral and financial support from major powers was also increased. Mandela was able to achieve this thanks to his charisma and the respect that world leaders and the international community in general had for him. The South African icon helped leaders look at the negotiations from a different perspective and this resulted in much more consistent support.

Arusha Negotiation Rounds and their Achievements

The Burundi negotiation process consisted of two major phases. The first phase began with the resuming of peace talks in June 1998 in Arusha, Tanzania under the facilitation of Mwalimu Julius Nyerere and his team. Nyerere, as facilitator, played an important role in gathering all the parties that were key players in advancing the process. Nevertheless, Nyerere was contested by UPRONA and the army. They accused him of being partial and of defending the Hutu cause. This undermined his action and delayed the process.

In 1999 Nyerere died and was replaced by the former South African President Nelson Mandela. The second crucial phase of the negotiations began with Mandela's facilitation. In August 2000, the Arusha Peace and Reconciliation Agreement was signed. The ceremony saw the participation of a number of renowned leaders including Bill Clinton and numerous African heads of state.

Despite controversies over the successes and shortcomings of the Arusha Peace Process, some significant achievements were made; these include the creation of a platform for a transitional government that would implement the agreement's key provisions. Among other provisions, the power sharing arrangements played an important role in transforming the Burundi conflict, and in changing how it was perceived. After implementing power sharing arrangements, the conflict shifted from being perceived as solely ethnic to a political conflict, which in turn contributed to easing tensions.

Power Sharing Arrangements

The Burundi conflict has been mainly connected to problems of monopolization of power by a small group of Tutsi minority and the unequal distribution of wealth and opportunities by the existing establishment. During the Arusha negotiations, the provision of power was aimed at addressing this problem and fostering inclusiveness. In the past, several attempts of power sharing have been tested without significant success. These include the Convention of Government agreed upon between 1994 and 1995 (the tandem UPRONA-FRODEBU) and the Partnership for Peace (Pro-FRODEBU National Assembly and the Buyoya Government).

The Arusha power sharing deal awarded the Tutsi minority an over-representation in the different institutions. The 2000 Arusha Peace and Reconciliation Agreement aimed to institutionalize a democratic system of power sharing between Burundi's Hutu and Tutsi political parties, and initiated a three-year transitional period with a grand coalition government.[8] One of the major shortcomings of the power sharing arrangements was the fact that armed groups seemed to have been left out. As a consequence, war continued unabated, causing many casualties.

With regards to power sharing, Burundi explicitly indicated ethnic differences as a necessary condition to reconcile minority rights with the demands of the majority. The aim was to strike an appropriate balance between Hutu and Tutsi in the executive and legislative organs of government, and in the communal councils.

The Arusha Peace Agreement served as a reference in crafting a new constitution for Burundi, laying the foundation for power sharing. According to the constitution, the National Assembly would be composed of 60 percent Hutu and 40 percent Tutsi. The same quota would be respected in the formation of the Cabinet's ministerial portfolios.

Gender was also taken into consideration, as no less than 30 percent of all members of parliament were to be women. In the Senate, the representation is equal between the two ethnic groups. The parity was also evident within the defense and security forces, where all the groups need to be equally represented in order to increase confidence in these bodies – the army and the police (50 percent for each side). In the case of imbalances, the law provides the use of co-optation as an instrument for correction.[9]

Following implementation, the Burundi transitional government was unable to effectively work in the context of ongoing violence. This prompted the stakeholders to call the armed groups to the negotiating table. On the one hand the CNDD-FDD agreed to negotiate only under specific conditions. On the other hand the FNL Palipehutu decided to continue fighting. This resulted in a potential deadlock avoided thanks to South African leaders Thabo Mbeki and Jacob Zuma's diplomatic efforts.

In 2003, after signing the Global Accord, the armed wing of CNDD-FDD stopped operating. In 2004, the CNDD-FDD entered the transitional government in which its leaders obtained some key positions, including the Ministry of Good Governance. In the same year the cantonment was implemented in eleven sites throughout the country. In November 2004, the demobilization operation began.

Challenges of the Negotiation Process

In the beginning of the negotiation rounds the peace process was delayed because of several factors. One of them was the radical position held by UPRONA leaders, backed by high ranking army officers, according to which there was no need to negotiate with the rebels. This was a position of extremist Tutsis who preferred the status quo. For a long time, the negotiation process was carried out without involving the armed groups such as the CNDD-FDD or the FNL. As a result, when the Arusha Peace and Reconciliation Agreement was signed, there was no ceasefire on the ground. This made it impossible to implement the provisions of the Arusha Accord. Calling the principal armed groups to the negotiation table became an imperative; as Lemarchand pointed out, "The inability or unwillingness of the facilitators to admit to the negotiating table some of the key players, the CNDD-FDD and Palipehutu, is where the role of external actors appears to have been singularly counterproductive."[10] The differing interests of key stakeholders for the peace process constituted another challenging factor.

Since the 2005 elections, which brought to power the former armed group CNDD-FDD, the Arusha Agreement implementation monitoring diminished. The only mechanism that was involved in a follow up of the implementation was the UN Office in Burundi (Bureau des Nations Unis au Burundi – BNUB), whose main task is to monitor the security situation. Its focus has shifted towards the transitional justice process.

One of the enduring challenges is the linkage between the Burundi political and security situation to that of the Great Lakes Region as a whole. Currently, there are two core tendencies which are not only preventing the consolidation of the peace building process, but are impeding democracy. As Judith Vorrath points out, there is a continuing or increasing authoritarian tendency in the ruling governments on the one hand, and emerging divisions and fragmentations (especially among the opposition's political leaders) that indicate new sources for conflict and political gridlock on the other. If these problems are not properly addressed, the gains of the peace talks could be lost.[11] This region remains highly militarized due to availability and uncontrolled flow of weapons across borders. This could be a factor of new tensions.

Conclusion and Key Lessons

Burundi's peace process was very important not only for Burundians but also for the Great Lakes Region as a whole. Regional actors tried to bring a viable solution to this crisis in the framework of "African solutions to African problems." However the process demonstrated that this policy would be difficult to implement because of lack of financial support. It thus became obvious that collaboration with the international community was necessary. One of the challenges related to this collaboration is that the two visions on problem-solving approaches compete in some situations. In addition, the differing interests of key stakeholders hindered the success of the negotiation process.

Some important lessons derived from the Arusha peace process are that it is imperative to be inclusive when this is likely to break the deadlock or to push forward a negotiation process. The second lesson is that under pressure, those involved in negotiations can achieve some success but this doesn't mean the implementation of the agreed principles will follow as stated. There is a need to create follow up mechanisms in order to ensure that agreements are implemented on the ground. It is also worth noting that one person's recognized authority and wisdom can bring new energy into a process that was deemed a likely failure. Nelson Mandela's charisma was crucial for the negotiation process. However, no one element is sufficient to bring about needed changes; the combination of efforts in resolving problems like ethnic conflict is imperative. One must note that the agreement reached during a negotiation process may be considered as a temporary solution. Ongoing checkups are needed in order to identify new emerging issues and limit their impact.

When facing the mission of establishing and maintaining a peace process, the mediators of facilitators must take several measures.

a.   First, they should ensure that all key players are on board in the peace process, including those perceived as spoilers, when such a move can help in breaking the deadlock of negotiations.

b.   Second, they should create follow up mechanisms in order to ensure that what was agreed on is being implemented on the ground.

c.   Third, they should combine efforts in resolving protracted ethnic conflict.

d.   Finally, they should ensure ongoing checkups after the agreement has been implemented, in order to identify new emerging issues and limit their negative impact on peace after a country has truly started emerging from the gridlock of the conflict.

Notes

1   Jane Boulden, ed., *Dealing with Conflicts in Africa* (London: Palgrave Macmillan, 2003).

2   Burundi's constitution was adopted on March 9, 1992.

3   Irvin Staub, *The Roots of Evil* (Boston: Massachusetts University Press, 1989).

4   International Crisis Group, *Africa Report* No. 131, August 2007.

5   Adonia Ayebare, "Peacemaking in Burundi: A Case Study of Regional Diplomacy Backed by International Peacekeeping and Peace Building," *International Peace Institute* (2010): 81-86.

6   René Lemarchand, "Consociationalism and Power Sharing in Africa: Rwanda, Burundi and the Democratic Republic of Congo," *African Affairs* 106 (2006): 1-20.

7   Ayebare, "Peacemaking in Burundi."

8   Ashild Falch and Megan Baker, "Power Sharing to Build Peace: The Burundi Experience of Power Sharing Agreements," *Centre for the Study of Civil War Papers* (Oslo: PRIO, 2008).

9   Arusha Peace and Reconciliation Accords for Burundi, 2000.

10 René Lemarchand, *The Dynamics of Violence in Central Africa* (Philadelphia: University of Pennsylvania Press, 2009); René Lemarchand, *Burundi: Ethnic Conflict and Genocide* (New York: Woodrow Wilson Center Press, 1995).

11 Judith Vorrath, "Political Trends in the African Great Lakes Region," Special Report 279 (United States Institute of Peace, 2011), http://www.usip.org/sites/default/files/Political_Trends_Great_Lakes.pdf.

Liberia: How Diplomacy Helped End a 13-Year Civil War

Alan J. Kuperman

The end of Liberia's long running civil war in 2003 reveals that smart diplomacy is at least as important as military intervention if the international community seeks to save lives under the Responsibility to Protect (R2P) doctrine. This article, drawing on field interviews in Liberia and Washington, finds that enlightened diplomacy succeeded in Liberia for two main reasons. First, unlike in several other recent conflicts, the international community refused to reward Liberia's rebels for provoking a humanitarian emergency. Instead, diplomats threatened the rebels with prosecution unless they halted their offensive, and peacekeepers were deployed to prevent their advance. This mitigated the "moral hazard of humanitarian intervention" that has emboldened rebels and escalated violence in other conflicts. Second, the international community refrained from demands that Liberia's leaders surrender all power or face quick elections or prosecution. Instead, negotiators promised asylum to Liberia's president and a share of power to his political circle, thereby averting a potentially violent backlash from the regime. Proponents of R2P should incorporate these lessons in future international efforts to protect civilians.

The end of Liberia's long running civil war in 2003 demonstrates that smart diplomacy is at least as important as military intervention if the international community seeks to save lives under the Responsibility to Protect (R2P) doctrine. Indeed, the nuanced international action in Liberia stands in stark contrast to typical calls for military intervention to help rebels overthrow vilified regimes, which has backfired miserably in other cases.[1] Although Liberia has some distinctive features that facilitated the success of international diplomacy, it also offers more general lessons for future implementation of R2P.

This article starts with a brief overview of Liberia's civil wars from 1990 to 2003. Then, based on field research, it details the origins and strategy of the two rebel groups that escalated fighting in 2003, triggering a humanitarian crisis and international action. Next, it describes how a combination of diplomatic and military intervention over the course of three months successfully ended Liberia's civil war in a durable manner, and explains how this effort differed from failed attempts to protect civilians in other civil wars. Finally, the article presents lessons for future international efforts to implement R2P.

The Rise of LURD & MODEL

Liberia's first civil war raged from 1989 until 1997, at which time the militarily strongest rebel, Charles Taylor, was elected president. Stability was achieved, at least temporarily, but only after years of war that had cost tens of thousands of lives in both Liberia and neighboring Sierra Leone. Newly elected President Taylor generated cooperation with opponents by including them in government, but during 1997 and 1998 he ordered the arrest or execution of other former adversaries. Some of these ex-rebels fled the country – ethnic Mandingos typically went to Guinea, and ethnic Krahn went to Nigeria and the Ivory Coast – where they eventually formed new armed movements that returned several years later with a vengeance.

In 1999, an exiled Liberian rebels meeting in Guinea formed the Liberians United for Reconciliation and Democracy (LURD).[2] Unwilling to be perpetual refugees and seeing no prospect for peaceful return, they decided to fight their way back into Liberia. From 2001 to 2003, LURD expanded rapidly to as many as 5,000 trained fighters, including former Liberian army soldiers, supplemented by another 25,000 ragtag forces.[3] By late 2002, LURD controlled about one third of Liberia in the country's northwest, bordering Guinea and Sierra Leone.[4] In March 2003, a second militant movement, calling itself the Movement for Democracy in Liberia (MODEL), emerged on the other side of the country. These Liberian refugee rebels invaded from the Ivory Coast and made rapid progress. In just three months, from March to June

2003, MODEL expanded from 15 fighters to a force that controlled virtually the entire eastern half of Liberia (figure 1).[5]

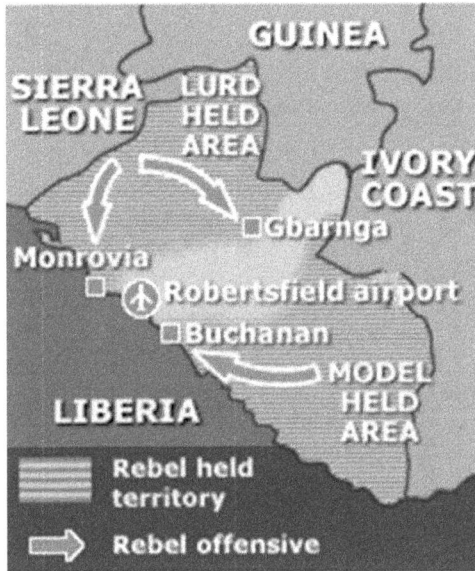

Figure 1. LURD and MODEL Rebels Converge on Monrovia
Source: Reliefweb

2003 Crisis and Soft Landing

A humanitarian crisis emerged by June 2003, as the LURD and MODEL rebels advanced toward the capital, compelling tens of thousands of terrified civilians to flee ahead of them into Monrovia, which overwhelmed the government's capacity to provide aid (figure 2). The regime could not fend off the rebels for several reasons: a UN arms embargo hampered its resupply efforts; economic sanctions had reduced government revenue and, in turn, the ability to pay troops and maintain equipment;[6] and Taylor's fear of a coup had led him to hollow out the army in favor of personal security forces and various militias.[7] Ostensibly, Taylor had up to 40,000 troops at his disposal, but less than one quarter were paid and equipped well enough to rely upon.[8] Moreover, by early 2003, his tiny air force had been grounded due to lack of spare parts and maintenance. In the capital, the specter loomed of an imminent three-way battle for control between government forces and

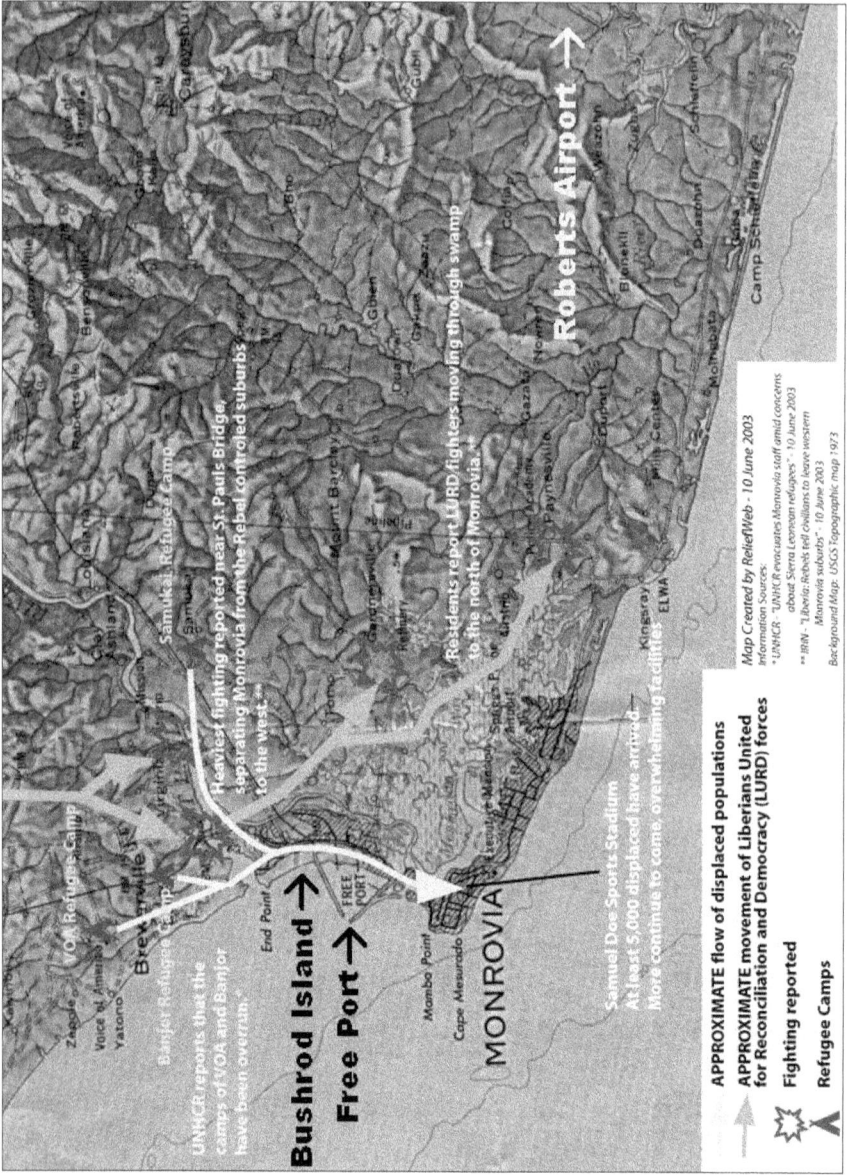

Figure 2. June 2003: Humanitarian Crisis as Rebels Displace Civilians. Source: Reliefweb, June 10, 2003

the two rebel groups.[9] The last time a scenario of that sort had occurred, in 1990, a disaster ensued – devastating the city, killing thousands, injuring and displacing tens of thousands, failing to yield a winner, and perpetuating the civil war for years to come.

Confronting this impending disaster, the international community launched a multi-track effort that in just three months successfully ended Liberia's civil war in a durable manner. First, peace negotiations commenced between Taylor and rebel leaders on June 4, 2003 in Accra, Ghana, organized by the regional Economic Community of West African States (ECOWAS). On that same day, a special international court released its indictment of Charles Taylor for sponsoring war crimes in neighboring Sierra Leone. As Taylor returned to Liberia the next day, LURD launched a new offensive ("World War I," in the rebels' vernacular) toward the capital. On June 17, in Accra, the two rebel groups and Liberia's government signed a ceasefire that effectively called for Taylor's departure from office, by pledging to reach a peace agreement within one month that would establish a transitional government without him.[10]

Barely a week later, on June 25, as negotiations continued in Accra, LURD broke the ceasefire and launched another offensive ("World War II") that reached the edge of the capital. The international community complained, so the rebels retreated temporarily, and Taylor's forces then reoccupied the area and punished suspected collaborators. On July 17, LURD launched its final offensive ("World War III"), successfully occupying Bushrod Island and its Free Port, the capital's lifeline, but failing to cross either of the two bridges into downtown Monrovia (figure 2). LURD had large supplies of ammunition, including mortars that they fired indiscriminately while trying to capture the bridges, endangering civilians in the densely populated urban area.[11] From the east, meanwhile, MODEL launched its own offensive, capturing the country's second biggest sea port of Buchanan, about 75 miles from the capital. MODEL then proceeded northwest toward its next two objectives: the Firestone plant in Harbel – which provided an opportunity for looting but also was the refuge for thousands of displaced civilians – and the international airport just east of the capital.[12]

At that moment, international action succeeded in halting the fighting. On August 4, Taylor announced that he would accept asylum in Nigeria the following week, and a Nigerian-led peacekeeping force of 5,000 troops – the ECOWAS Mission in Liberia (ECOMIL) – began to arrive at the airport. Soon after, a U.S. task force of 2,000 Marines, stationed offshore, commenced overflights of the capital area and briefly deployed 320 troops ashore. The African peacekeepers marched west and took control of the Free Port from the LURD rebels, who had agreed to retreat, enabling resumption of humanitarian deliveries. On August 11, Taylor went into exile as promised. One week later in Accra, on August 18, the rebels and Liberian officials signed a comprehensive peace agreement, providing for an interim power sharing government to be followed by democratic elections within two years. All U.S. forces departed the area by the end of September 2003, and on October 1, the UN took control of the peacekeeping force from ECOWAS, gradually expanding its UN Mission in Liberia (UNMIL) to 15,000 troops and police. Except for a few minor skirmishes over the next few months, between and within the three Liberian armed factions, everything went according to plan: the peace agreement was implemented, the civil war ended, the factions disarmed, the interim government served its term, elections were held, and Liberia remains a peaceful democracy at the time of this writing in April 2015. After 13 years of brutal and nearly incessant violence, the remarkable success of this international peacemaking effort without resort to large scale military force offers important lessons regarding intervention.

Interveners Avoided Past Mistakes

The key to success in Liberia was that the international community avoided many mistakes it has made in other attempts to implement R2P.[13] First, the intervention did not reward the rebels for provoking a humanitarian emergency, and thus did not embolden them to seek military victory. To the contrary, the international community warned the rebels that they would never be recognized – but instead prosecuted – if they attempted to seize power militarily. Rather than helping the rebels militarily, the peacekeeping intervention interposed between the armed factions, thereby compelling the rebels to retreat and discouraging them from further attacks. The U.S. military also minimized its ground presence, reducing the danger of mission creep.

Second, humanitarian assistance was delivered in ways that avoided bolstering the rebels – for example, it arrived via government-controlled areas. Third, the interveners rewarded Liberia's nonviolent opposition by including them in the peace negotiations and ensuring them a share of power in the interim government, thereby bolstering their prospects in subsequent elections. This also reduced the incentive for future rebellion, in Liberia or elsewhere, by demonstrating that nonviolent opposition groups can obtain political power without the costs and risks of resorting to violence. Fourth, humanitarianism was not mere window dressing for self-interested Western meddling. The intervention was sincerely motivated by concern for Liberia's civilians – who were displaced, and targeted indiscriminately, and facing a humanitarian emergency in Monrovia.

Fifth, and perhaps most important, the interveners did not demand that Liberia's government surrender all power, or that Taylor face immediate prosecution, or that the country hold quick elections – any of which could have threatened the security and welfare of loyalist factions and thereby provoked a violent or even genocidal backlash. Instead, international diplomats forged a power sharing deal that guaranteed a portion of authority and wealth during the interim government to each of the four main societal factions – the Taylor regime, the two rebel groups, and the nonviolent opposition – while also permitting Taylor to receive asylum (table 1). In the transitional legislature, the 76 seats were divided as follows: 12 each for Taylor's regime, LURD, and MODEL; one each for 18 political parties; one each for the 15 counties; and seven for civil society. Of the political parties, one was Taylor's own and 9 others were affiliated with him, so the old regime effectively controlled at least 22 seats (almost 30 percent) in the new legislature, making it the largest faction.[14] This illustrates how the peace deal incorporated potential spoilers, rather than alienating them by demanding wholesale regime change, which has backfired in other cases.

Government ministries likewise were divvied up. The regime was permitted to maintain control of the National Defense and Internal Affairs ministries, among others, to address its security concerns. To share wealth (via corruption), LURD was granted the Finance Ministry, while MODEL was awarded the Ministry of Agriculture, as well as that of Lands, Mines, and Energy. The nonviolent opposition predictably obtained less lucrative ministries, such as Education, Gender and Development, and Youth and Sports. To further distribute wealth among the factions, the state's key public corporations were divided as follows: electricity, broadcasting, and petroleum refining to the regime; ports and telecommunications to LURD; agriculture and forestry to MODEL; and mining, rubber, and the national oil company to the nonviolent opposition.[15]

Table 1. Power Sharing in 2003 Comprehensive Peace Agreement

	Seats	Key Ministries	Key Parastatals
Regime	12	National Defense	Electricity
		Internal Affairs	Broadcasting
			Petroleum Refining
LURD	12	Finance	Ports
			Telecommunications
MODEL	12	Agriculture	Agriculture
		Lands, Mines, and Energy	Forestry
Civ Society	7	Education	Mining
		Gender and Development	Rubber
			National Oil Company
Pol Parties	18		
Counties	15		
TOTAL	76		

The other international action to ensure stability was provision of peacekeepers, which stanched incipient violence within and between the armed factions following the peace accord.[16] Despite Taylor's departure, renewed war remained a considerable risk, especially initially. In the weeks after the peace deal, the MODEL rebels kept advancing toward the capital's international airport, and both rebel groups continued to obtain weapons. On October 1, 2003, LURD clashed briefly with the ex-regime in the Monrovia suburb of Paynesville. Later that month, when the LURD's chief of staff was denied the top position in the new army, he threatened renewed war.[17] When the ex-rebels were not incorporated into the country's new army as they had been promised, many of them also considered a return to war.[18] Illustrating this threat to peace, in December 2003, former rebels in one camp launched a riot.[19] Many ex-rebel commanders were also disgruntled at facing travel bans and not receiving high government posts, which were reserved for a select few.[20] In early spring 2004, LURD factions even fought each other over who would control the group's lucrative positions in the interim government.[21]

The peacekeepers successfully prevented these minor disputes from escalating into renewed war. According to LURD's senior surviving military officer, Ophoree Diah, the power sharing deal "would not have worked" without the international troops. Although the two rebel groups could have cooperated because they both descended from Liberia's former army, he says, they would have continued fighting against the ex-regime, resulting in a bloodbath.[22] Likewise, MODEL's commanding general at the end of the war, Kai Farley, says "it would be a different story" if the peacekeepers had not mediated disputes during implementation.[23] MODEL's senior military planner, Boi Bleaju Boi, agrees that the peacekeepers were "essential to monitor the peace" and to prevent the armed factions from fighting over "who was in charge."[24] The peacekeepers mainly achieved their goals in two ways that did not require the actual use of force: deterring aggression, and reducing the need for any faction to lash out in fear of surprise attack. However, the peacekeepers also engaged forcefully at times, including quashing the skirmish between the LURD and regime forces in early October 2003.[25]

The peacekeepers may also have been crucial in the weeks after the 2005 elections, which ended the transitional government. Only a few former members of the armed factions were able to remain in government by being elected. For example, LURD's original Secretary General, Isaac Nyenabo, became the senior senator from Grand Gedeh County.[26] Both senators elected from Nimba County were former military commanders associated with Taylor: Adolphus Dolo, a retired army general; and Prince Johnson, who had assassinated Liberia's president in 1990.[27] Taylor's ex-wife, Jewel Howard-Taylor, was elected to the Senate from Bong County.[28] But the large majority of former fighters lost access to wealth and power. The fact that they did not then return to violence is best explained by the peacekeeping presence. However, other factors also contributed, including the extensive demobilization and two years of peaceful power sharing prior to elections. As a leading member of Liberia's civil society recalls, "Initially, we all thought war would resume, but the peacekeepers deterred it, and then the expectation faded over time."[29]

Was Liberia Easy?

Before generalizing lessons for future intervention, it is necessary to consider whether particular characteristics of Liberia or its conflict enabled the successful outcome, making it difficult to replicate elsewhere. One helpful factor was that the region's armed factions were relatively weak, which also facilitated interventions in neighboring Sierra Leone and the Ivory Coast. Despite that, most peacemaking efforts in West Africa's civil wars have failed, so there are lessons to learn from Liberia's relatively rare success.[30] A second consideration is that for historical reasons the United States has a special aura in Liberia that enhanced its coercive abilities.[31] More generally, however, coercive leverage is available whenever interveners are more powerful than the parties to the conflict, which is the typical balance.[32]

A third factor is that Liberia's rebels may have been unusually willing to compromise, because their stated goal was to remove Taylor, not seize power.[33] However, when LURD approached the capital, its civilian authorities lost control to military commanders, who then attempted to cross the final bridge into downtown Monrovia to take control. Accordingly, the rebels' ultimate acceptance of a negotiated compromise cannot be explained by any lack of desire for victory.

A fourth claim is that neither LURD nor MODEL were confident that they could prevail against each other and Taylor's forces, so that both rebel groups had incentive instead to accept power sharing. However, uncertainty about relative power is common in civil wars and generally believed to prolong the fighting,[34] as it did in Liberia for most of 1990 to 2003. Indeed, the only previous pause in Liberia's war occurred in 1997, when the dominance of Taylor's forces reduced uncertainty about relative power. It is thus unlikely that an increase in such uncertainty explains the peace of 2003. A fifth assertion is that Liberia's residents were exhausted by the long running civil war and thus ready to embrace peace. While that may be true, the two rebel groups were relatively fresh and making rapid progress, so exhaustion cannot explain their willingness to accept a peaceful outcome.[35]

A sixth factor was that neighboring Nigeria was willing and able to quickly provide a few thousand relatively well-trained troops to interpose between the armed factions prior to deployment of the larger UN mission.[36] Although such a rapid deployment may indeed have been crucial, other forces including the U.S. Marines poised offshore could have performed this function if necessary. More generally, the United States is physically capable of inserting a vanguard peacekeeping force of a few thousand troops anywhere in the world within a matter of days,[37] and can often airlift forces from neighboring countries as it did in Liberia. Nigeria's ability and willingness to provide suitable forces, however, was undoubtedly helpful.

A seventh factor was that Liberia had only 3 million people, which reduced the peacekeeping requirements that correlate with population and level of instability. However, this was not atypical, because many violent civil conflicts occur in countries with relatively small populations.[38] A final claim is that Liberia's civil war was not really an ethnic conflict because the opposing groups did not harbor the "ancient hatred" or existential fear that has precluded power sharing in other conflicts. However, scholars have demonstrated that ethnic conflict is not an insurmountable barrier to power sharing and that non-ethnic civil wars are also difficult to end in a lasting manner via negotiated agreement.[39] Thus, the allegedly low level of ethnic animosity and fear in Liberia is neither necessary nor sufficient to explain the success of peacemaking efforts in 2003.

In summary, no unique characteristic of Liberia appears to have determined the peaceful outcome. However, at least four characteristics discussed above may have been helpful, which suggests that replicating such success elsewhere might be facilitated by the presence of these factors: relatively weak local forces; diplomatic interveners with significant coercive leverage; a small population; and suitable peacekeepers able to deploy quickly. By contrast, there is no evidence that peace was enabled by the other ostensible causes: rebels with limited goals; the absence of an armed faction that was stronger than the others combined; a populace exhausted by war; and relatively low levels of inter-ethnic animosity.

Lessons and Conclusions

Given that Liberia's peaceful outcome cannot be attributed to unique characteristics of the conflict, this case offers lessons for future implementation of R2P. Four international policies were the key to success in Liberia: (1) enabling the rise of the rebels to pressure the brutal Taylor regime; (2) incorporating all armed factions, including the government, in the temporary power sharing deal; (3) announcing the indictment of Taylor and then offering him amnesty; and (4) deploying a small scale military intervention to deter and prevent renewed fighting. Washington also made tactical decisions that facilitated the peaceful outcome, most importantly, by reining in the rebels to compel them to accept a compromise. The most questionable, and perhaps shortsighted, U.S. tactic was to double-cross Taylor by subsequently persuading Nigeria to revoke his asylum. In theory, that step reduced impunity and thereby deterred future crimes. More likely, however, it will backfire by discouraging tyrants from accepting future offers of asylum, thereby perpetuating civil wars and leading to even more violence against civilians.

These lessons from the successful international action to end Liberia's civil war in 2003 reinforce the five recommendations for humanitarian intervention that I identified in previous work.[40] First, the international community did not reward the rebels for provoking a humanitarian emergency, but rather threatened them (including with prosecution) unless they halted, thus minimizing the moral hazard that inadvertently has escalated other conflicts. Second, humanitarian assistance was delivered in ways that avoided bolstering or emboldening the rebels, which further reduced the moral hazard and deescalated the conflict. Third, the diplomacy rewarded Liberia's nonviolent opposition by ensuring it a share of power in the interim government and the opportunity to win subsequent elections, thereby further reducing the moral hazard that can encourage rebellion and perpetuate civil war. Fourth, humanitarianism was not merely a cover story but the actual motivation for the intervention, which thus did not artificially raise hopes of future humanitarian-inspired intervention. Fifth, the interveners did not demand that Liberia's leaders surrender all power, or risk quick elections, or face immediate prosecution – but rather promised asylum to the President and a share of power to his political circle – thereby averting a potential violent backlash from regime elements.

When civil wars endanger civilians, proponents of R2P often promote forceful international action: military intervention, regime change, and prosecution of senior state officials. However, such actions have backfired repeatedly, escalating civil war and humanitarian suffering in cases such as Bosnia, Kosovo, Darfur, and Libya. By contrast, Liberia reveals that more diplomatic international action – relying on power sharing, golden parachutes for departing leaders, and peacekeepers rather than offensive military action – can end civil war and save thousands of lives. The goal of R2P is admirable, but its proponents should embrace these lessons to enhance future international efforts to protect civilians.

Notes

The author gratefully acknowledges the valuable research assistance of Jill Pokorney and financial support from the following: The U.S. Institute of Peace's Jennings Randolph Senior Fellowship in 2013-2014; the Woodrow Wilson International Center for Scholars' fellowship in 2009-2010; the University of Texas at Austin's Faculty Research Assignment; the Policy Research Institute at the LBJ School of Public Affairs; and the U.S. Army Research Office grant number W911NF-09-1-0077 under the Minerva Initiative of the U.S. Department of Defense.

1   Examples are Bosnia, Rwanda, Kosovo, Darfur, and Libya. See Alan J. Kuperman, "Provoking Genocide: A Revised History of the Rwandan Patriotic Front," *Journal of Genocide Research* 6, no. 1 (2004): 61-84; Alan J. Kuperman, "The Moral Hazard of Humanitarian Intervention: Lessons from the Balkans," *International Studies Quarterly* 52, no. 1 (2008): 49-80; Alan J. Kuperman, "Darfur: Strategic Victimhood Strikes Again?" *Genocide Studies and Prevention* 4, no. 3 (2009): 281–303; and Alan J. Kuperman, "A Model Humanitarian Intervention? Reassessing NATO's Libya Campaign," *International Security* 38, no. 1 (2013): 105-36.

2   Joe Wylie, interview with author, Monrovia, August 2, 2012. Wylie says that he and Nigerian Gen. Maxwell Colby helped form LURD by uniting four existing groups: Organization of Displaced Liberians, Islamic Justice Coalition for Liberia, Islamic New Horizon, and Freetown Coalition of Liberians. Wylie advocated that the new organization, unlike its predecessors, should put "Liberia" first in its name.

3   Ophoree Diah, interview with author, Monrovia, August 2, 2012. He appears to be the most senior LURD military officer still alive (as of early 2014), having served in 2003 as the rebel group's deputy chief of staff. His military career started in 1990 and took him from Liberia's army, to ULIMO, back to the army, and then to LURD. James Brabazon, "Liberia: Liberians United for Reconciliation and Democracy (LURD)," Armed Non-State Actors Project, Briefing Paper No. 1,

Royal Institute of International Affairs, February 2003, pp. 7, 9-10, estimates that in late 2002, LURD had up to 3,000 troops; 90 percent of the command and 60 percent of the ranks were ex-ULIMO; about 10 percent of the force were fighters from Sierra Leone, whom he viewed as mercenaries.

4   Brabazon, "Liberia: Liberians United," p. 6.

5   Boi Bleaju Boi, interview with author, Monrovia, August 3, 2012, claims that MODEL controlled 7½ of Liberia's 15 counties. International Crisis Group, "Liberia: Security Challenges," *Africa Report* No. 71, November 3, 2003, p. 8, says that when foreign-owned businesses retreated from Buchanan, they stopped paying government troops, who thereby became easy for MODEL to defeat or coopt.

6   The sanctions may have been decisive in the war. Nicole Itano, "Liberating Liberia," Institute for Security Studies, Paper 82, November 2003, p. 4, quotes Sam Jackson, Liberia's minister of state for financial and economic affairs, in mid-2003: "If we had the ability to buy arms openly, LURD would not be at the Freeport today." Taylor provoked these sanctions by angering both the UK (by meddling in Sierra Leone) and France (by meddling in the Ivory Coast), according to Amos Sawyer, interview with author, Washington, DC, November 12, 2009. Sawyer was President of Liberia's Interim Government of National Unity from late 1990 to March 1994. William S. Reno, "Liberia: The LURDs of the New Church," in *African Guerrillas*, eds. Morten Boas and Kevin C. Dunn (Boulder, CO: Lynne Rienner, 2007), p. 75, and Colin M. Waugh, *Charles Taylor and Liberia*, (London: Zed Books, 2011), p. 263, report that the sanctions originally were triggered by a UN report, in December 2000, accusing Taylor of aiding the RUF rebels in Sierra Leone, and were expanded to encompass diamond exports in March 2001. But Waugh, *Charles Taylor and Liberia*, p. 268, notes that even after Taylor cut off aid to those rebels, in April 2002, the UN did not lift the sanctions. Monie Captan, interview with author, Monrovia, August 3, 2012, and Waugh, *Charles Taylor and Liberia*, pp. 263, 266-67, report that France helped protect Taylor at the UN until he aided anti-government rebels in the Ivory Coast in 2002, after which Paris supported further expanding the sanctions to include timber exports. Ironically, according to these sources, Taylor believed that France and the United States supported the rebels in the Ivory Coast, so he expected to be rewarded – not punished – for doing likewise. Taylor may have been tricked into aiding the rebels by Burkina Faso's president Blaise Compaoré, who was backing them.

7   Itano, "Liberating Liberia," pp. 3-5, notes that the army still was viewed as dominated by Krahn, the same ethnic group as many of the rebels, especially in MODEL. After LURD seized the Free Port in July 2003, the government could not obtain fuel to operate its vehicles or the power generator of its radio station.

8   International Crisis Group, "Liberia: Security Challenges," pp. 7-8, lists the regime's most reliable forces: 6,000 in the Anti-Terrorism Unit (led by Taylor's son, "Chuckie," until he was removed in 2002 for human rights abuses), 1,500 in the Jungle Lions (led by Roland Duo), 300-800 in the Special Security Service (the elite unit, led by Benjamin Yeaten), 300 Marines (led by Gen. Gonda), and an unspecified number in the Special Strike Force. Much less reliable were the 7-11,000 army troops and the 20-30,000 pro-government militia. Brabazon, "Liberia: Liberians United," pp. 7-8, estimates that Taylor could deploy only 500 troops outside the capital.

9   Former interim President Sawyer, interview, says that without a power sharing deal the outcome would have been protracted fighting, since neither rebel group was strong enough to defeat the other, and each likely would have splintered, as such groups in Liberia had in the past.

10 "Agreement on Ceasefire and Cessation of Hostilities Between the Government of the Republic of Liberia and Liberians United for Reconciliation and Democracy and the Movement for Democracy in Liberia," June 17, 2003, signed by Defense Minister Daniel Chea for the government, Kabineh Janneh for LURD, and J. D. Slanger for MODEL, http://kms1.isn.ethz.ch/serviceengine/Files/ISN/21541/ipriadoc_doc/b0be53f1-8452-4b77-a58b-a3230c6656a5/en/040.pdf.

11 A former U.S. official, who requests anonymity, says the rebels would falsely tell Guinea that they had expended their ammunition, in order to get more, when in fact they were stockpiling it in Liberia for their offensives.

12 International Crisis Group, "Liberia: Security Challenges," p. 4; Itano, "Liberating Liberia," pp. 1, 3, 5-7; Priscilla Hayner, "Negotiating Peace in Liberia," International Center for Transitional Justice, November 2007, p. 11; Wylie, interview.

13 Alan J. Kuperman, "Rethinking the Responsibility to Protect," *Whitehead Journal of Diplomacy and International Relations* 10, no. 1 (2009): 33-43. See also footnote 1.

14 "The Comprehensive Peace Accord (CPA): Status of Implementation," Prepared by the Office of the Advisor to the Chairman on the Scrupulous Implementation of the Accord, December 18, 2005, in author's possession. Hayner, "Negotiating Peace in Liberia," p. 12.

15 "Allocation of Cabinet Positions, Public Corporations and Autonomus [sic] Agencies/Commission Under the NTGL," Annex 4 of the Comprehensive Peace Accord, August 18, 2003, http://www.usip.org/sites/default/files/file/resources/collections/peace_agreements/liberia_08182003.pdf. International Crisis Group, "Liberia: Security Challenges," pp. 3-4, notes that "each warring faction was given key public corporations and autonomous agencies, which promises to allow them to continue old habits of siphoning off state resources." Hayner, "Negotiating Peace,"

p. 14, reports that, in order to obtain the posts that it sought in the peace agreement, LURD escalated its military pressure in Monrovia until it was appeased in Accra.

16   John Blaney, phone interview with author, November 3, 2009, says that after the initial intervention, his staff had to go put out "two dozen firefights all over."

17   International Crisis Group, "Liberia: Security Challenges," pp. 4-7, 10.

18   Joe Gbalah, interview with author, Monrovia, August 1, 2012. Boi, interview. Hayner, "Negotiating peace in Liberia," p. 19.

19   Blaney, interview, says that one of his tactics to keep ex-rebels from returning to war was to employ them in Liberian public works teams, which he called "Blaney Brigades."

20   Diah, interview. Kai Farley, interview with author, Monrovia, August 3, 2012.

21   Sekou Conneh, interview with author, Monrovia, July 31, 2012, says that after the interim government replaced his appointees, "ex-rebels came to me and said 'let's fight.'" See also Reno, "Liberia: The LURDs," p. 80; Kendra Dupuy and Julian Detzel, *Power Sharing and Peace-building in Liberia* (Oslo: Center for the Study of Civil War, PRIO, 2007), p. 19.

22   Diah, interview. He says that LURD and MODEL were compatible despite tribal differences, but that they had no military coordination during the civil war.

23   Farley, interview.

24   Boi, interview.

25   Col. Sue Ann Sandusky, interview with author, Washington, DC, November 30, 2009.

26   Diah, interview.

27   This point was noted by Sawyer, interview.

28   Waugh, *Charles Taylor and Liberia*, p. 280.

29   Kabah Trawally, interview with author, Monrovia, July 31, 2012. He leads the Inter-Religious Council of Liberia.

30   More than a dozen peace efforts had failed in Liberia alone. See Lansana Gberie, "Liberia's War and Peace Process: A Historical Overview," in *A Tortuous Road to Peace: The Dynamics of Regional, UN and International Humanitarian Interventions in Liberia*, eds. Festus Aboagye and Alhaji M S Bah (Pretoria, South Africa: Institute for Security Studies, 2005), pp. 58-61. For a comparison of failed and successful intervention in a neighboring country, see Leslie Hough, "A Study of Peacekeeping, Peace Enforcement and Private Military Companies in Sierra Leone," *African Security Review* 16, no. 4 (2007): 8-21.

31   For example, at the time of the US intervention, one young Liberian was quoted as follows: "We wish they'd stay until peace would come. Their presence here puts fear in our fighters. It makes them think if they carry on hostilities, they'll be handled by the Americans." Major James G. Antal and Major R. John Vanden

Berghe, *On Mamba Station: U.S. Marines in West Africa 1990-2003* (Washington, DC: U.S. Marine Corps, 2004), p. 116.

32 The United States sometimes may be unwilling to use that leverage, such as if it would require withholding support from an ally. For example, in Afghanistan in 2001, the United States did not want its ally the Northern Alliance to seize the capital Kabul, but Washington refrained from using its leverage to deter that outcome. (My thanks to Jill Hazelton for this observation.)

33 Four months prior to the peace talks, and six months prior to the peace agreement, LURD declared objectives similar to those of the international community. As reported by Brabazon, "Liberia: Liberians United," p. 4, in February 2003: "If Taylor is removed, Conneh and LURD claim they will cease fighting. . . . [A] non-elected interim government (comprised of LURD, current opposition parties and certain members of Charles Taylor's government) would oversee a transitional phase of political authority in conjunction with an international stabilization force, preferably provided by the United Nations . . . . [Then, LURD would] help the international community to oversee free and fair elections." Gbalah, interview, says that in June 2003 he expressed similar objectives to a U.S. delegation that was visiting Guinea, led by Gen. Thomas Turner and including approximately six U.S. defense intelligence officials.

34 Geoffrey Blainey, *The Causes of War,* 3rd ed. (New York: Free Press, 1988), pp. 108-24.

35 For a summary and critique of "ripeness" theory, see Alan J. Kuperman, "Ripeness Revisited: The Perils of Muscular Mediation," in *Conflict Management and Africa: Negotiation, Mediation, and Politics*, eds. Terrence Lyons and Gilbert Khadiagala (Abingdon: Routledge, 2008), pp. 9-21.

36 Nigeria also provided asylum. But some country could be found to provide asylum for virtually any head of state, especially if encouraged by the United States.

37 Alan J. Kuperman, *The Limits of Humanitarian Intervention: Genocide in Rwanda* (Washington, DC: Brookings Institution Press, 2001). The time requirements can be substantially greater if the force is larger or must be equipped for extended combat.

38 For example, Bosnia (1995), Kosovo (1999), and East Timor (1999) had populations even smaller than that of Liberia (2003) when international forces were deployed. A larger populace would increase peacekeeping requirements, potentially prohibitively so, as explained by James T. Quinlivan, "Force Requirements in Stability Operations," *Parameters* (winter 1995-96): 59-69.

39 Alan J. Kuperman, "Is Partition Really the Only Hope? Reconciling Contradictory Findings About Ethnic Civil Wars," *Security Studies* 13, no. 4 (2004): 314-49.

40 Kuperman, "Rethinking the Responsibility to Protect."

The 1996 "Grapes of Wrath" Ceasefire Agreement and the Israel-Lebanon Monitoring Group: A Model of Successful Negotiations in Conflict Management

Marc Finaud

From 1985 to 2000, Israel maintained a military presence in a so-called "security zone" in South Lebanon, where it supported the South Lebanese Army (SLA). Hizbollah fighters not only engaged Israeli and SLA forces in that zone, but also occasionally fired rockets into Israeli territory, causing civilian casualties and destruction. In 1993 and 1996, Israel conducted a massive offensive against Lebanon, leaving damage and destruction in its aftermath. The United States mediated ceasefire arrangements between Israel and Hizbollah (through the Lebanese and Syrian governments). As opposed to the 1993 ceasefire agreement, the 1996 agreement following Israel's Operation Grapes of Wrath was mutually accepted and provided for a mechanism to monitor its implementation (the Israel-Lebanon Monitoring Group, co-chaired by the US and France, with the participation of Israel, Syria, and Lebanon). It functioned until February 2000, shortly before Israel completely withdrew its forces from South Lebanon. Two decades later, this instrument remains a model of successful negotiation for conflict management, both with respect to the process that led to the agreement and monitoring of the ceasefire. Its success in reducing civilian casualties on both sides during its four-year implementation has caused some to advocate the use of a similar model for other purposes (an Israeli-Lebanese peace agreement, a conflict prevention mechanism, or Israeli-Palestinian peace negotiations).

Historical Background

The origins of the conflict between Israel and Lebanon go back to the creation of the Jewish state in 1948, though after their 1949 Armistice Agreement, relative stability between both countries prevailed, including during the 1967 and 1973 wars in which Lebanon was hardly involved. Nevertheless, Lebanon was increasingly drawn into tensions with Israel when its territory was used as a base by Palestinian militants fighting Israel during the Lebanese civil war (until 1982) and later by Hizbollah, supported by Syria and Iran, conducting a proxy war against Israel. In response, Israel launched several operations aimed at stopping attacks on its northern territory.

In 1978, Operation Litani led the United Nations (UN) Security Council to establish Resolution 425 (UNSCR 425), calling for the withdrawal of Israeli forces and deployment of the United Nations Interim Force in Lebanon (UNIFIL); Israel handed over its outposts to its ally, the Free Lebanon Army (FLA), that later became the South Lebanon Army (SLA). In 1982, Operation Peace for the Galilee ended with the evacuation of PLO forces from Lebanon mediated by the United States and France. Israel maintained residual forces in a "security zone" in southern Lebanon along with the SLA.

In 1993, Operation Accountability included aerial strikes against Hizbollah bases, which had replaced the Palestinians, as well as shelling villages in South Lebanon, Tyre, and Sidon to force the Lebanese government to pressure the guerrilla movement[1] and send a strong signal to its Syrian sponsor.[2] Hizbollah, in retaliation, fired a number of indiscriminate Katyusha rockets into northern Israel. As it did in 1981, the U.S. government stepped in and negotiated a ceasefire through Bill Clinton's Secretary of State Warren Christopher, who spent a whole week calling the leaders of Israel, Syria, and Lebanon and making indirect contacts with Iran.[3] The resulting July 1993 agreement boiled down to applying the "red lines" already spelled out by Hizbollah and de facto accepted by Israel: Hizbollah pledged to stop firing rockets at northern Israel while Israel agreed to refrain from attacking civilian targets in Lebanon. This arrangement was oral and based on each party's commitment to the arrangement. All the parties believed that the agreement would be honored because of American involvement. But the ceasefire arrangement was far from being respected by both sides, though most of the time they insisted that they were following their "red lines."

Regular exchanges of fire lasted until April 1996, when Israel decided to launch a new operation named Grapes of Wrath.

The 1996 Ceasefire Agreement and the Israel-Lebanon Monitoring Group

In the context of the 1996 campaign for general elections, Prime Minister Shimon Peres was hoping to obtain a full ceasefire, which would serve to protect Israeli forces in South Lebanon in exchange for a commitment to negotiate a complete withdrawal from Lebanon after a trial period of nine months.[4] Consequently, he decided to send a request that Damascus impose restraint upon Hizbollah, conveyed through the Lebanese government.[5] From April 11 to 26, 1996, Operation Grapes of Wrath took the form of a massive air and artillery attack on alleged Hizbollah military infrastructure as well as civilian infrastructure such as power stations. The Israeli Defense Forces (IDF), through the SLA radio, sent warnings to the civilian population in South Lebanon to evacuate their towns and villages, causing the displacement of some 400,000 Lebanese civilians.[6] Some 30,000 people in northern Israel were also forced to seek shelter.[7]

A dramatic turning point in the offensive occurred on April 18, 1996, when Israeli artillery shells landed on a UN military compound in Qana, near Tyre, killing 106 civilian refugees and injuring another 116.[8] Whereas for the UN it was unlikely that the shelling resulted from a procedural or technical error,[9] Israel stressed that Hizbollah was to be blamed for having fired at an Israeli outpost from the vicinity of a populated area.[10] UNSCR 1052 of April 18, 1996[11] called for an immediate cessation of hostilities. Once again, U.S. President Bill Clinton sent his Secretary of State Warren Christopher to the region to mediate a ceasefire. In a weeklong negotiation marathon, Christopher visited Damascus, held intensive meetings in Jerusalem as well as telephone consultations with Egyptian and Saudi leaders, and went to Beirut when an agreement was practically finalized.[12] During the U.S. mediation efforts, other countries also dispatched envoys to the region: French President Jacques Chirac, a personal friend of Lebanese Prime Minister Rafik Hariri, sent his Foreign Minister Hervé de Charette. The Foreign Ministers of Russia, Italy, Spain, and Ireland also travelled to the Middle East.[13] Israel expressed some discontent regarding those attempts and insisted that the U.S. remain the principal mediator.[14] Christopher also made it clear that the U.S. should take the lead.[15]

There were serious differences between the French and U.S. ceasefire proposals despite their common goal (protecting civilians) and provision for a standing monitoring mechanism. The French based their plan on UNSCR 425, though it was not intended to substitute the peace negotiations. For its part, the U.S. proposal was closer to Israel's requests.[16] Due to the strong international pressure on Israel after the Qana massacre, the U.S. could not impose Israel's desired goals (full ceasefire in exchange for a pledge to negotiate withdrawal) and the parties settled on a "package" that was close to the French proposal. The Ceasefire Agreement was made public simultaneously on April 26, 1996 in Jerusalem[17] and in Beirut. Hizbollah Secretary General Hassan Nasrallah announced that his organization would consider itself bound by it.[18]

Contrary to the 1993 agreement, this was a written text with straightforward commitments. Formally, it recorded what both Israel and Lebanon would ensure: "armed groups in Lebanon" would not carry out attacks against Israel; Israel and SLA forces would not fire any kind of weapon at civilians or civilian targets in Lebanon; civilians will never be the target of any attack, and civilian populated areas and industrial and electrical installations will never be used as launching grounds for attacks; nothing precluded any party from exercising the right for self-defense but "without violating this Agreement." An Israel-Lebanon Monitoring Group (ILMG) composed of the U.S., France, Israel, Lebanon, and Syria would monitor the implementation of the agreement by addressing complaints in case of alleged violations.

The Agreement was not intended as "a substitute for a permanent solution" but only as an instrument "to bring the current crisis to an end."[19] However, the U.S. did propose the resumption of negotiations between the parties "with the objective of reaching comprehensive peace" and understood that those negotiations should be "conducted in a climate of stability and tranquility."[20] This stressed the difference between a temporary ceasefire and a full-fledged peace process. This agreement was confirmed by Syria's Foreign Ministry, which stated that the agreement would "stop the cruel assault against the lives of the civilians without abandoning the legitimate right of the Lebanese resistance to confront the Israeli occupation."[21]

The parties then negotiated the ILMG rules of procedure. Diplomatic talks held in Washington were interrupted by the general elections in Israel in May 1996. The negotiations led to the adoption of a Protocol on the Working Rules for the ILMG on July 12, 1996.[22] The operation of the ILMG was considered by the Clinton administration as "a useful indicator that both the new [Israeli] government and the Syrians and Lebanese were interested in finding ways to defuse tensions and... showing that they could do business."[23]

For nearly four years, from July 1996 to February 2000, the ILMG met regularly at UNIFIL headquarters at Naqura to address complaints of alleged violations of the Agreement from either Lebanon or Israel or both, and issued public statements often pointing in practice to the responsibility of Israel (or the SLA) or Hizbollah (as represented by Lebanon). In total, the Group issued 103 press statements after having examined 607 complaints (298 from Israel and 309 from Lebanon).[24] Although most complaints related to actual incidents, there may have been a secret competition between Israel and Lebanon in order to maintain some balance in the number of complaints submitted.[25] In regards to the functioning of the ILMG, the following points are worth mentioning:

a. For the purpose of decision making, a consensual approach was eventually preferred to a voting system.[26] Press statements containing indirect admission of guilt or responsibility by one or the other party would carry more weight than unilateral accusations rejected by the other side. After hearing evidence from the complaining party and a response from the accused, and possibly conducting its own on-site verification mission,[27] the Group drafted a factual, confidential, internal report registering the various positions. It included results from verification visits, and the agreements or disagreements about the findings. Such reports were detailed, including locations of incidents, types of weapons used, resulting damage to people or property, and mentioned by name the accused forces (IDF, SLA, or Hizbollah) or even commanders, combatants, victims, or witnesses.[28] Then the parties negotiated a public press statement, usually also prepared by the chair. Obviously, this exercise was often time consuming, since the accused party generally attempted to deflect the blame for the charges. If there was unanimity in identifying the non-complying party, the report would mention it; if not, the report would contain a factual description of the group's discussions and possibly the outcome of the verification visit.

b. The chair and co-chair positions were rotated between the U.S. and France for periods of five months. Both were supposed to "work together closely in a spirit of full coordination and cooperation."[29] Despite some initial competition,[30] this coordination worked well.[31] Both delegations were active in drafting the internal and public reports. However, the expected roles were sometimes reversed:[32] although viewed as Israel's ally and protector, a U.S. chair would occasionally exert pressure on the Israeli delegation to admit its responsibility, while the French, considered as defenders of the Lebanese, often convinced the latter to accept blame for Hizbollah's behavior.[33] An Israeli delegate even admitted in private that the French chairs were more impartial because the Americans over-compensated for a perceived bias in favor of Israel.[34]

c. The Monitoring Group appeared as a model of civil-military cooperation. Officially, it consisted of "delegates headed by military representatives." In practice, the chair and co-chair were always diplomats, with military advisors in their delegations, while the Israeli, Lebanese, and Syrian delegations were headed by high-ranking military officers alongside hosted civilian advisors.[35] This mixture of cultures and backgrounds as well as networks and communication channels contributed to a professional, non-polemical approach to the discussions. The military expertise was useful in examining and possibly rebutting the submitted evidence,[36] while the diplomatic skills were put to a test in the arduous negotiations on the public statements. The role of the military in the implementation of the 1996 Agreement was the most important, and an actual change of tactics and modus operandi of the IDF resulted from the restraint imposed by the agreement.[37] Even when military commanders complained in Israel about those constraints, the Israeli political leaders always ruled in favor of strict compliance with the Agreement.[38]

d. The Monitoring Group also offered a framework for discreet communication between Israel and Syria. Officially, during meetings the Arab participants did not speak directly to the Israelis but through the chair; the Lebanese wanted to avoid the impression of cooperating with the enemy.[39] However, on several occasions, the chair left Israeli and Syrian delegates alone in a room ostensibly in order to negotiate a public statement but in fact to discuss other issues such as an exchange of prisoners,[40] a ceasefire to recover bodies of Israeli soldiers[41] or in exchange for the transfer of a town to Lebanese control.[42] Despite public denials, personal amicable ties and mutual trust were even forged between Israel and Arab delegates who met on a regular basis.[43] The fact that Israel and Syria used this back channel to avoid escalation of tensions that could have led to an all-out war between them, was all the more crucial given that U.S. mediation efforts to resume peace negotiations were unsuccessful during the whole duration of the ILMG. An Israeli delegate went as far as claiming that Syrian and Israeli representatives occasionally used complaints to the ILMG as pretexts for meeting each other.[44]

e. The functioning of the ILMG was also affected by domestic political developments. Albeit intended to spare civilians, military operations were causing the IDF and SLA increasing losses, and this was occasionally used in the political debate, especially during electoral campaigns. Some Israeli politicians advocated a negotiated Israeli withdrawal from Lebanon, which seemed logical after UNSCR 425 had been formally accepted by the Netanyahu government on April 1, 1998.[45] In the run-up to the 1999 early general elections, Labor candidate Ehud Barak promised that he would unilaterally withdraw Israeli forces from Lebanon if negotiations with Syria failed. During the last weeks of the Netanyahu government, Israel announced that it was no longer bound by the 1996 Agreement and would cease its participation in the ILMG.[46] However, soon after Ehud Barak assumed his position as Prime Minister on July 6, 1999, Israeli delegates resumed their participation in the Monitoring Group (only interrupted from June 24 to July 13, 1999).[47] On February 11, 2000, when the ILMG met to examine an Israeli complaint regarding a Hizbollah attack from a civilian area, the Israeli delegation interpreted this incident as evidence of ill will by Syria, and left Naqura as a sign of protest, marking the last meeting of the Monitoring Group.[48] Eventually, with the actual Israeli withdrawal from South Lebanon completed on May 25, 2000, the ILMG had lost its main *raison d'être*.

Lessons Learned from the Israel-Lebanon Monitoring Group

Assessing the effectiveness of the 1996 Agreement requires reference both to the facts regarding their main purpose – protecting civilians from a continuing armed conflict – and the public appraisal in Israel and Lebanon about achievement of this goal. A precise count of actual civilian victims is difficult because Lebanese statistics do not distinguish between "real" civilians and "resistance" combatants.[49] Nevertheless, a study did compare casualties between 1996 and the first eight months of 1997: the number of Katyusha attacks had dropped from 25 to 8; Israeli civilian casualties from 34 to 4; Israeli military fatalities from 26 to 17; Lebanese civilian casualties from 640 to 123; and Hizbollah casualties from 50 to 45.[50] From 1985 to 2000, the 4,000 rockets launched by Hizbollah onto northern Israel killed nine Israeli civilians.[51] After the 1996 Agreement had entered into force, statements on both sides admitted[52] that as a result, the number of civilian casualties had been considerably reduced.[53] Even the leader of Hizbollah recognized that "despite our annoyance with the continuing Israeli violations, the Agreement did curb the attacks on civilians."[54]

The success of the 1996 Agreement explains why it was considered a model for fulfilling similar missions in other contexts. In 2001, negotiators from the Palestinian Authority examined the experience of the ILMG in light of the Mitchell Report (containing recommendations on the Israeli-Palestinian peace process): while taking a skeptical view of its relevance to the Palestinian track, they recognized the value of a multilateral monitoring structure.[55] In 2002, in view of the fragility of the situation along the Lebanese border, the International Crisis Group (ICG) recommended that both Israel and Hizbollah respect the "spirit of the April 1996 Agreement" by refraining from attacking civilians and that "regular talks" be held between U.S., European Union, UN, Russian, Syrian, and Lebanese representatives.[56]

During the 2006 Lebanon war, which caused some 1,300 civilian deaths in Lebanon[57] and killed 165 Israelis,[58] Israel asked the US to establish a new ILMG to "coordinate" a ceasefire with a "UNIFIL-Plus force" and "prevent a vacuum in South Lebanon."[59] The 4,000 Katyusha rockets launched by Hizbollah during the war onto Israel killed 40 Israeli civilians.[60] Most probably, had the 1996 Agreement survived Israel's withdrawal, civilian casualties would have been avoided, and the ILMG could have served as a basis for a future peace agreement between Israel and Lebanon, especially for the monitoring of possible border incidents.[61] In 2010, Daniel Kurtzer, former U.S. Ambassador to Israel and Egypt, proposed a plan to prevent a new war between Israel and Lebanon that included the option of "resurrecting in some form" the ILMG to "restore credibility to the effort to implement" UNSCR 1701 (calling for a total cessation of hostilities in Lebanon and the future disarmament of Hizbollah).[62] According to an Israeli commentator, a de facto framework similar to the ILMG was used "for meetings of IDF and Northern Command officers with senior Lebanese and UNIFIL officers."[63]

Of course, in the 2006 Lebanon war, the general context had dramatically changed compared to 1996: after the withdrawal of Syrian troops from Lebanon in 2005, Bashar al-Assad's influence on Hizbollah was reduced;[64] Hizbollah had acquired sophisticated weaponry mainly from Iran,[65] which made this war look more like an Israel-Iran proxy confrontation;[66] because Hizbollah had two cabinet ministers in the Lebanese government, Israel considered the latter responsible for the abduction of Israeli soldiers that triggered the offensive; Israel also believed that should it suffer the consequences of war, the Lebanese population would turn its back against Hizbollah;[67] finally, Israel enjoyed unconditional support on the part of the U.S. Bush administration, which stressed Israel's right to self-defense and left it to the UN to painfully conduct a month-long ceasefire negotiation.

A former advisor to the Israeli ILMG delegation also advocated a "resurrection of the monitoring group and the establishment of a parallel Israeli-Palestinian body." For him, such a renewed ILMG could be tasked to monitor the disarmament of Hizbollah by the Lebanese Army and "create a constructive new channel of communication among Israel, Lebanon, Syria and the Palestinian Authority." The Israeli-Palestinian monitoring group, with the possible inclusion of Egypt and Jordan, could immediately convene in the event of any spike in Israeli-Palestinian violence.[68]

In 2007, the idea of European civilian border assistance mission to help Lebanon ensure security along its border with Israel was considered. But voices from the region suggested rather to "revamp" the ILMG to "provide verification measures for the projected downsizing of" UNIFIL.[69] This new institution would "report and reprimand any violations of Resolution 1701 from all involved parties." This "new EU-led group could act as a means of diplomatic dialogue, and, most imperative for Lebanon's sovereignty, could be a verification mechanism to condemn Israel's overflight violations and Syrian trans-border transgressions."[70]

Obviously, in the current context of the Syrian civil war, it is difficult to imagine any relevance for resurrecting a mechanism similar to the ILMG before some stabilization and de-escalation of armed violence occurs among the warring parties. However, in a future scenario of reconstruction and the interim phase towards a regional peace settlement, this idea should be kept alive.

Conclusions and Recommendations

The success incurred by the 1996 Agreement and the ILMG, which makes them appear as a possible model to solve similar problems, can suggest the following recommendations:

a. *In most cases, multilateral approaches are more effective than unilateralism.* The history of the Middle East, in particular the relations between Israel and the Palestinians or Hizbollah, abounds in cases when unilateral moves by either actor led to a worse situation than the status quo, while most attempts of multilateral solutions were successful and sustainable.[71] With the 1993 and 1996 agreements, the U.S. mediation based on UN resolutions established a situation of relative calm with fewer casualties. In both cases, the limited ceasefire collapsed due to Hizbollah actions, followed by unilateral military actions by Israel instead of joint action with external actors. Similar situations occurred when Israel expelled some 400 Palestinians to Lebanon in 1992,[72] withdrew from South Lebanon in 2000 without an agreement with Lebanon and Syria, unilaterally pulled out from the Gaza Strip in 2005, or conducted its offensive on Lebanon in 2006. In contrast, two multilateral peacekeeping operations resulting from negotiated multilateral arrangements, the UN Disengagement Force (UNDOF) on the Golan Heights deployed in 1974 and the Multinational Force of Observers (MFO) established in the Sinai in 1981, still contribute to maintaining relative calm in these regions of strategic importance for Israel.

b. *In some cases, preference should be given to realistic, short-term goals over ambitious peace plans.* Often in the Middle East "the avoidance of war is a far more achievable goal" than getting the parties to make peace.[73] The success of the 1996 arrangement was mainly due to its well-delineated, rather short-term and limited ambition: protecting civilians from the military conflict waged between the parties. This restricted purpose was clearly separated from the political aim of resuming peace negotiations between Israel and Syria, mentioned in the Agreement as a U.S. "proposal." The U.S. mediation efforts failed not because the belligerents found it more convenient to continue the fighting while keeping it under control, but rather due to the lack of readiness by both sides to make the necessary concessions for achieving full peace. Nonetheless, the parties had an interest in keeping the 1996 mechanism alive for avoiding escalation into a direct military confrontation, a more costly alternative, and keeping a communication back channel open. Of course, in today's context of the civil war in Syria, that consideration seems quite irrelevant. However, in a different situation, one could imagine that a system of conflict management between two enemies not yet ready to negotiate full cessation of hostilities could serve their common interest to spare civilians and avoid escalation of tensions. This would probably require, like the 1996 agreement, a powerful mediator enjoying trust from the belligerents.

c. *Mediation has a better chance of success if it seeks balanced results.* The search for mutual obligations was critical to the success of the 1996 ceasefire negotiations. Perhaps as a result of a regional culture of revenge for harm suffered, the fighting between Hizbollah and Israel was characterized by a cycle of violent acts and responses. Of course, the conflict was also marked by asymmetry that made it difficult to put the belligerents on the same footing. Israel, as a State Party to the 1949 Geneva Conventions[74] and equipped with sophisticated weapon systems, was bound by the obligations of international humanitarian law applicable in armed conflict (IHL), in particular not to target civilians and to take additional precautions as an occupying power. Hizbollah, a non-state actor, claimed that it was only carrying out acts of resistance against occupation and was not bound by IHL. This is why it was so important for the U.S. mediator to seek the adherence of states, Syria and Lebanon, held responsible for the acts of Hizbollah. But the U.S. and French mediators were also aware of the constant need for consensus that required mutual concessions and sometimes face-saving devices (such as a public apology for an unintentional casualty or the procedural fiction that the belligerents did not talk to each other but only through the chair).[75] This explains why most of the public statements were so carefully crafted, often reaffirming the rules for the benefit of all. This was perceived as superior to a zero-sum game approach consisting in scoring points but losing human lives. In any similar situation, mediators should strive to find the proper balance between designating a belligerent responsible for a clear breach of a ceasefire or IHL and consensus language reaffirming commitments to abide by the agreements.

d. *Timing is critical in most crisis negotiations.* In 1993 and 1996, the U.S. mediator initiated negotiations without delay with all parties in the absence of direct communications between them. In both cases, it took a week to achieve an agreement and de-escalate the military confrontation, which by most standards is a rather short time. The 1996 negotiations were facilitated by the previous ones and their unwritten outcome. Time was of the essence in 1996 because of the electoral campaign in Israel, and the domestic uproar about casualties and constraints on the population in northern Israel. The sense of urgency was also part of the monitoring system: when complaints of alleged violations were submitted, the Chair was supposed to call for a meeting "immediately." In many cases, the meetings were convened within 24 or 48 hours. Outside meetings, the Chair also served as an intermediary for emergency communication between the parties, as for instance in the December 1999 unintentional Israeli shelling of a Lebanese school.[76] In a similar conflict situation, rapid communication and intervention of mediators can be critical in preventing escalation of tensions and saving civilian lives. In contrast, in the 2006 Lebanon war, for 18 days, the U.S. did not support any ceasefire.[77] The irony was that just like in 1996, the abstention which resulted in hundreds of casualties was reversed after new bloodshed in Qana due to indiscriminate Israeli shelling.[78]

e. *When third-party mediators are involved in negotiations, they must agree to work intensively with all the parties, and focus on achieving the desired result.* In 1996, contrary to 1993, the U.S. mediator travelled to the region and conducted full-time shuttle diplomacy for one week between the parties. He also held active telephone consultations with other leaders who could exert influence. The French Foreign Minister also spent 13 days shuttling between Beirut, Damascus, and Jerusalem, an unprecedented duration for a French politician also active on the domestic scene.[79] Despite disadvantages of competition, insufficient coordination, and irritation of some parties, it seemed that only personal involvement and perseverance of high-level political figures (backed by strong national interests and competent teams of advisors) can deliver successful agreements.

f. *Leaders involved in negotiations on an agreement to stop violence should also assume the responsibility of implementation of the accord through a verification mechanism.* Especially in contexts of total lack of trust between the parties, respect for any agreement cannot be assumed and left to their good faith. This is why the ILMG was so successful: it involved powerful third-party mediators backed by the UN and capable of leveraging respect for the agreement, and it gave the parties a chance to hold the responsible party accountable for violations. Thus, the mechanism enjoyed both credibility and ownership of the parties, and its operation contributed to strengthening confidence in compliance with the agreement.

g. *The choice of mediators and negotiators, both on national and professional criteria, can be decisive.* In 1996, on the U.S. side, Warren Christopher benefited from his own experience of the 1993 negotiations and the personal knowledge of most of his interlocutors. He also relied on a team of competent experts in Middle East affairs, such as Dennis Ross, Special Middle East Coordinator at the State Department,[80] or Martin Indyk, the U.S. Ambassador to Israel.[81] Among U.S. delegates to the ILMG, a few American diplomats were later rewarded for their work: David N. Greenlee, Chairman of the ILMG in 1996-1997, then Ambassador to Bolivia and Paraguay; Joseph G. Sullivan, his successor in 1997-1998, then Ambassador to Angola and Zimbabwe; Theodor Feifer, deputy head of the U.S. delegation in 1996-1997, then Adviser to the Special Middle

East Coordinator. On the Israeli side, the most prominent negotiator was Dore Gold, a close advisor to Benjamin Netanyahu;[82] although not directly involved in the negotiations, Itamar Rabinovich, the Israeli Ambassador to the UN and delegate to the Israel-Syria peace talks, also played an influential role.[83] Another key Israeli expert was Uri Lubrani, the Ministry of Defense Coordinator on Lebanese Affairs for decades, considered as the Israeli official with the strongest connection to the Syrians and the Lebanese.[84] The Israeli delegation to the ILMG was headed by Brigadier General David Tzur, Chief Israeli Liaison Officer to Foreign Forces, who had an impressive record in the Israeli security establishment and was later elected to the Knesset. The Syrian Ambassador to the U.S., Walid Muallem, involved in the negotiations on the ILMG rules, later became Deputy Foreign Minister and then Foreign Minister in 2005.[85] The Lebanese delegate, Colonel Maher Toufeili, and his Syrian counterpart, General Adnan Balloul, deputy chief of Military Intelligence in Lebanon,[86] were more "traditional" military officers with limited initiative but they proved to be effective communication channels. On the French side, the two successive Chairmen of the ILMG, Jean-Michel Gaussot and Laurent Rapin, also had some experience in Middle East affairs: both from their tenures at the Permanent Mission of France to the UN and the latter as Desk Officer for Egypt and the Levant. Both of them also relied on a solid team of experts, starting with the Director for North Africa and the Middle East, Denis Bauchard, a tough negotiator.[87] In a similar context, it is important to select the individuals involved in the talks carefully, preferably for their experience and knowledge of the issues but also their skills in actual negotiation, legal argumentation, and imaginative solutions, as well as ability to withstand psychological pressure.

h. *Negotiations involving both military and diplomatic/political actors are effective when the division of tasks between them is clear.* Indeed, the military generally accepts the authority of the political level, and the civilians are willing to rely on the expertise of the military on defense, equipment, and situation on the ground. Communication seems more straightforward among the military, including from opposing sides, due to the commonality of culture, shared sense of duty, and discipline within the chain of command. This was demonstrated repeatedly within the negotiations of the ILMG. Often, the military delegates from opposing sides accepted the technical evidence related to alleged violations while their diplomatic advisors continued to argue on the merits of the case.[88] In a similar context, it is important to ensure that a clear division of tasks is maintained and that each group trusts the expertise of the other.

i. *Confidentiality is critical during the whole negotiation process.* This mitigates media pressure, posturing, and damaging leakages. But possible recourse to publicity, not of debates but of results, may play a useful role in achieving positive outcomes. This dual approach explained the success of the 1996 Agreement. The discussions conducted within the ILMG remained confidential: the Chair and Co-Chair were careful to collect written statements but not to leak them to the media, and to abstain from publicly mentioning national positions. The delegates themselves generally followed this rule, perhaps out of fear of backfire. Even several years after the fact, most testimonies in Adir Waldman's book remained anonymous.[89] This assurance that only agreed language would be made public, even if it included admission of responsibility by one or the other party, contributed to the building of confidence at least in the credibility of the mechanism. It did not stop each party from politically exploiting critical language towards the "enemy" or highlighting its own conduct as legitimate. But it had the merit of restricting the conflict to the level of propaganda or ideological warfare, always safer in the short term for both military and civilian lives.

Notes

1   Human Rights Watch, "Civilian Pawns: Laws of War Violations and the Use of Weapons on the Israel-Lebanon Border," May 1996, p. 2.

2   Adir Waldman, "Clashing Behavior, Converging Interests: A Legal Convention Regulating a Military Conflict," *Yale Journal of International Law* 27, no. 2 (2002): 249.

3   David Hoffman, "Israel Halts Bombardment of Lebanon," *Washington Post*, August 1, 1993.

4   Zvi Barel, "Katyushas Have a Course of their Own," *Haaretz*, February 16, 2000, cited in Adir Waldman, *Arbitrating Armed Conflict – Decisions of the Israel-Lebanon Monitoring Group* (Huntington: JP Juris, 2003), p. 23.

5 Itamar Rabinovich, *The Brink of Peace* (Princeton, N.J.: Princeton University Press, 1998), p. 231.
6 Human Rights Watch, "Civilian Pawns," p. 9.
7 Amnesty International, "Unlawful Killings during Operation 'Grapes of Wrath,'" July 23, 1996, p. 3.
8 United Nations Security Council, Letter from the Secretary-General to the President of the Security Council, Document S/1996/337 of May 7, 1996.
9 Ibid.
10 Israeli Ministry of Foreign Affairs, "Response to the UN Secretary-General's Report on the Kana Incident," July 1996.
11 United Nations, Security Council, Resolution 1052 (1996), April 18, 1996.
12 Waldman, *Arbitrating Armed Conflict,* p. 25.
13 Ibid., p. 23.
14 Israeli Ministry of Foreign Affairs, "Press Stakeout with PM Peres and Secretary of State Christopher," op. cit.
15 Ibid.
16 Hala Jaber, *Hezbollah: Born with a Vengeance* (New York: Columbia University Press, 1997), p. 195.
17 Israeli Ministry of Foreign Affairs, "Israel-Lebanon Ceasefire Understanding," April 26, 1996.
18 Alan Sipress, "Hezbollah, Israel Agree to Cease-fire. The Two Sides Said They Would Halt Attacks on Civilians. They Also Won't Launch Armed Operations from Populated Areas," *The Enquirer*, April 27, 1996.
19 Israeli Ministry of Foreign Affairs, "Israel-Lebanon Ceasefire Understanding."
20 Ibid.
21 Alan Sipress, "Hezbollah, Israel Agree to Cease-fire."
22 Full text, made public in 1998, available in Waldman, *Arbitrating Armed Conflict,* pp. 129-31.
23 "Accord Sets Up Five-Nation Monitoring Group for Lebanon Cease-Fire," *Reuters*, July 13, 1996.
24 Waldman, "Clashing Behavior, Converging Interests," p. 280.
25 Ibid., p. 276.
26 Waldman, *Arbitrating Armed Conflict,* pp. 33-34.
27 Article 1 B and C of the Working Rules amounted to requiring consensus for carrying out verification missions; the latter would be conducted jointly by the U.S., France, and Israel in the case of attacks on Israeli territory, and by the U.S., France, Lebanon, and Syria (if Syria so wished) in case of alleged violations on Lebanese territory.

28 For an example of such internal reports, see Waldman, *Arbitrating Armed Conflict,* pp. 135-40.
29 Ibid., p. 130.
30 Ibid., p. 108.
31 Author's interview with anonymous French diplomat, Tel Aviv, July 1998.
32 Ibid.
33 Khalil Fleihan, "Rapin Hits Out at Israeli Occupation," *Daily Star*, September 25, 1998.
34 Waldman, *Arbitrating Armed Conflict,* p. 47.
35 Waldman, "Clashing Behavior, Converging Interests," p. 271.
36 Waldman, *Arbitrating Armed Conflict,* pp. 46-47.
37 Alan Philips, "Israel's Military Might Cannot Quell Lebanese," *Telegraph*, September 25, 1998, cited in Charles Spain et al., *Conceptual Monitoring Options for a Southern Lebanon Withdrawal Agreement* (Albuquerque, NM: Sandia National Laboratories, 2000), p. 14.
38 David Rudge, "Mordechai: We Will Stick to Grapes of Wrath Understandings," *Jerusalem Post*, October 28, 1997.
39 See for instance "A Diplomatic Assessment of the Monitoring Group's Work – Discussions in Limbo," *al-Safir*, November 6, 1996 (in Arabic), cited in Waldman, *Arbitrating Armed Conflict,* p. 119.
40 Ibid., p. 116 and 119.
41 Ibid., p. 119.
42 Nicolas Blanford, "Syria 'Seeks Arnoun Deal,'" *Daily Star*, April. 30, 1999.
43 Ibid.
44 Waldman, *Arbitrating Armed Conflict,* p. 120.
45 "Lebanon Rejects Israeli Pullout Plan," *CNN World News*, April 1, 1998.
46 Waldman, *Arbitrating Armed Conflict,* p. 99.
47 Ibid.
48 Ibid., p. 101.
49 "Lebanon Sees More than 1,000 War Deaths," *Associated Press*, December 28, 2006.
50 Adam Frey, "The Israel-Lebanon Monitoring Group – An Operational Review," *Research Note* No. 3, Washington Institute, September 1997, p. 13.
51 Human Rights Watch, "Israel-Lebanon – Persona Non Grata: The Expulsion of Civilians from Israeli-Occupied Lebanon," 1999, p. 2.
52 Waldman, *Arbitrating Armed Conflict,* p. 36.
53 "Foreign Ministry Comments on ILMG Meeting," *Beirut Radio Lebanon*, December 12, 1996, cited in Waldman, *Arbitrating Armed Conflict*, p. 37.

54 "Nasrallah Interviewed on ILMG," *al-Safir*, January 31, 1997, cited in Waldman, *Arbitrating Armed Conflict*, p. 37.

55 Nabil Shaath and Basil Jabir, "Israel-Lebanon Monitoring Group Assessment," *Palestine Papers*, *al-Jazeera*, July 21, 2001.

56 International Crisis Group (ICG), "Old Game, New Rules: Conflict on the Israel-Lebanon Border," *Middle East Report* No. 7, November 18, 2002.

57 Robert Fisk, "Lebanon's Pain Grows by the Hour as Death Toll Hits 1,300," *Independent*, August 17, 2006.

58 Yaacov Katz, *Israel vs. Iran: The Shadow War* (New York: Potomac Books, 2012), p. 17.

59 "Spiegel Urges Rapid USG Stand-up of Israel-Lebanon Monitoring Group Team," Cable Ref. 06TELAVIV3151, *Wikileaks*, August 9, 2006.

60 Robin Wright and Thomas E. Ricks, "Bush Supports Israel's Move against Hezbollah," *Washington Post,* July 19, 2006.

61 Efraim Karsh et al., eds., *Conflict, Diplomacy and Society in Israeli-Lebanese Relations* (London: Routledge, 2013), p. 140-43.

62 Daniel C. Kurtzer, "A Third Lebanon War," *Contingency Planning Memorandum* No. 8, Council on Foreign Relations, July 2010.

63 Amir Oren, "If Lebanon Erupts Again," *Haaretz*, August 2, 2010.

64 Shlomo Brom, "Political and Military Objectives in a Limited War against a Guerrilla Organization," in *The Second Lebanon War: Strategic Perspectives,* eds. S. Brom and M. Elran (Tel Aviv: Institute for National Security Studies, 2007), p. 18.

65 Yiftah Shapir, "Observations on Hizbollah Weaponry," in *The Second Lebanon War,* pp. 223-32.

66 Eyal Zisser, "Iranian Involvement in Lebanon," *Military and Strategic Affairs* 3, no. 1 (2011): 3.

67 Wright and Ricks, "Bush Supports Israel's Move against Hezbollah."

68 Adir Waldman, "Lebanon's Force for Good," *New York Times*, August 2, 2006.

69 Stuart Reigeluth, "EU Monitoring not the Best Option," *al-Arabiya News*, December 6, 2007.

70 Ibid.

71 See detailed arguments in: Marc Finaud et al. *Multilateralism and Transnational Security: A Synopsis of Win-win Solutions* (Geneva: Slatkine, 2009), pp. 268-84.

72 B'Tselem, "The Mass Deportation of 1992," January 1, 2011, http://www.btselem.org/deportation/1992_mass_deportation.

73 David C. Wrobel, "Review of Arbitrating Armed Conflict: Decisions of the Israel-Lebanon Monitoring Group," *New York Law Journal* 2 (January 2004): 21-37.

74 Israel is not party to the 1977 Additional Protocols to the Geneva Conventions, but the International Committee of the Red Cross (ICRC) considers that those

instruments mainly codify pre-existing rules of customary law at least regarding the protection of civilians. See: ICRC, "Commentary on the Additional Protocols of 8 June 1977 to the Geneva Conventions of 12 August 1949," 1987.

75 "Sud: Action Limitée du Groupe de Surveillance de la Trêve," *La Revue du Liban*, April 31, 1997.

76 Waldman, *Arbitrating Armed Conflict,* p. 117.

77 "Rice Says 'Time to Get a Ceasefire in Lebanon,'" *Forbes*, July 30, 2006.

78 Ibid.

79 Pierre Haski, "Hervé de Charette, 58 ans, giscardien et ministre des Affaires étrangères," *Libération*, March 20, 1997.

80 Daniel Pipes and Patrick Clawson, "Interview with Dennis Ross: Living the Peace Process," *Middle East Quarterly* (June, 1996): 71-78.

81 Daniel Pipes and Patrick Clawson, "Interview with Martin Indyk: I Must Be Optimistic about Arab-Israeli Relations," *Middle East Quarterly* (March, 1999): 65-72.

82 See Ambassador Dore Gold, Jerusalem Center for Public Affairs, http://www.jcpa.org/dgold.htm.

83 Waldman, "Clashing Behavior, Converging Interests," pp. 256, 259.

84 Ibid., p. 294.

85 Robert G. Rabil, *Syria, The United States, and the War on Terror in the Middle East* (Westport: Praeger, 2006), p. 191.

86 Frey, "The Israel-Lebanon Monitoring Group," p. 12.

87 Waldman, *Arbitrating Armed Conflict,* p. 33.

88 Waldman, "Clashing Behavior, Converging Interests," p. 273.

89 Waldman, *Arbitrating Armed Conflict.*

Overcoming Socio-Psychological Barriers: The Influence of Beliefs about Losses

Ruthie Pliskin, Eran Halperin, and Daniel Bar-Tal

Overcoming socio-psychological barriers entails a long process of persuasion and cognitive change. In other words, society members and leaders must implement a process of mobilization for peacemaking in the same way the process of mobilization for supporting and participating in the conflict was implemented at the conflict's onset. In both cases, society members matter. The society members themselves initially developed the ideas that led to the conflict's onset, and they can also develop ideas about the necessity of peacemaking. In both cases they must persuade fellow society members in the "justness" of the proposed path. Thus any analysis of intractable conflicts necessitates the use of a socio-psychological perspective alongside other perspectives. Humans are the decision makers; therefore, the psychological aspects embedded in human characteristics must be addressed in order to change the social context. Addressing the socio-psychological repertoire can assist in the creation of various socialization and mobilization mechanisms for peacemaking and peacebuilding. It is thus of crucial importance to advance knowledge that will shed light on the conditions, contents, and processes that not only lead society members to embark on peacebuilding processes in times of conflicts, but also socialize them to actively prevent the outbreak and maintenance of vicious and destructive conflicts and costly hate cycles.

Peacemaking focuses on societal actions towards reaching an official settlement of an intergroup conflict, in the form of a formal agreement between the rival sides to end the confrontation.[1] Such actions are real and concrete, but the essence of peacemaking is psychological, as it requires changing the societal repertoire that has fueled the conflict, into a repertoire that is in line with the new goal of peacefully resolving the conflict. The new peace-supporting repertoire should include an approach to peaceful resolution, as well as humanization and legitimization of the rival. It should also involve changing previous views of the conflict as being of zero sum nature and unsolvable, changing the goals that fueled the conflict, accepting compromises, building trust, constructing beliefs that the agreement can be implemented, and developing new goals related to peaceful relations with the rival. Eventually, this process should lead to recognition of the need to reconcile and the construction of a new climate that promotes these new ideas about peacemaking and peacebuilding.[2]

Peacemaking usually involves "bottom-up" processes in which groups, grassroots organizations, and civil society members support the ideas of peacebuilding and act to disseminate them among leaders. On the other hand, peacemaking requires "top-down" processes in which emerging leaders join such efforts, initiate a peacemaking process, act to persuade the society members of the necessity of resolving the conflict peacefully, and carry it out. In both cases, unfreezing is the key process leading to change in the conflict-supporting repertoire.

The Unfreezing Process

According to the classical conception offered by Lewin in 1947,[3] every process of societal change must begin with cognitive change. In individuals and groups, this indicates "unfreezing." Hence, a precondition for the acceptance and internalization of any alternative beliefs about the conflict or peacebuilding depends on the ability to destabilize the rigid structure of the aforementioned dominant socio-psychological repertoire about the conflict. This endeavor is especially challenging because in many conflict situations, the unfreezing process begins with a minority that must have the courage to present the alternative ideas to fellow society members, as well as to decision makers that may eventually effect change on the political level. Indeed, all steps described below must occur among opinion leaders and other individuals in positions of leadership. Such top-down processes must join societal level processes, so as to support and accelerate shifts in public opinion, while also directly influencing changes in policymaking relevant to the conflict.

Step 1: An Instigating Belief

In such a social climate, peacemaking requires a new perspective on the necessity of a peace process. Indeed, on the individual psychological level, the process of unfreezing usually begins pursuant to the appearance of a new idea (or ideas) inconsistent with held beliefs and attitudes, thus causing tension, a dilemma, or even an internal conflict, which may stimulate a reexamination of one's basic position.[4] This new idea is termed "an instigating belief," because it motivates a reevaluation of held societal beliefs regarding the culture of conflict. Consequently, it may lead to the unfreezing of these beliefs.[5] The content of the instigating belief may come from different domains, and may pertain to the image of the rival, the history of the conflict, the group's goals, new threats to the group, and so on. Regardless of its content, the belief must contradict existing beliefs.

The instigating belief must also be of high validity and/or coming from a credible source, otherwise it may be easily rejected. Additionally, it must be strong enough to cause dissonance, as described by Festinger.[6] In other words, this belief must force an individual to pause and think before he or she can reconcile between the colliding beliefs. This may not mean that every society member will consider the instigating belief once it emerges, but it is possible that at least a few will be motivated to reconsider. The belief may emerge from personal experience or from external sources, but once it is acknowledged and considered it can eventually lead to an unfreezing process, in which at least some of the held beliefs are rejected.

Step 2: A Mediating Belief

This process paves the way for a new "mediating belief" that calls for changing the context of intractable conflict. The mediating belief is the logical outcome of dissonance, if it is resolved in the direction of accepting the instigating belief as valid.[7] Mediating beliefs are usually stated in the form of arguments, such as "we must change strategies or we are going to suffer further losses," "some kind of change is inevitable," "we have been going down a self-destructive path, so we must alter our goals and strategies," and "the proposed change is clearly in the national interest, it is necessary for national security."[8] These statements prompt a discussion of alternatives and thereby deepen the process of unfreezing initiated by the instigating beliefs.

Step 3: A Peaceful Alternative

At least one alternative that may emerge at the end of this process is the suggestion that the peaceful settlement of the conflict may change the direction in which society is heading. The emergence of this idea marks the beginning of the journey towards peacemaking. For instance, in South Africa, a number of unequivocal indicators (internal violence, deterioration of the South African economy, demographic growth of the Blacks, South African isolation, and so on, all of which have served as instigating beliefs) led Pieter Willem Botha, the conservative leader of the South African National Party who came to power in 1978, to realize as early as the 1980s that the situation cannot continue and that the leadership must implement reforms and initiate negotiation with the African National Congress. This logic indicated the appearance of mediating beliefs.[9]

Conditions for Change

While unfreezing is an individual process that may transpire in different individuals at different times, the likelihood of this process beginning and fully developing is increased when certain societal conditions are met. Some scholars of conflict resolution argue that the success of peacemaking processes and consequential conflict resolution depend on specific conditions that make the conflict ripe for a peaceful resolution. For example, Zartman proposed that "if the parties to a conflict (a) perceive themselves to be in a hurting stalemate and (b) perceive the possibility of a negotiated solution (a way out), the conflict is ripe for resolution (i.e., for negotiations toward resolution to begin)."[10] Furthermore, ideas about terminating the conflict peacefully often emerge and are successfully disseminated when changes in the context of the conflict are observed. These changes pertain to major events and/or information that may facilitate the process of peacemaking, and this stage can therefore be termed "the emergence of facilitating conditions." This may happen at any point during the peacemaking process.

Among the most salient facilitating conditions, trust-building actions by the rival lead to a perceived change in the opponents' character, intentions, and goals. Another facilitating condition pertains to information about the state of society. A realization of the costs to society in continuing the conflict may lead to the crystallization of beliefs in the need to change the views of the conflict and the rival, reconsider the intransigent policy, and even adopt conciliatory positions that could allow a peaceful resolution of the conflict. Sometimes the intervention of a powerful third party pushing for a peaceful resolution of the conflict may also serve as a determining condition in changing these views about the conflict. In some cases, such an intervention may include a proposed mega-incentive by a third party. If this incentive is highly valued by at least one party to the conflict, it may affect its views on the conflict and move it towards more conciliatory views. Changed conflict-related beliefs may also result from global geopolitical processes and events that are not directly related to the conflict (for example, the collapse of a superpower or new global realignments). In such cases, global change may affect a party in conflict and move it to adopt more conciliatory positions, thus acting as a facilitating condition.

The noted conditions are neither exhaustive nor exclusive. Each condition, as well as possible combinations of conditions, may generate new needs and new goals that become more important than the goals that led to the conflict's eruption. As a result, a set of beliefs may emerge that can contribute to the unfreezing of the long-held conflict-supporting repertoires. As we have discussed above, different beliefs can lead to unfreezing, but the main idea influencing unfreezing is probably the recognition that the losses incurred if the conflict continues are greater than the losses incurred with the acceptance of a particular opportunity for peaceful solution.[11] This recognition is a potent idea that may push the peacemaking process forward to its successful conclusion, and can therefore be a highly effective condition for change. In essence, such recognition refocuses the individual on the losses that the society may incur should it not resolve the conflict peacefully under the present conditions.

Effects of Information about Losses as a Facilitating Condition

Information about losses is a uniquely important condition, as individuals living in conflict zones are usually focused only on fear of loss, and may therefore underestimate or overlook losses incurred as a result of the continued conflict. Such information is of even greater importance when considering unfreezing processes among decision makers, since a miscalculation of possible losses may inhibit them from actively advancing conflict resolution. Our view on the importance of these considerations is partly based on Kahneman and Tversky's prospect theory,[12] which has been adapted to apply to conflict situations.[13] According to prospect theory, people are more reluctant to lose what they already have than they are motivated to gain what they do not have.[14] In the language of prospect theory, the value function is steeper on the loss side than on the gain side.

Reframing the Point of Reference

One way to emphasize the potential losses associated with continuing a conflict and to reduce the emphasis on possible losses associated with a peaceful settlement is to reframe the reference point. Prospect theory proposes that people react more strongly to changes in existing assets than to net asset levels; that is, they react to gains and losses from their subjective reference point rather than referring to the absolute values of gains or losses.[15] In most cases, the reference point is the status quo, but in some situations it can be an "aspiration level"[16] or a desired goal.[17] Often, individuals residing in conflict zones are socialized to believe in the feasibility of future gains from the conflict or even their group's possible victory over the rival.[18] The alternative possibility of paying a heavy price for continuing the conflict or being defeated is often ignored. As a result, when the compromises demanded in the context of a peaceful settlement of the conflict are compared with the society's aspirations, or even the status quo (mostly for the stronger party in the conflict), they are perceived as involving an enormous loss. In other words, the motivation to reevaluate firmly-held beliefs and consider alternatives depends on a new realization that continuing the conflict will not lead to a better or desired future, but may in fact drastically reduce the chances of achieving it.[19] Moreover, as noted, the conflict's continuation may lead to losses that are greater than the sacrifices needed in order to achieve a peaceful resolution to the conflict via compromises.

Real-World Transformations Driven by Beliefs about Losses

Two noteworthy examples of changes driven, at least to some extent, by the described processes can be found in the peacemaking efforts in Northern Ireland and South Africa. In Northern Ireland, MacGinty and Darby[20] have recently argued that in the early 1990s, the understanding that future change is inevitable and that such change might consist of fundamental losses to the unionist side of the conflict was one of the central motivations for reconsidering their intransigent position, and finally joining the negotiations in order to gain influence when formulating a future agreement. The writers quote a statement by a senior Orangeman, which they believe reflected a common view shared by the unionists: "Every time something comes along it is worse than what came before."[21] Within the context of the South African conflict, Mufson[22] has pointed to a similar example of the unfreezing process, suggesting that de Klerk and his people realized that "white South Africans' bargaining position would only grow weaker with time," leading them to launch negotiations and make every effort to move towards a viable agreement as soon as possible.

The Israeli-Palestinian conflict, while yet unresolved, also offers ample examples for the importance of beliefs about losses to unfreezing processes among leaders. In fact, Israeli leaders whose positions on the conflict moved towards support for conflict resolution, cited instrumental cost-benefit considerations, that is, information about potential losses should the conflict continue, rather than moral or ideological considerations. In fact, when heading into the Oslo peace process, the only strategic goal voiced by then-Israeli Prime Minister Yitzhak Rabin was his fear of continued Israeli sovereignty "over a large number of Arabs, which could lead to a binational state." For many Jewish Israelis, this meant the loss of a Jewish state. Rabin's former Foreign Minister Shimon Peres often echoed this sentiment, adding that "Rabin knew that the absence of decisiveness was likely to bring about a situation in which events would lead us, instead of us leading them."[23] Several right wing Israeli leaders underwent a similar process, bringing them closer to a realization of the importance of peacefully resolving the conflict. Former

Prime Minister Ariel Sharon, for instance, decided to evacuate settlements out of a desire to avoid the loss of a Jewish majority in the State of Israel, and the next leader of the Likud Party, Prime Minister Benjamin Netanyahu, also stated the end goal for a peace agreement would be avoiding a binational state,[24] not mentioning any moral or ideological goals alongside this fear of a loss of Jewish sovereignty.

Empirical evidence of this process can be found in work conducted together with other colleagues,[25] in which the perception of the proposed process was examined among Jews in Israel. The investigation found that instigating beliefs that include information about future losses in various aspects of life (e.g., economic aspects, demographic aspects, as well as Israel's future position in potential negotiations with Palestinians) may help unfreeze Israelis' predispositions about the peace process with the Palestinians.

The ultimate outcome of unfreezing is detachment from the repertoire that supports the continuation of the conflict, its reevaluation, and a new-found readiness to entertain alternative beliefs.[26] The repertoire can then be replaced by alternative societal beliefs that promote a peaceful resolution to the conflict.[27] Nonetheless, the examples described illustrate more than unfreezing. In most of these examples, the leaders arrived at the point of being able to formulate a coherent set of compromising beliefs, and these served as a holistic plan acceptable to the rival party. Indeed, the ultimate objective is to go beyond an agreement that settles the conflict peacefully, to the formulation, acceptance, and internalization of a new ethos of peace. This ethos must act to counter the conflict-supporting repertoire in terms of both content and structure. However, in the absence of peace and reconciliation, the attempt to form the new socio-psychological repertoire that will fulfill these needs and aspirations is a great challenge for every society that strives to end the conflict peacefully. Fulfilling these needs in each of two clear-cut situations – intractable violent conflict or a viable peace – is much easier than doing so in the "transitional" period between violent conflict and peace, rife with uncertainty and often with continuing violence and active opposition by some groups within society.

Conclusion

Disagreements over tangible and non-tangible commodities influence harsh and violent conflicts that engage society members and cause continuous suffering and hardship, as well as considerable losses in human lives. Such conflicts inflict serious problems and challenges upon the involved societies and the international community. A resolution requires not only addressing the tangible issues that lie at the heart of the disagreements, but also necessitates finding ways of overcoming the socio-psychological barriers that underlie and magnify the disparities. Moreover, these barriers often become the major obstacles to resolving intractable conflicts. They reject new ideas and prevent the possibility of alternative views. These are essential steps in embarking on the road to peace, possessing the potential to unfreeze the highly-entrenched conflict-supporting societal beliefs.

One cannot underestimate the fact that at the foundation of these barriers lie ideological beliefs supporting the conflict that were formed on the societal level and then imparted to society members via societal institutions and major communication channels. Such ideological beliefs play a major role in maintaining the conflict, feeding its continuation, and preventing its peaceful resolution. Socio-psychological barriers and the mechanisms employed by society to maintain the above views are potent inhibitors of any potential peace process. Only a determined group employing activism and innovative ideas can lay the groundwork for overcoming the human tendency to adhere to known patterns of thought and action, and overcoming inherent reactions to threat and danger in order to build a better world, free of violence, suffering, and destruction. Overcoming these barriers is a major challenge for every society involved in harsh and violent conflict, if it aspires to embark on the road to peace.

The present paper suggests that overcoming these socio-psychological barriers is not beyond reach, but it is a long process of persuasion and cognitive change. In other words, society members and leaders must implement a process of mobilization for peacemaking in the same way the process of mobilization for supporting and participating in the conflict was implemented at the conflict's onset. Sadly, while it often takes a very short time to mobilize society members for participation in a conflict under the umbrella of patriotism, it usually takes a very long time to mobilize society members to reject the way of conflict and replace it with new ways of peacemaking. In both cases, society members matter. The society members themselves initially developed the ideas that led to the conflict's onset, and they can also develop ideas about the necessity of peacemaking. In both cases they must persuade fellow society members in the "justness" of the proposed path.

From these observations we can learn that any analysis of intractable conflicts necessitates the use of a socio-psychological perspective alongside other perspectives. Human beings perceive, evaluate, infer, and act; they are active participants in events taking place around them. Human psychological processes are an integral part of conflict interactions, as human beings are the only real actors on the conflict stage. Humans make the decisions regarding the dissemination of information about the conflict's necessity, the mobilization of society members, and their children's socialization to maintain the conflict, violently persist in it, and reject its peaceful resolution. In essence, humans are the decision makers; therefore, the psychological aspects embedded in human characteristics must be addressed in order to change the social context. Later, if people begin to view the conflict situation differently, they may make the decision to disseminate ideas about the necessity of peacemaking and to mobilize society members at large to act to achieve this goal. Hopefully, addressing the socio-psychological repertoire can assist in the creation of various socialization and mobilization mechanisms for peacemaking and peacebuilding. It is thus of crucial importance to advance knowledge that will shed light on the conditions, contents, and processes that not only lead society members to embark on peacebuilding processes in times of conflicts, but also socialize them to actively prevent the outbreak and maintenance of vicious and destructive conflicts and costly hate cycles.

Notes

1 I. William Zartman, ed., *Peacemaking in International Conflict: Methods and Techniques* (Washington, DC: United States Institute of Peace, 2007).

2 Michelle I. Gawerc, "Peace-building: Theoretical and Concrete Perspectives," *Peace & Change* 31 (2006): 435-78.

3 Kurt Lewin, "Frontier in Group Dynamics: I," *Human Relations* 1 (1947): 5-41.

4 Robert P. Abelson, ed., *Theories of Cognitive Consistency: A Sourcebook* (Chicago: Rand McNally, 1968); Jean M. Bartunek, "The Multiple Cognitions and Conflict

Associated with Second Order Organizational Change," in *Social Psychology in Organizations: Advances in Theory and Research*, ed. John Keith Murnighan (Englewood Cliffs, NJ: Prentice Hall, 1993), pp. 322-49; and Arie W. Kruglanski, ed., *Lay Epistemics and Human Knowledge* (New York: Plenum, 1989).

5   Daniel Bar-Tal and Eran Halperin, "Overcoming Psychological Barriers to Peacemaking: The Influence of Beliefs about Losses," in *Prosocial Motives, Emotions, and Behavior: The Better Angels of Our Nature*, eds. M. Mikulincer and P. R. Shaver (Washington, DC: American Psychological Association Press, 2009), pp. 431-48.

6   Leon A. Festinger, *A Theory of Cognitive Dissonance* (Evanston, IL: Row, Peterson, 1957).

7   Kruglanski, *Lay Epistemics.*

8   Yaacov Bar-Siman-Tov, "Value-Complexity in Shifting from War to Peace: The Israeli Peace-Making Experience with Egypt," *Political Psychology* 16 (1995): 545-65.

9   William Beinart, *Twentieth-Century South Africa (*Oxford: Oxford University Press, 2001).

10   I. William Zartman, "Ripeness: The Hurting Stalemate and Beyond," in *International Conflict Resolution After the Cold War,* eds. P. C. Stern and D. Druckman (Washington DC: National Academy Press, 2000), pp. 228-29.

11   Bar-Tal and Halperin, "Overcoming Psychological Barriers."

12   Daniel Kahneman and Amos Tversky, "Prospect Theory: An Analysis of Decision under Risk," *Econometrica* 47 (1979): 263-91.

13   William A. Boettcher III, "The Prospects for Prospect Theory: An Empirical Evaluation of International Relations Applications of Framing and Loss Aversion," *Political Psychology* 25 (2004): 331-62; Jack S. Levy, "Loss Aversion, Framing, and Bargaining: The Implications of Prospect Theory for International Conflict," *International Political Science Review* 17 (1996): 179-95; and Nehemia Geva and Alex Mintz, eds., *Decision-Making on War and Peace: The Cognitive-Rational Debate* (Boulder, CO: Lynne Rienner, 1997).

14   Amos Tversky and Daniel Kahneman, "Rational Choice and the Framing of Decisions," *Journal of Business* 59, no. 4 (1986): 251-78.

15   Kahneman and Tversky, "Prospect Theory: An Analysis of Decision under Risk"; and Tversky and Kahneman, "Rational Choice and the Framing of Decisions."

16   John W. Payne, Dan J. Laughhunn, and Roy Crum, "Further Tests of Aspiration Level Effects in Risky Choice," *Management Science* 27 (1981): 953-58.

17   Chip Heath, Richard P. Larrick, and George Wu, "Goals as Reference Points," *Cognitive Psychology* 38 (1999): 79-109.

18 Daniel Bar-Tal, "Sociopsychological Foundations of Intractable Conflicts," *American Behavioral Scientist* 50 (2007): 1430-53.

19 Bartunek, "The Multiple Cognitions."

20 Roger MacGinty and John Darby, *Guns and Government: The Management of the Northern Ireland Peace Process* (Houndmills: Palgrave Macmillan, 2002).

21 Ibid., p. 23.

22 Steven Mufson, "South Africa, 1990," *Foreign Affairs* 70 (1991): 120-41.

23 Quoted by JPost.com staff, "PM, Peres Remember Rabin's Legacy of)eace," *Jpost. com,* October 28, 2012, http://www.jpost.com/Diplomacy-and-Politics/PM-Peres-remember-Rabins-legacy-of-peace.

24 Aaron Kalman, "Netanyahu Calls for Peace Deal to Avert Binational State," *Times of Israel,* May 1, 2013, http://www.timesofisrael.com/netanyahu-calls-for-peace-deal-to-avert-binational-state/.

25 Corinna Carmen Gayer, Shiri Landman, Eran Halperin, and Daniel Bar-Tal, "Overcoming Psychological Barriers to Peaceful Conflict Resolution: The Role of Arguments about Losses," *Journal of Conflict Resolution* 53 (2009): 951-75.

26 Bar-Tal and Halperin, "Overcoming Psychological Barriers."

27 Arie W. Kruglanski and Donna M. Webster, "Motivated Closing of the Mind: 'Seizing' and 'Freezing,'" *Psychological Review* 103, no. 2 (1996): 263-83.

Overcoming Relational Barriers to Agreement

Byron Bland and Lee Ross

Perhaps the greatest obstacle to the achievement of peace between the Israelis and Palestinians is the widespread conviction within both societies that the other side's true goals and aspirations, if realized, would create an unbearable future for their own side. Insofar as traditional peace processes focus on negotiating and implementing "efficient" agreements without addressing a standard "enemy relationship" and the distrust and fear it encompasses, those processes are unlikely to succeed. The Four-Question Framework developed by the Stanford Center on International Conflict and Negotiation (SCICN) offers a new and different design for a peace process that would address the relational barriers that prevent progress toward peace.

The biggest obstacle to the achievement of peace between Israel and the Palestinians may not be the numerous intractable issues (Jerusalem, borders, refugees, and security) or, what is a major subtext within the talks, the activities of various spoiler factions (e.g., jihadists and the radical violent element among the Israeli right) seeking to impede, if not block, progress. Rather, it is likely the widespread conviction among both Israelis and Palestinians that the other side's true goals and aspirations, if ever reached, would create an unbearable future for their own side. Israelis fear (with some justification) that the ultimate Palestinian and broader Arab goal would be the demise of a Jewish state in the Middle East, and Palestinians fear (also with some justification) that Israel's real preference would be a greatly enlarged Israeli state with a greatly reduced Palestinian presence.[1]

The appropriate term for the relationship between the two parties today is, thus, "enemies" – a term that suggests more than the antagonistic disagreements that comprise the difficult but nevertheless standard political engagements of adversaries. We would reserve the term enemies for a state of affairs in which either or both sides in the conflict believe that the other seeks its destruction – if not as individuals, then as a sovereign and functioning political community.[2] In an enemy relationship, each side feels that what prevents the other side from pursuing its maximalist goals is not a lack of will but the lack of means (or at least means that have acceptable political costs).

Enemy relationships mean that a process focusing on negotiating and implementing an agreement between the parties is unlikely to produce the peace that it is ostensibly designed to create. In enemy relationships, the primary consideration is not how much any agreement improves the immediate circumstances of the two parties, but an agreement's impact on the relative balance of power between them and the prospects of eventual domination. The goal of minimizing the risk of such future domination, indeed, the guarantee of future social and political survival, is what assumes paramount importance.

This state of affairs differs from more standard adversarial relationships in which the parties try to package and trade interests such that each party, because of its needs, priorities, existing resources, or perceived opportunities, cedes what it values less than the other party in order to gain what it values more than the other party. The goal is that of an "efficient" agreement, one that exhausts the possibilities of trades that would simultaneously or even sequentially improve the position of both sides.[3] In this regard, the difference between enemy and adversarial relationships is the differences between zero sum and non-zero sum interactions.

Another important difference between enemy and adversarial relationships is the effectiveness of conciliatory gestures. Overtures that might be welcomed in adversarial relationships fail in enemy relationships because they don't address the existential concerns that arise from each side's assessment of what it feels the other's true intentions are. One hears many Palestinians protest that they only want an end to the occupation and the recognition of their human rights; many Israelis respond that what the Palestinians see as legitimate entitlement is actually the first step in a slippery slope toward unacceptable ultimate Palestinian objectives. One hears many Israelis claim that they have made numerous generous offers and expressed a willingness to make difficult concessions to the Palestinians in the past without receiving meaningful concessions in return. In turn, many Palestinians respond that what the Israelis consider generous is humiliating and actually only the first step in a process that will ensure continued Israeli domination and denial of justice. Each side views what it offers and what it receives against a background of fear with respect to the other side's maximalist goals. Both sides, with some justification, claim that the other side is not a "serious" negotiating partner.[4]

In such circumstances, the first barrier to be overcome in the pursuit of peace is a psychological or relational one. The following statement by President Anwar al-Sadat of Egypt before the Knesset in November 1977 eloquently captures this relational barrier and the road to its successful resolution:

> Yet, there remains another wall. This wall constitutes a psychological barrier between us, a barrier of suspicion, a barrier of rejection; a barrier of fear, of deception, a barrier of hallucination without any action, deed or decision. A barrier of distorted and eroded interpretation of every event and statement. It is this psychological barrier which I described in official statements as constituting 70 percent of the whole problem. Today, through my visit to you, I ask why don't we stretch out our hands with faith and sincerity so that together we might destroy this barrier.[5]

To overcome that barrier and create a climate wherein the parties' priority shifts to that of drafting terms that address the well-being of the citizenries, a reduction in enmity and establishment of greater trust is essential. Work on the interface of theory and practice at the Stanford Center on International Conflict and Negotiation suggests that having representatives of the two parties address the following four interrelated questions provides an important starting point:[6]

a. *The question of a shared future.* Are the parties able and willing to articulate a future for the other side that it would find bearable? No agreement, or at least no lasting agreement or even the achievement of substantial progress toward stable politics is possible unless each party feels it could live a reasonably tolerable existence if the other side's basic aspirations were to be realized. The vision of a shared future is not necessarily a shared vision of the future. Disagreement about the specific policies, institutions, and political arrangement is bound to persist. Indeed, the future that one or both sides seek may be far from what the opposing side wants or would deem fair. But each side must recognize the need to consider and articulate the place the other side will fill in the future it seeks. Furthermore, it must communicate that vision to the other side with an awareness that if it is likely to be deemed intolerable – if the day-to-day life of the individuals and communities on the other side will not offer both dignity and a lifestyle that if not better than the present in most respects is at least not appreciably worse – no amount of persuasion or appeals to principle are likely to bear fruit. This question, we feel, is the most fundamental one, and unless it is addressed, the process of negotiation or even the attempt to create good will is almost certain to be an exercise in futility.

b. *The question of trustworthiness.* Can the two sides trust each other to honor commitments and take (all of) the intermediate steps necessary toward that shared future? In the context of longstanding conflict, each side feels that it is the other that bears responsibility for the onset of the conflict, has broken past promises, and has otherwise proven unable or unwilling to make the types of difficult compromises necessary for progress toward a settlement. Given these sentiments, both sides face a critical question: why should we trust you now? What has changed to make things different? In other words, both parties need to be convinced that there is some new basis for trust, some new awareness on the part of the other side or perhaps some change in circumstance that means that the other side now will both agree to and honor, even if not unreservedly embrace, terms it previously rejected. Hearing the other side propose a future in which one is offered a bearable place, and above all seeing the other side act in a way that suggests it accepts that vision of a shared future, can be that change.

c. *The question of loss acceptance*. Can the parties accept the losses that a settlement will inevitably entail for them; are they truly ready to make the necessary compromises, including ones that they said they never would make? A deep mutual sense of loss pervades the aftermath of virtually every negotiated peace agreement. This is because a real peace achieved by negotiated agreement, as opposed to one achieved by outright victory, demands an abandonment of the hopes and dreams that fueled the conflict and that allowed them to reduce their dissonance about the price they were paying in that conflict. Both sides, furthermore, are bound to feel that they are the ones making the more painful and difficult concessions while the other side is surrendering nothing of consequence – certainly nothing to which they were ever entitled. One important purpose served by dialogue prior to agreement is that it can help both sides come to appreciate the extent to which the concessions being made by the other side for the sake of peace are truly painful – that they, no less than their own concessions, represent the abandonment of cherished hopes and dreams.

d. *The question of just entitlements.* Can the parties work to accept an agreement that does not meet what they perceive to be the requirements of justice; and are they willing to work together to alleviate or rectify the most serious injustices that are apt to remain in the aftermath of agreement? Every peace agreement imposes not only losses but seemingly unjust losses on the parties. The goal of reaching a settlement that is deemed to be just by the parties and by the different constituencies comprising the two sides is impossible to achieve. The question therefore is not whether the agreement will be deemed just – it will not be – but whether the parties feel that the injustices the agreement imposes are bearable. No less important, both parties, and especially those constituencies within each party that could become "spoilers," must come to feel that the benefits of the peace at hand are likely to outweigh the injustices it imposes. The common task challenging both parties is to work together to make the answer to this question "yes," which in turn demands that they also work together to address the needs of those most likely to be adversely affected by the terms of that peace.

Conclusion

A peace process constructed around this four-question framework thus would focus less on reaching conclusive outcomes than on reshaping relationships to achieve more positive interactions and both the existence and awareness of shared peaceful intentions. This shift in focus points to a change in conception of what creating peace entails. Rather than assuming that stable peaceful futures will result from exchanges of concessions and agreements, we suggest that the reverse is true. In other words, rather than agreements producing peaceful relationships, it is peaceful, trusting, relationships that make agreements possible.[7]

In the Israeli-Palestinian context, the four-question framework would not change the substance of the issues that divide Israelis and Palestinians. What it would change is the relational context in which the parties approach these issues. The specific core issues that appear intractable when viewed through the current lens of distrust about ultimate intentions and willingness to honor commitments – borders, security, Jerusalem, and refugees – can become quite tractable if the proposed four-question framework transforms the existential stakes for the two parties.

For example, the peaceful relationships envisioned by the four-question framework might alter the negotiating climate in the following ways:

a. Borders would become less important because they are not seen as a defense against the incursion of the other.
b. Sharing holy places would become more feasible because the prospect does not heighten fears of either terrorism or humiliation.
c. The return of refugees would become less threatening because one imagines them living in peace and becoming good neighbors. Moreover the acceptance of compensation for lost property rather than exercising a right of return might become more acceptable if it were seen not as a humiliating surrender but as a step toward a better life in a new sovereign state.

The goal in tackling and transforming enemy relationships through the four-question framework is not to replace negotiation but to make the negotiation of efficient agreements that improve the immediate and long-term prospects of the two sides a realistic possibility. The shift in approach called for in this short essay will not be easy to accomplish, and frustrating setbacks will be inevitable. It will require leadership on both sides that is not only astute but courageous. Those who call for moderation, accommodation, realism, and ultimately peace generally do so at considerable personal risk. But we believe that addressing relational dynamics addressed by four questions is the most fruitful path to follow in traveling the long road to a peaceful shared future.

Notes

1   A study by Ifat Maoz and Clark McCauley documents the fact that respondents who perceived high collective threat and zero-sum relations were markedly less willing than their peers to support possible agreements that included concessions to Palestinians. See Ifat Maoz and Carl McCauley, "Threat Perceptions and Feelings as Predictors of Jewish-Israeli Support for Compromise with Palestinians," *Journal of Peace Research* 46, no. 4 (2009): 525-39.

2   Carl Schmitt, *The Concept of the Political* (New Brunswick, NJ: Rutgers University Press, 1932).

3   Roger Fisher and William Ury, *Getting to Yes* (Boston, MA: Houghton Mifflin, 1981).

4   We have seen this dynamic at play many times in Northern Ireland regarding parades, flags, housing, policing, and just about every other contentious issues that arise between unionists/loyalist and republicans.

5   Anwar al-Sadat, *Peace with Justice*, International Relations Archive, Mount Holyoke College, http://www.mtholyoke.edu/acad/intrel/speech/sadat.htm.

6   For a more extensive presentation of this framework, see Byron Bland, Brenna Powell, and Lee Ross, "Barriers to Dispute Resolution," in *Understanding Social Action, Promoting Human Rights,* eds. R. Goodman, D. Jinks, and A. Woods (Oxford, UK: Oxford University Press, 2012), pp. 265-91, http://www.law.stanford.edu/sites/default/files/child-page/370999/doc/slspublic/Powell,%20Bland,%20Ross,%20Relational%20Barriers.pdf.

7   A recent study by Kahn, Halperin, Liberman, and Ross explored the role of negative intergroup sentiments play, beyond that of political affiliations and identities, in creating and exacerbating barriers to agreement in the context of the Israeli-Palestinian conflict. The authors conclude: "The most obvious implication of our studies is that hatred and anger, and the absence of positive intergroup sentiments and or moral sentiments of guilt or shame, may be an important obstacle both to the type of interest-based agreements that would benefit all concerned and to the type of relationship-building programs that can humanize adversaries and create the trust necessary for more comprehensive agreements. Indeed, trying to produce

such agreement through careful crafting of efficient trades of concessions, without attending to relational barriers may be an exercise in futility." See Dennis T. Kahn, Eran Halperin, Varda Liberman, and Lee Ross, "Intergroup Sentiments, Political Identity, and their Influence on Responses to Potentially Ameliorative Proposals in the Context of an Intractable Conflict," *Journal of Conflict Resolution* (May 2014).

The Israeli-Palestinian Conflict: Is There a Zone of Possible Agreement ("ZOPA")?

Robert H. Mnookin

Is a negotiated resolution of the Israeli Palestinian conflict possible? Can the parties fashion a comprehensive permanent status agreement at the bargaining table that puts an end to the dispute? To put the question in the jargon of negotiation theory: is there a Zone of Possible Agreement, or "ZOPA"? The article seeks to determine the existence of a ZOPA in regards to the Israeli-Palestinian conflict, and if so, the manner in which it can be emphasized and utilized. The article begins by using a simple example to define ZOPA, along with other basic negotiation terms. The second part refers to the feasibility of a ZOPA in the Israeli-Palestinian conflict, and the final section identifies the barriers to an agreement.

Conventional wisdom would suggest that a Zone of Possible Agreement (ZOPA)[1] does exist in regards to the Israeli-Palestinian conflict. More than a decade ago, at Camp David, President Clinton identified the basic parameters of a resolution that would appear to better serve the interests of most Israelis and most Palestinians, rather than continued conflict. However, repeated attempts by the Palestinian Authority and the Israeli government to reach a deal have all failed, despite mediation efforts on behalf of the Clinton, Bush, and Obama administrations, including personal efforts by Tony Blair, George Mitchell, and most recently, Secretary of State John Kerry. How can one understand this paradox?

The answer lies in recognizing two apparently contradictory ideas; on the one hand, there are a variety of ways to resolve issues that would better serve a majority of Israelis and a majority of Palestinians. Nevertheless, such a deal cannot be achieved through negotiations because of barriers that, at present, are insurmountable. In short, conventional wisdom is only partly correct; while there are deals with respect to the final status issues that would probably better serve the interests of most Israelis and most Palestinians than the long-term risks associated with a continuation of the conflict, at least in the short run, such outcomes cannot be reached through negotiation.

Terminology

A simple example can be used to explain the term Zone of Possible Agreement. Suppose Jim recently changed jobs and as a consequence no longer needs a car commute to work. He wants to sell his 10-year-old Honda Accord which has 68,000 miles on it. He takes the car to three different dealers to see what they would offer, and the best offer he got was $6900. Jim is going to leave for vacation in France in less than a week and he wants to sell the car before he leaves. From his research, he knows that the dealer would sell a similar used car for $9600. Jim decides to list the car for sale on eBay for $9200.

Sarah responds to the ad. She is in the market for a used car and once owned a Honda Accord and likes them, and is confident about their reliability. Based on the age and condition of Jim's car she estimates that a dealer would charge about $10,000 for it. She has already visited several dealers and found only two other used Hondas for sale: a 2006 Honda with lower mileage than Jim's for which the dealer's firm price was $11,500, and a 2000 Honda Accord with much higher mileage which she could buy for $6500. Sarah would much prefer to buy Jim's car than the 2000 car, even though it costs more.

To determine whether there is a ZOPA, one must determine the reservation value of each party. Jim's reservation value is the least Jim would accept at the bargaining table rather than pursuing an alternative away from the table. Sarah's reservation value is the most she would pay rather than pursue her alternatives. If Jim's reservation value is less than Sarah's, the Zone of Possible Agreements represents all those deals in which the price would be in between.

Let's assume that Sarah's best alternative, if she does not buy Jim's car, is to buy the 2006 Honda for $11,500. This does not mean, of course, that she is willing to pay that much for Jim's 2004 Honda. Jim's Honda is an older model with more mileage. Instead, to determine her reservation value, Sarah would have to ask herself at what price would she be indifferent to the choice between paying Jim that amount and instead buying the 2006 Honda. Assume Sarah sets this amount at $8700. This means that if Sarah can buy Jim's car for less than $8700 she would prefer buying Jim's car. But if she would have to pay more, she would instead walk away.

To determine whether there is a ZOPA, we must determine Jim's reservation value. This depends on Jim's "no-deal" alternatives. Jim must assess the range of possible outcomes if he makes no deal. In light of that assessment he must decide the least he would accept at the bargaining table rather than pursue one of the alternatives. Assume Jim decides that if Sarah does not buy the car, he will continue to try to sell the car to another private party for four more days, and failing that, to sell it to the dealer for $6900. Once again, Jim needs to translate this alternative into a reservation value. Suppose Jim is mildly optimistic that in the next few days he is likely to find another buyer who will pay more than the $6900 by the dealer. In that case he might set a reservation value of $7200. This is the lowest price he would accept from Sarah.

Any sale for a price between $7200 and $8700 would make both parties better off than their no-deal option. This is the Zone of Possible Agreement or ZOPA. The important point here is that a party's reservation value depends on its perception of how well the "no deal" alternatives compare to what is being offered by the other side at the table. Each must assess the range of outcomes if no agreement is reached in terms of his or her underlying interests.

The existence of a Zone of Possible Agreement does not guarantee a deal. Rational parties may sometimes fail to reach an agreement when there are deals that could make them both better off than continued conflict. One reason negotiations fail relates to strategic opportunism. In this example, Sarah wants to pay as little as possible, and Jim wants to be paid as much as possible. Typically, neither party knows the other party's perception of its "no deal" options or his or her reservation value. Sarah probably does not know, for example, that Jim has to get rid of the car one way or another within the next few days. Nor does Jim know precisely what alternatives Sarah has or the extent to which she might prefer a Honda to other cars. Negotiators rarely honestly reveal the reservation value. They are often reluctant to disclose the full range of their alternatives if no deal is made.

With respect to the distributive dimensions of bargaining, a seller typically tries to assess the buyer's highest price. Indeed, in many negotiations, parties do not know in advance whether a ZOPA even exists. If Sarah only cared about finding the answer to whether a ZOPA existed, she could offer Jim $8700, her reservation value. Even if she did, however, Jim might incorrectly assume that if he holds out she would pay more. More generally, as part of the negotiation processes each negotiator often attempts to shape the other party's perceptions of its "bottom line." Indeed, negotiators sometimes employ a variety of tactics to influence the other side's perceptions – some misleading, some outright dishonest. In all events, even when a ZOPA exists, "rational" parties may fail to achieve a deal because one or both engage in hard bargaining tactics in the hope of securing an even better deal.

In short, the existence of a ZOPA is a necessary but not sufficient condition for a successful negotiation. If no ZOPA exists, it means that no matter how hard the parties try – even if neither side engaged in strategic behavior and was completely open about its underlying interests and alternatives – there could be no deal. The most the willing buyer would pay is less than the least a willing seller would take, and one or the other has a no deal alternative that is superior to the most the other party could rationally offer.

Framework for the Resolution of the Final Status Issues

Conventional wisdom suggests that a variety of arrangements with respect to the final status issues would probably better serve the interests of most Israelis and most Palestinians, rather than the long-term risks associated with a continuation of the conflict. The basic parameters of such an agreement would include the following:

Two states: the establishment of an independent and sovereign Palestinian state alongside the State of Israel engaged in peaceful security cooperation. The states of Israel and Palestine would recognize each other. The full implementation of this agreement in its entirety will mean the end of conflict between the two states, and the end to all claims. A UN Security Council Resolution to that effect would also ensure the release of all prisoners.

Territory: the borders of the two states will be based on the 1967 lines with mutual agreed exchanges. Land annexed by Israel would be compensated by an equivalent land swap and a permanent corridor linking the West Bank and the Gaza Strip. Guidelines for the exchange would include a small 2-6 percent exchange in which most Israeli settlers would live under Israeli sovereignty, the least number of Palestinians would be affected, and Palestinians would have territorial continuity.[2]

Through a land swap, a substantial majority of the 500,000 Jewish settlers living beyond the Green Line could remain in their homes which would now be in Israel proper. Israel could be confident that the Jewish state would retain a Jewish majority and the demographic "time bomb" would be permanently diffused. The swap would not require Israel to give up vital infrastructure, nor would it jeopardize Israeli security.

Israeli settlements: in accordance with an agreed implementation timeline, all Israeli civilians would be evacuated from the territory of the State of Palestine. Individual Israeli citizens could apply for residency and/or citizenship in the state of Palestine. The parties would reach agreement on the disposition of all fixed assets and infrastructure within Israeli settlements, with the goal of transferring such assets and infrastructure in good condition to the state of Palestine in return for fair and reasonable compensation.

Security: the state of Palestine would be defined as a "non-militarized state" but would have a strong security force. Both sides would agree to exercise comprehensive and complete commitment to fighting terrorism and incitement. For deterrence and border security, an international presence that could only be withdrawn by mutual consent would be deployed in Palestine. An Israeli presence would be allowed in early warning station facilities for a limited period of time. The state of Palestine would have sovereignty over its airspace but special arrangements would be made for Israeli training and operational needs. No foreign army would enter Palestine, and its government would not engage in military agreements with a country that does not recognize Israel.

Israel's vital interest in security provides the primary justification for the continued occupation of the West Bank. The occupation provides strategic territorial depth against the risk of invasion from the east, through the use of tanks and ground troops. However, the current serious threat to Israel comes from missile and air attacks, and from terrorism. The new Palestinian state would be non-militarized and would have no army that could conceivably threaten Israel. The deal would provide for phasing and benchmarking in terms of implementation to provide Israel with greater confidence that the internal security would be sufficient to minimize the threat of terrorist attacks emanating from the new state. Part of the deal would prohibit alliances with countries hostile to Israel and the end of incitement to violence in Palestinian schools.

Many security analysts believe that continued occupation of the West Bank is neither necessary nor effective, and that counter-insurgency rather than a counter-terrorism approach would better serve Israel's long-term security.[3] Critics of the occupation ask: What are the long-run security costs of not creating a viable Palestinian state? They suggest that the occupation emboldens extremists, undermines moderates, prevents regional cooperation, fuels the international campaigns to delegitimize Israel, and alienates allies, especially in Europe.

Jerusalem: Jerusalem would be the capital of the two states and will remain united with two municipalities and a coordination body. Arab areas in East Jerusalem would come under Palestinian sovereignty and Jewish under Israeli. Palestinians would have effective control over the Haram (Temple Mount) and Israelis effective control over the Western Wall. An international committee made up of Jordan, Saudi Arabia, the U.S., Israel, and Palestine would serve as a custodian managing matters related to holy places in the Old City and other agreed areas adjacent to the city wall. The committee would maintain the holy sites, oversee relevant cooperation and conflict resolution, and guarantee access for all religions. It would oversee the implementation of special arrangements barring excavation under the Haram and behind the Western Wall, requiring consent of all parties before any excavation can take place. International monitoring would provide mutual confidence.

Jerusalem is embedded in the narratives of three great religions, and the old city has many important religious sites. Conventional wisdom envisions that Jerusalem would become a "condominium" of sorts. It would serve as the capital of Israel and the future state of Palestine. The Jewish neighborhoods would be part of Israel, the Arab areas would be part of the new Palestinian state, and a special regime would be established for certain areas.

At present, most Jerusalem neighborhoods have uniform ethnicity. Most of the Jewish neighborhoods in East Jerusalem are mostly contiguous with West Jerusalem. Of the 193,000 Jews who live in East Jerusalem, it is estimated that only about 1 percent would be required to move.[4] Three different types of regimes for Jerusalem have been identified: 1) territorial sovereignty border models,[5] in which effective borders would both separate and connect a divided city; 2) a special regime with either joint management by Israel and the new Palestinian state or management by an international body; or 3) a mixed regime that contains elements of both, as each has advantages and disadvantages.[6] The regime outlined above is a "mixed regime."

Refugees: Israel would acknowledge the Palestinian people's moral and material suffering as a result of the 1948 war. The solution to the refugee problem would be consistent with the two-state approach: the two states as the homelands of their respective peoples. The Palestinian state would be the focal point for the Palestinians who choose to return to the area while Israel would accept some of these refugees. Refugees would have five possible homes: the state of Palestine; the areas in Israel being transferred to Palestine in the land swap; host countries; third countries; and in Israel. Right to return to the Palestinian state and the swapped areas would be granted to all Palestinian refugees. Settlement in host and third countries and absorption into Israel will depend upon the policies and sovereign decisions of those countries and would be implemented in a manner that would not threaten the national character of the State of Israel. An international body would be established to process claims and manage the process of location, resettlement, return, and compensation. The parties would agree that this implements Resolution 194.

The challenge with respect to refugees is to provide for a "just solution"[7] for the Palestinian refugee problem while preserving Israel as a Jewish-majority state. The arrangement described above would provide refugees with options, including a right to compensation and return to the new Palestinian state. While there is no easy reconciliation of the profoundly conflicting Israeli and Palestinian narratives concerning "who is to blame" for the refugees' plight, some Israeli acknowledgment of the suffering of the refugees would be included. As part of the arrangement, subject to Israeli control, some Palestinian refugees may be allowed to resettle in Israel.[8] Moreover, as the International Crisis Group suggested, "Palestinians will assess any comprehensive settlement as a package deal, and compromise on the refugee question will be facilitated if core needs are met elsewhere."[9] In this regard, cash or vouchers for training, and the prospect of decent housing and future employment would be of substantial importance.[10]

Discussion

A two-state arrangement along these lines would better serve the long term interests of most Israelis and most Palestinians than a continuation of the conflict. The Israeli occupation would end and Palestinians would have a viable and contiguous state of their own with territory equivalent to 100 percent of the West Bank and Gaza.

Polling data suggest that a deal along these lines might well be ratified by a majority of Israelis and Palestinians.[11] On the Israeli side, recent polling suggests that 59 percent of the public supports a Palestinian state; 69 percent support a solution of "two states for two peoples." Since 2006, a majority of the Jewish public "expressed consistent support for the establishment of a Palestinian state"[12] and opposed ending the negotiation process despite the fact that less than a third of the population believes a negotiated settlement is possible.[13] On the Palestinian side, polling data similarly suggest that a majority supports a peace agreement. Although approximately 70 percent of Palestinians are pessimistic about the chances for success, 53 percent of the public supports the two-state solution, two thirds oppose a one-state solution, and 57 percent believes that if [President] Abbas reaches a peace agreement with [Prime Minister] Netanyahu, a majority of the public would vote in favor of that agreement.[14] Indeed, 50 percent of the Palestinian public supports the resumption of direct Palestinian-Israeli negotiations.[15]

The Paradox Unraveled: Barriers to a Negotiated Resolution

If the final status issues could be resolved in a way that would better serve the long run interests of most Israelis and most Palestinians, why is a negotiated resolution not possible?

The first section of this article described how even when a ZOPA exists, strategic barriers – i.e., hard bargaining to maximize one's own competitive gain – can lead to bargaining failures. The following section describes several other barriers that currently make a negotiated resolution along the lines described above impossible.

A variety of barriers have been discussed as causes for failed negotiations, despite deals that would make both parties better off than maintaining the status quo.[16]

For negotiators to establish reservation values to inform wise decision-making, they need to be able to accurately assess the value of reaching a negotiated agreement and compare that value with the value of their "no deal" options. These values are often subject to considerable uncertainty, where parties must assess the probability of a variety of possible outcomes. Research suggests that individuals routinely use decision making heuristics that are systematically biased in predictable ways. One is called the "self-serving bias," suggesting that on average, decision makers will be too optimistic about the likelihood of favorable outcomes in the future. These misperceptions can reduce or even eliminate altogether a bargaining zone that would exist if parties had unbiased and accurate perceptions. George Lowenstein and his colleagues demonstrated the existence of self-serving assessments and how they may influence lawsuit settlement negotiations.[17]

A second potential barrier is characterized as "reactive devaluation."[18] A negotiator should set his reservation value, according to rational choice theory, by determining in advance the conditions for being indifferent to the choice between reaching agreement and pursuing his "no deal" alternative. There is some evidence, however, that "the very offer of a particular proposal or concession – especially if the offer comes from an adversary – may diminish its apparent value or attractiveness in the eyes of the recipient."[19]

"Loss aversion" is yet another reason parties may fail to reach a deal even though there are set negotiated agreements that would better serve the underlying interests than continued conflict. Building on Kahneman and Tversky's prospect theory,[20] individuals will demonstrate a stronger preference for avoiding something they perceive to be a loss than for achieving something that appears to be a gain of the same magnitude.

An important characteristic of the Israeli-Palestinian conflict is that the deal based on the Clinton parameters would be perceived as imposing considerable losses on important stakeholders within each constituency. This proposal, for example, does not give all Palestinian refugees an individual or collective right of return that would involve a choice of whether to resume domicile within Israel proper. Refugees, in other words, would be forced to relinquish the dream of exercising their choice embedded in what they see as a legal entitlement embedded in the right of return. The proposal would also require Israelis who are national religious settlers to give up the dream of "Eretz Israel" and indeed require many of them to relocate from the West Bank to Israel proper. In short, for many on each side, territorial losses would loom large and loss aversion might as a consequence encourage risk-taking behavior at the negotiation table that gives too little weight to the potential gains of resolution.

A final barrier relates to internal or "behind the table" conflicts among the Israelis, and among Palestinians. Among Palestinians, for example, there is a profound conflict between Fatah and Hamas about whether the Palestinians should be prepared to negotiate a two state resolution at all. Analogously, among Israelis, there are profound internal conflicts concerning the settlement project, and the extent to which Israel should aspire to have and retain West Bank settlements. A consequence of these internal conflicts is that it is extraordinarily challenging for a political leader on either side to build a sufficient consensus that a particular deal should be made. The incentives facing the leader who is responsible for carrying out the negotiations may well be different than those for a majority of his or her own constituents.

Conclusion

By exploring whether a ZOPA exists, the goal of this article was to provide an explanation for a seeming paradox: how is it possible that an agreement that better serves the interests of a majority of both Israelis and Palestinians exists, and yet despite repeated efforts, such a resolution cannot be achieved through negotiation?

The answer relates to the existence of a number of barriers – strategic, psychological, relational, and institutional.

Other papers in this volume suggest some of things that might be done if a resolution is not possible through direct negotiations between Israelis and Palestinians. One possibility would be to address the relational issues in the hope that over time these might diminish to the point that effective leaders arise who can manage the internal conflicts on both sides.[21] As Bland and Ross note, a peace process may need to "focus less on reaching conclusive outcomes than on reshaping relationships to achieve more positive interactions and both the existence and awareness of shared peaceful intentions."[22] This approach rests on the view that "rather than agreements producing peaceful relationships, it is peaceful, trusting relationships that make agreements possible."[23]

A second possibility relates to unilateral initiatives. In an earlier article I suggested that the evacuation of Gaza served the interests of the Israeli government, Hamas, and Fatah but could never have been achieved through negotiations. But it was achieved unilaterally.[24] The same may be true here. Someday there may be a way for Israel to unilaterally establish its own borders with respect to the West Bank in a way that serves the interests of a majority of Israelis and Palestinians. As Gilead Sher argues, Israeli decision makers could pursue "an independent and gradual withdrawal from Palestinian territory in the West Bank" and, in doing so, "begin a process of taking independent step towards turning the two state solution into a reality."[25]

Another possibility may relate to strong-armed mediation. The United States, for example, might publicly propose a deal along the lines outlined above on a "take-it-or-leave-it" basis, combined with sufficient carrots and sticks that the Israeli government and the Palestinian authority may be convinced to agree.[26] It is worth noting that in the recent negotiations involving Secretary of State Kerry, no American framework was ever tabled.

Notes

1   Roger Fisher, William Ury, and Bruce Patton, *Getting to Yes* (New York: Simon & Schuster, 1987).

2   David Makovsky, Sheli Chabon, and Jennifer Logan, "Imagining the Border: Options for Resolving the Israeli-Palestinian Territorial Issue," Washington Institute for Near East Policy, 2011. This paper outlines several land-swap options that could achieve such objectives: the Geneva Initiative involved a land-swap of about 2.2 percent and included an estimated 71 percent of the Jewish settlers; the most troublesome

areas with respect to a land swap relate to Ariel and the Jerusalem envelope of settlements. For an interactive map, visit www.ispeacepossible.com.

3   Daniel Byman, *A High Price: The Triumphs and Failures of Israeli Counterterrorism* (New York: Oxford University Press, 2011); Yaakov Amidror, *Winning Counterinsurgency War: The Israeli Experience* (2010), http://www.jcpa.org/text/Amidror-perspectives-2.pdf.

4   Zvia Kriger, "Is Peace Possible: The Future of Jerusalem," *Atlantic*, November 14, 2011, http://www.theatlantic.com/personal/archive/2011/11/transcript-for-is-peace-possible-chapter-4-jerusalem/248437/.

5   "The Border Regime for Jerusalem in Peace," SAYA (2010), http://www.sayarch.com/the-border-regime-for-jerusalem-in-peace/389/; "The Geneva Accord: A Model Israeli-Palestinian Peace Agreement," Geneva Initiative, http://www.geneva-accord.org/mainmenu/english.

6   Kriger, *"Is Peace Possible."*

7   Note that the Arab Peace Initiative now uses this language.

8   At Taba and as part of the Camp David negotiations Israel offered an absorption plan for some Palestinian refugees to return to Israel; Lex Takkenberg, "The Search for Durable Solutions for Palestinian Refugees: A Role for UNRWA?" in *Israel and the Palestinian Refugees,* eds. E. Benvenisti, C. Gans, and S. Hanafi (Berlin: Springer-Heidelberg, 2007), pp. 373-86; Elhanan Miller, "Israel Agreed to Absorb 200,000 Refugees, ex-Fatah Leader Says," *Times of Israel*, December 4, 2013, http://www.timesofisrael.com/dahlan-israel-agreed-to-absorb-200000-refugees/; Jeremy Pressman, "Visions in Collision: What Happened at Camp David and Taba?" *International Security* 28, no. 2 (2003): 5-43.

9   International Crisis Group, "Palestinian Refugees and the Politics of Peacemaking," Middle East Report 22, February 5, 2004, http://www.crisisgroup.org/en/regions/middle-east-north-africa/israel-palestine/022-palestinian-refugees-and-the-politics-of-peacemaking.aspx.

10   The AIX group suggested the total economic costs would be from \$55-85 billion, and while Israel might be expected to contribute and get credit for the value of those settlements that would be evacuated, plainly there would need to be substantial contributions from other nations. Elizabeth Dwoskin, "Trying to Put a Price on Middle East Peace," *Bloomberg Businessweek*, August 11, 2011, http://www.businessweek.com/magazine/trying-to-put-a-price-on-middle-east-peace-08112011.html.

11   Yehuda Ben Meir and Gilead Sher, "Israeli Public Opinion" in *Strategic Survey for Israel 2013-2014,* eds. S. Brom and A. Kurz (Tel Aviv: Institute for National Security Studies, 2014), p. 161. Two caveats are in order when discussing polling data that assess public support amongst Israelis and Palestinians for a potential

peace deal. First, polling data on the question of final status negotiations tend to be highly sensitive to the questions' exact wording. As Yehuda Ben Meir and Gilead Sher assert in their discussion of Israeli polling data, "similar questions that are formulated in different terms are likely to paint different pictures and lead to correspondingly different conclusions." Second, caution should be exercised when drawing comparing Israeli and Palestinian polls assessing support for hypothetical peace agreements, given the number of variables subsumed in any such agreement.

12 Ibid.

13 Y. Ben Meir and O. Bagno-Moldavsky, eds., *The Voice of the People: Israeli Public Opinion on National Security 2012*, Memorandum 126 (Tel Aviv: Institute for National Security Studies, 2013).

14 Palestinian Center for Policy and Survey Research, "Palestinian Public Opinion Poll No. 50." December 19-22, 2013, www.pcpsr.org/en/node189.

15 Ibid.

16 Lee Ross and Constance Stittinger, "Barriers to Conflict Resolution," *Negotiation Journal* 7, no. 4 (1991): 389-404.

17 George Lowenstein, Samuel Issacharoff, Colin Camerer and Linda Babcock, "Self Serving Assessments of Fairness and Pretrial Bargaining," *Journal of Legal Studies* 135 (1993).

18 Lee Ross, "Reactive Devaluation in Negotiation and Conflict Resolution," *Barriers to Conflict Resolution* (1995): 26-42.

19 Ibid.

20 Daniel Kahneman and Amos Tversky, "Prospect Theory: An Analysis of Decision under Risk," *Econometrica* 47, no. 2 (1979): 263-92.

21 Byron Bland and Lee Ross, "Overcoming Relational Barriers" (current volume).

22 Ibid.

23 Ibid.

24 Robert H. Mnookin, Ehud Eiran, and Shula Gilad, "Is Unilateralism Always Bad? Negotiation Lessons from Israel's 'Unilateral' Gaza Withdrawal," *Negotiation Journal* 30, no. 2 (2014): 131-56.

25 Gilead Sher, "When Negotiations Fail to Bear Fruit: The Case For Constructive Independent Steps," (current volume).

26 Russell B. Korobkin and Jonathan Zasloff, "Roadblocks to the Roadmap: A Negotiation Theory Perspective on the Israeli-Palestinian Conflict after Yasser Arafat," *Yale Journal of International Law* 30 (2005): 1-80.

When Negotiations Fail to Bear Fruit: The Case for Constructive Independent Steps

Gilead Sher

Despite decades of negotiations aimed at resolving the Israeli-Palestinian conflict, a peace agreement between Israel and the Palestinians has not yet been achieved. Efforts to conclude a two-state solution have been the central aim of direct bilateral negotiations for over twenty years, and agreements, most notably the Oslo Accords, have been signed by both PLO and Israeli government leaders. However, with frequent rounds of violence, the 50-day Operation Protective Edge against Hamas in Gaza being the latest to-date, and the recurring decision to postpone negotiation of core issues, no plan has been successfully implemented. Early in 2014, the Palestinian Authority's strategy shifted to the legal and diplomatic international arena. Designed to curb Israel's military power and right to self-defense through exploitation of the media, diplomatic channels, international institutions, and international law, it fuels the de-legitimization campaign against Israel, erodes its international standing, and invites an internationally imposed solution to the conflict. Since then, Palestinian lawfare has been building momentum. This paper first briefly outlines the main problems of the Gaza withdrawal and explains how a gradual evacuation of parts of the West Bank could be more successful and avoid many of its pitfalls. It then outlines how independent Israeli steps could be conducive to the conflict resolution process, advancing both Israeli and Palestinian vital interests. Finally, the paper presents a set of policy recommendations on key issues: borders, security, economics, and garnering support among Israelis, Palestinians, and the international community.

The most recent nine-month round of Israeli-Palestinian talks, arranged by U.S. Secretary of State John Kerry, ended with the parties no closer to an agreement. With growing apathy among the civilian populations, increasing distrust of the other, and the impasse on any resolution of the core issues, it is questionable whether the conflict is ripe for a negotiated settlement. Indeed, the recent developments would suggest that bilateral negotiations as a standalone process towards resolving the conflict are unlikely to bear fruit in the near future.

Among supporters of a two-states-for-two-peoples solution, there is wide consensus that a negotiated settlement is the best way to resolve the Israeli-Palestinian conflict. However, when negotiations fail and the status quo is no longer viable or desirable, leaders must examine constructive alternatives toward a peace agreement. This paper argues that there are complementary and ultimately alternative options to the "negotiations only" notion. These include, inter alia, a broader spectrum of gradual, partial, and regional steps, first and foremost an independent and gradual withdrawal from Palestinian territory in the West Bank. The Israeli government needs to begin a process of taking independent steps toward turning the two-state solution into a reality, thus securing the future of Israel as the democratic nation-state of the Jewish people.

As early as 2002, the idea of "proactive separation" from the Palestinian territories was presented in a policy paper drafted by the Van Leer Jerusalem Institute and intended for public debate.[1] From 2003 the policy was debated in the public sphere,[2] and withdrawal from the Gaza Strip was even included within the Israeli Labor Party's platform in its unsuccessful bid in the 2003 elections. In late 2003, Prime Minister Sharon, who earlier that year publicly criticized the policy, embraced it, stating that if peace talks with the Palestinians were not successful, "Israel will initiate the unilateral step of disengagement with the Palestinians."[3] In 2005, Sharon implemented the policy with the unilateral withdrawal from Gaza and four settlements in the northern West Bank.[4]

This paper contends that for independent steps to be effective and yield the desired results, they must be carried out gradually. The impact of each respective step must be evaluated before any successive measure is taken. From Israel's perspective, it should attempt to coordinate steps with the

Palestinians and garner support from the U.S. and as many members of the international community as possible. In addition, while implementing the independent approach, which relies solely on Israel's own decision making, Jerusalem should continue genuine efforts to revive the negotiation process with the Palestinians. It must present an initiative expressing its clear willingness to end the Arab-Israeli conflict while securing its vital national interests.

Israel should design and prepare for a two-state solution on its own, challenging the Palestinians to do the same and seeking to impart convincingly that it intends to live side by side with them as two nation-states. That could begin motivating each side to try to unify its constituents behind a peaceful future, as opposed to waiting for spoilers to decide that periodic war is inevitable. In tandem, Israel should also explore coordination and possibly below-the-surface negotiations on points of common interest with the Palestinians, Egypt, Jordan, Saudi Arabia, a number of the Gulf principalities, the United States, the European Union, and others. All share a common concern: to counter the spread of violent Islamic fundamentalism, led by ISIS and other radical Islamic jihad terrorist organizations and Iran's nuclear race.

However, if bilateral, regional, or secret multilateral negotiations do not produce a two-state reality, Israel must do whatever it can in the meantime to advance the peace process and create a situation ripe for negotiating a final end to the Israeli-Palestinian conflict. Independent Israeli action has the power to create visible progress toward a two-state solution and generate momentum toward reviving negotiations.[5] It can offer the parties a renewed sense of progress and hope, and facilitate a rapid return to negotiations. And indeed, ensuing negotiations will have to address core issues that an independent withdrawal from areas in the West Bank does not begin to tackle – including the future of Jerusalem and the issue of the Palestinian refugees.

Lessons Learned from the Gaza Withdrawal

The Israeli withdrawal from the Gaza Strip that was implemented in 2005 in the absence of an agreement with the Palestinians was – and still is – highly controversial among the Israeli public. The disengagement saw the dismantling of Israeli settlements, which included the eviction of more than

8,000 Israeli civilians in Gaza, as well as the evacuation of the residents of the four isolated settlements in the West Bank.[6] It also saw Israel's 38-year military rule come to an end with the withdrawal of all IDF troops from the Gaza Strip. However, the context of the disengagement was unclear. Whether Prime Minister Sharon's aim was to begin a process of creating a two-state solution, or to sever the Gaza from the West Bank while strengthening Israel's presence in the West Bank, was not stipulated.

The plan, which required the uprooting of thousands of Israeli citizens from their homes by their own government on an unprecedented scale and destroying communities and infrastructures, met strong opposition within the Israeli public. Yet while the Israeli government went to great lengths to persuade the public of the advantages of independent withdrawal and convince it of the soundness of the measure, little proceeded as planned.[7] Following the disengagement, in part due to a shortsighted George W. Bush administration that insisted on holding elections in the Palestinian Authority, Hamas assumed control of the government, and the terrorist organization was now in a more favorable environment to strengthen its terrorist capacity and build a larger militia. Within the first year after Israel's withdrawal, Hamas intensified its rocket fire from the Gaza Strip into Israel and captured Israeli soldier Gilad Shalit; in response Israel launched Operation Summer Rains. Similar cycles of violence have repeated themselves since, leading to numerous deaths and casualties and constant insecurity in bordering Israeli towns and villages. In addition to these new security concerns, rehabilitation measures for the evacuated Israeli civilians proved inadequate. The state-commissioned report headed by retired Supreme Court Justice Eliyahu Matza concluded that "the State's handling of the evacuees has been riddled with failures."[8] Many of those evicted resided in mobile homes for a significant period before being resettled, remained unemployed, or found work but at a far lower salary, faced the dissolution of their community, and did not receive the compensation they were expecting.[9] To avoid a recurrence of these serious problems, Matza also instructed the Israeli government to begin preparing itself for the eventual relocation of Israelis residing in the West Bank settlements.

Given the experience of the Gaza withdrawal, the notion of withdrawal from additional Palestinian territory, perhaps predictably, conjures up visions of self-destruction, chaos, and war in the minds of many Israelis today. However, Israel can learn lessons from the Gaza withdrawal and construct a plan that circumvents many of the pitfalls. With these lessons in mind, a policy for independently delineating the provisional border between Israel and the Palestinian state in-the-making should:

a. Be implemented in the wider context of a two-state solution resulting from direct Israeli-Palestinian and regional negotiations that will hopefully be revived during the process.

b. Be launched as a gradual process, allowing Israel to assess the impact of each step, including the repercussions for security, before undertaking the next measure.

c. Allow for a continued IDF presence in the West Bank and the Jordan Valley even after the relocation of Israeli civilians, until a time when Israel feels confident handing over the responsibility to an international force.

d. Consider not withdrawing from all West Bank land in order to retain some bargaining chips and give the Palestinians incentives to resume or continue negotiations.

e. Ensure mechanisms for proper compensation of Israeli civilians.

f. Be coordinated with the Palestinians and the international community as much as possible.

g. Address wider issues of the occupation, including borders, airspace, infrastructure, power, and commerce.

h. Be implemented at a time of relative quiet and stability and not in response to violence or pressure from Palestinian terrorism.[10]

If these elements are included in the policy, then Israel is likely to see a much better outcome than that of the Gaza disengagement.

Meeting the National Aspirations of Both Peoples

A majority of Israelis and Palestinians still support resolving the conflict through a two-state solution,[11] the only solution that allows both parties to fulfil their respective aspirations for a sovereign state for their people. However, support for this option, particularly among the Palestinian population, is waning in the name of historic justice, morality, and realism, and a one-state or bi-national state solution is gaining popularity.[12] As the Jewish settlements become increasingly entrenched in the West Bank, the idea of separating the populations is becoming less viable.

For Israel, continuing its current policy of occupation and settlement expansion is actually far riskier than implementing a policy of gradual, measured, independent steps. Although Israel may feel safer continuing with what it deems to be the status quo, no such status quo actually exists, as Israel has no control over adverse developments. Adopting a "wait and see" approach would be based on an illusion: there is no way to maintain the status quo, as the situation on the ground continues to evolve, Arab and Jewish populations become increasingly entangled, and the two-state solution moves farther out of reach.[13] Of course, not all risks will be eliminated through a policy of independent steps. Israel will still face threats with enemies such as Iran and its proxies, Hizbollah and Hamas, seeking its destruction. Implementing this policy is likely, however, to create a new and auspicious horizon for Israel to meet its national aspirations and secure its vital national interests.

It is unlikely that the Palestinians will support Israel's independent gradual steps. Meantime, though, PA President Mahmoud Abbas has laid out his own unilateral plan, which consists of three alternatives. The first involves U.S.-led negotiations between Israel and the PA for a limited time period, which would begin with Israel's presentation of its idea of permanent borders. The goal is to determine the borders of the Palestinian state and achieve Israeli recognition of the state, all within four months. Little is new in this idea. In case this alternative fails or is not tried at all due to Israeli and U.S. opposition, as indeed has happened, the second alternative would be activated, whereby the PA, through the Arab League, would demand that the UN Security Council instruct Israel to withdraw from Palestinian territory within three to five years. Should both the first and second alternatives fail, the PA would join all international institutions and organizations, sign the Rome Statute of the International Criminal Court in The Hague, and subsequently file a suit against Israel and its leaders. By now, all alternatives have been activated.

One could argue how constructive this threat-driven Palestinian plan is. Regarding an Israeli unilateral plan, however, even if the proposed timeframe is not optimal for the Palestinians, it would still remove settlements and many of the problems associated with them, such as restrictions on freedom of movement within the West Bank and extremist settler violence. Furthermore, the occupation has existed for almost fifty years and there is no sign that it is becoming any less entrenched. Therefore, surely a ten year framework per se is far better than no framework.

Palestinians have also opposed the notion of independent steps, arguing that they allow Israel to dictate the framework and outcome.[14] Rather than viewing withdrawal as an opportunity for peace, they view it as an attempt by Israel to delineate the final borders of a two-state solution. However, without the pressure of an agreement with the Palestinians, Israel only needs to consider its own interests.

To be sure, withdrawing the Jewish population from the settlements outside the main settlement blocs in the West Bank is in both parties' interests. Even if independent withdrawal is not the optimal solution for neither the Israelis nor the Palestinians, the policy proposed here would still mark an improvement. In addition, each move will be coordinated with the Palestinian Authority as much as possible to advance the Palestinians' right to self-determination. As Israel withdraws its civilians there should be a gradual transfer of powers and authorities from Israel to the PA. Still, however, independent steps cannot replace a negotiated settlement and will not bring about an end to either Palestinian or Israeli claims related to the contested core issues. Ideally, independent steps will be taken in parallel with a negotiated process, or they will create a better set of circumstances in which negotiations can be revived and have a higher chance of success. As such, Israel will not be dictating the final agreement to the Palestinians.

Thus, there are several advantages of such a policy:

a. It allows Israel to remain a secure, Jewish, democratic state, with a strong Jewish majority under the State of Israel's jurisdiction.

b. It works toward realizing the Palestinian right to self-determination – the withdrawal of most settlers will create a more homogenous Palestinian territory in the West Bank and will allow Palestinians to have more control over their institutions.

c. It enables the establishment of provisional borders for the State of Israel and the future Palestinian state.

d. The dismantling of numerous Israeli settlements and the gradual withdrawal of IDF forces will strengthen Israel's international status.

The Policy

What would a policy of constructive independent Israeli steps look like? All the details of the policy must be carefully reviewed in advance to leave as little room for error as possible, and avoid the mistakes of the Gaza disengagement. At the same time, during the gradual implementation, there must be enough room for evaluation of the policy and its adaptation, if required. Simultaneously, the U.S. should adopt a paradigm that allows all stakeholders to take independent steps that will advance a reality of two states, by clearly spelling out the parameters of the end game.

Once the parameters – or even Secretary John Kerry's document comprising the U.S. insights from the latest negotiation round – are on the table, any independent step taken in the future can be clearly evaluated whether it moves the parties closer to the reality of two states, and thus considered constructive, or takes them further away.

The U.S. should announce that it will support constructive steps taken by either party, and will object to any destructive step.

Borders

Israel will independently withdraw its civilians to provisional and not final borders. The end of the conflict will of course require the demarcation of final borders, but these will be determined in negotiations between Israel and the Palestinians in either a bilateral or a multi-lateral framework. Even after withdrawing independently, it is advisable that Israel retains its settlements in Hebron, Kiryat Arba, Ariel, Ma'ale Adumim, and the Jordan River and not offer land swaps at that stage. The Israeli withdrawal from the majority of Palestinian territory (around 90 percent), but not of all of the territory, will allow Israel to retain bargaining power and provide incentive for the Palestinians to negotiate.

Security

Following decades of Palestinian terrorism, suicide bombing, hostilities, and rocket fire that have killed thousands of Israeli citizens and traumatized many others, security is a prime concern for Israel. Israel needs to be sure that withdrawing from any land will not compromise its own security. Arguably, the withdrawal from the majority of the West Bank may be viewed by the Palestinians as a sign of Israeli defeat and weakness, opening the country to further threats due to an erroneously perceived decreased deterrence. This is what many believed happened after Israel withdrew from Gaza in 2005, and from Lebanon in 2000. However, this independent action will differ fundamentally, and given the gradual nature of the process the IDF will remain in the West Bank for an extended time period after civilian withdrawal, retaining full freedom of action. Evacuated settlement outposts will be transferred initially to the Israeli army. Thus, there is no reason to assume that the security situation would worsen, as the IDF will be equally able to thwart any terrorist threats from within the territory. Only if and when Israel is confident that terrorist cells are not active within the West Bank, will it consider gradually replacing the IDF presence with that of an international military force.

The plan must also take into account the worst scenarios from the Israeli security perspective, including increased motivation by Palestinian and Islamic fanatics to attack Israel, with the Palestinian Authority unable to prevent it. On the one hand, it is hoped that progress on the ground toward a two-state solution will reduce motivations for violence; nonetheless, all circumstances should be considered. The preparations, therefore, must include a plan for the prevention of infiltration of rockets and missiles and defense against high trajectory weapons. Israel must also initially maintain control of the border crossings between the Palestinian Authority and Jordan, as well as movement between Gaza and the West Bank, in order to prevent the supply of weapons to potential Palestinian terrorists. Only following a long and monitored period of quiet will Israel consider replacing an IDF presence with an international force. Such a process that allows for the continued presence of the Israeli military will ensure the prevention of a security vacuum, avoiding the main security-related mistake that was made in the Gaza disengagement.

Absorption of Evacuated Israeli Citizens

Preparing a national plan for absorbing Jewish residents returning to Israel's recognized borders is essential. The plan must thoroughly address issues of compensation, employment, economics, security, psychological impact, and social planning. The process of being uprooted from one's home, community, social and religious environment, and workplace will be painful. Sufficient planning and provisions, however, could allow for a much smoother transition for evacuated residents than in the case of the Gaza withdrawal. A fringe benefit of such planning would be its serving a negotiated outcome as well.

The proposed policy requires the evacuation of up to 100,000 Jewish residents. Israel has never withdrawn a number of civilians approaching this scale. However, although circumstances are far different, Israel has successfully absorbed larger numbers into the state in the past. Since its establishment, Israel has received over three million immigrants, and in the early 1990s, Israel absorbed 200,000 immigrants per year and altogether one million in less than a decade. In addition, tens of thousands of Ethiopian Jews, whose absorption was especially costly, were taken in by the state. During these waves of immigration, the country's GDP was much smaller than it is today and the economy was far less robust. This suggests that a smooth absorption of the settler population is within Israel's means and is doable, subject to adequate preparations and planning.

A fair compensation scheme must be put in place, with a smooth bureaucratic process instituted so that those relocating can access easily what the state offers. There should also be legislation mandating that those living in the West Bank can relinquish their homes and/or their businesses, industrial plants, agricultural enterprises, and so on under state auspices, in exchange for an alternative home and related means of employment within Israel's borders. This law will ensure that those whose homes are of no real market value are not placed at a disadvantage.

Even with all these measures in place, the evacuated residents will still pay a very heavy personal price in the realization of a two-state solution. Nonetheless, the relocation, however difficult, in fact marks a step toward promoting Israeli fundamental interests and values, rather than the abandonment of Zionist ideals. It is to be hoped that with this higher goal in mind, the policy will gain the support of the majority of the Israeli public.

Economic Aspects

Any two-state solution necessitates the relocation of tens of thousands of Israeli citizens, whether it is the outcome of a negotiated agreement or whether it is preceded by an independent Israeli move. Israel's gradual, independent withdrawal from most of the West Bank will require the state to provide temporary and permanent housing solutions, including construction of new housing developments and community centers; compensate relocated residents, including for the loss of livelihood; redeploy its military forces in the area; and establish institutions to formulate, coordinate, and evaluate the policy. For the removal of over 8,000 residents of the Gaza Strip and four West Bank settlements, the government set aside NIS 3.8 billion (the equivalent of roughly $884 million) just for the compensation.[15] According to press reports, by 2012 the sum grew incrementally to NIS 5.5 billion. With the relocation of around ten times as many people, the estimated costs will be around $10-15 billion, but some of this will be offset by the savings from direct and indirect costs of the occupation.

Although costs for implementing an independent withdrawal will undoubtedly be high, with a combination of foreign aid and long term government bonds marketed overseas and in Israel to be purchased primarily by the pension and provident funds, Israel should be able to meet these costs. As Israel's policy of independent steps is likely to be internationally perceived as a move in the right direction, it can be expected that Israel will receive significant special aid from the U.S. and other countries. Despite the financial costs Israel will incur, a policy of well-planned constructive independent steps is financially viable. When it came to the building of the security fence separating Israel from the West Bank, it was said that Israel would not be able to sustain the expense, yet the barrier continued to be built – the state found a way.[16]

Moreover, in the long term, without the heavy costs of maintaining the West Bank settlements[17] (which averaged $215 million annually in 2004-2010[18]), Israel will be able to channel funds toward internal development and domestic issues. It can also be expected that as a result of Israel's efforts to advance the conflict resolution process, Israel will gain a better international reputation, and the BDS (divestment, boycott, and sanctions) campaign that could potentially have a serious impact on the country's economy would lose momentum. In the 2000s, the U.S. deducted over $2 billion from Israeli aid precisely because of continued settlement construction. There are thus financial gains to a policy of independent steps that go a long way to offset the losses. And in any event, the costs for resettling West Bank residents will have to be met, sooner or later, if Israel wants to realize a two-state solution and maintain a democratic Jewish state.

Garnering Support

For the policy to have maximum impact, Israel must put effort into amassing support for the policy within Israeli society, among Palestinians, and internationally.

Israel: the government will have to address many sectors of society, including those from lower socio-economic backgrounds that will oppose giving budgetary preferences to the residents of evacuated settlements. A campaign must focus on a clear presentation of the process and make full details of the policy accessible to the public. Government leaders must initiate serious preliminary discussion in order to build a consensus based upon confidence through an internal empathetic and respectful Israeli dialogue. The urgent and essential need for a two-state solution and the difference of the proposed policy from the Gaza disengagement must be explained. Strong leadership can thereupon amass adequate support behind this well calculated policy, which is motivated by Israeli interests.

Palestinians: although this policy is motivated by Israel's own interests, Israel should publically acknowledge its desire to see the establishment of a demilitarized Palestinian state living peacefully alongside the Jewish state. Israel should also end construction east of the security fence and in the Arab neighborhoods of East Jerusalem to show in both words and deeds its commitment to fostering a two-state solution.[19]

The process of disengagement needs to be given as much consideration as the end goal of a comprehensive final status agreement. In this vein, it is highly recommended that Israel coordinate its moves with the Palestinians as much as possible. Indeed, "independent" and "unilateral" do not necessarily mean uncoordinated. One reason cited for the instability after the Gaza disengagement is precisely this lack of communication and coordination. More than just the practical benefits of a coordinated withdrawal, coordination signifies Israeli respect of the Palestinian perspective. Moving toward a non-occupation reality, although it may meet Palestinian interests, does not necessarily fulfill other objectives of justice, respect, dignity, and rights. If the major action of withdrawal is carried out in the Palestinian territories without any coordination with the Palestinians, this would likely further entrench the imbalance of power between Israel and the Palestinians, which would in turn only exacerbate tensions and stall the peace process. However, this policy, if carried out well, could improve relations between the Israel government and the Palestinians leadership, perhaps leading to the resumption of more successful negotiations.

The international community: the U.S., European Union, and other members of the international community have consistently condemned Israeli settlement expansion within the West Bank, to the extent that it has at times even compromised the relationship between Israel and its main allies. This is an issue the world cares about. Therefore the support of foreign governments for this policy of gradually withdrawing from the territory is attainable. Support from the international community in several areas could assist the implementation of the policy. Special financial aid to assist Israel with the heavy financial toll of resettling West Bank Israeli residents will be essential, as will the deployment of a peacekeeping force after IDF withdrawal following a sustained period of quiet.

Conclusion

For the proposed policy to succeed, Israel must undertake three major policy efforts simultaneously:

a. Pursue a negotiated solution with the Palestinians, even partial or transitional, while mobilizing international and Arab support.
b. Take constructive, independent steps that delineate a border and promote the concept of two states for two peoples.
c. Launch an intensive, internal discourse to prevent domestic conflagration. Accordingly, the preferred negotiations model, if not viable on its own, should be complemented and eventually replaced by a new paradigm of constructive independent steps to create a reality of two states.

By promoting a two-state solution on the ground, Israel will deliver the message that it is taking action to advance the peace process, without jeopardizing its own security. Israel cannot afford to give up striving for a two-state solution because negotiations are not advancing, let alone yielding desired results. The intractable Israeli-Palestinian conflict is not close to resolution, and a new way to break the deadlock must be found. An independent gradual withdrawal from parts of the West Bank, planned carefully in a nation-wide process, represents progress and a renewed sense of opportunity. These independent steps will ideally help revive a negotiation process in order to begin tackling the core issues seriously. If not, Israel will at least be fulfilling its own interests of preserving the Jewish democratic nature of the state and gaining international support, as well as realizing a main Palestinian interest of dismantling settlements.

A process of disengaging from territory in such a politically volatile region brings with it a risk factor. However, doing nothing and just waiting for negotiations to eventually bear fruit may be the biggest risk of all. In addition, there are many expected advantages of this policy for both parties. Israel is likely to benefit in the long term from a stronger economy and heightened security, stronger national solidarity, and hopefully increased international legitimacy. With the relocation of Israeli civilians from the West Bank, the Palestinians are a significant step closer to the establishment of a sovereign state. After rounds of failed negotiations and deadlock on the same core issues, it is clear why both Israelis and Palestinians are close to giving up hope on a peaceful way out of this conflict. However, transitional arrangements, regional dialogue, and partial understandings can make complementary contributions along parallel tracks. Alternative options invite exploration, and decision makers can often find creative ways to begin resolving the conflict and lead the way toward peace.

Notes

The author wishes to thank Deborah Shulman, intern at the INSS Center for Applied Negotiations, for her important contribution to this article

1   Uri Sagie and Gilead Sher, "Policy Paper," Van Leer Jerusalem Institute, 2002, http://www.vanleer.org.il/sites/files/product-pdf/55_PDF.pdf.

2   Robert Zelnick, *Israel's Unilateralism: Beyond Gaza* (Washington, DC: Hoover Institution Press, 2006).

3   Address of PM Ariel Sharon, Fourth Herzliya Conference, December 18, 2003, http://www.mfa.gov.il/mfa/pressroom/2003/pages/address%20by%20pm%20 ariel%20sharon%20at%20the%20fourth%20herzliya.aspx.

4   In this essay, the term Gaza disengagement or Gaza withdrawal refers to the 2005 Israeli withdrawal from Gaza and four towns in the West Bank. In 2012, a research group at INSS studying Israeli-Palestinian issues presented a detailed policy recommendation of gradual, controlled, and measured implementation of independent withdrawal from the majority of the West Bank toward setting in place a two-state reality. From a comparative analysis of options, independent Israeli steps emerged as the most popular when taking into consideration its contribution to a two-state solution and to achieving political calm and security stability. See Shlomo Brom, "Israel and the Palestinians: Policy Options Given the Infeasibility of Reaching a Final Status Agreement," *Strategic Assessment* 15, no. 2 (2012). I was a member of the INSS working group that dealt with the Israeli-Palestinian arena and in that capacity contributed to the abovementioned policy options analysis.

5   See Amos Yadlin and Gilead Sher, "Unilateral Peace: It's Time for Israel to Move toward a Two-State Solution, Alone if Necessary," *ForeignPolicy.com* , March 18, 2013, http://www.foreignpolicy.com/articles/2013/03/19/unilateral_peace_israel_ palestine.

6   Jonathan Rynhod and Dov Waxman, "Ideological Change and Israel's Disengagement from Gaza," *Political Science Quarterly* 123, no. 1 (2008): 11.

7   Zaki Shalom, "From Vision to Reality," *Strategic Assessment* 13, no. 3 (2010): 86.

8   Aviad Glickman, "Inquiry Commission: State Failed in Rehabilitating Evacuees," *Ynet*, September 9, 2009, http://www.ynetnews.com/articles/0,7340,L-3783016,00.html.

9   William Booth, "Ariel Sharon Was No Hero for Israeli Settlers Evicted from Gaza," January 13, 2014, http://www.washingtonpost.com/world/ariel-sharon-was-no-hero-for-israeli-settlers-evicted-from-gaza/2014/01/12/aa56ee22-7bc9-11e3-9556-4a4bf7bcbd84_story.html.

10 Gilead Sher, "Op-Ed: Steps Israel Should Take to Control its Destiny," *Crescent City Jewish News*, October 11, 2012, http://www.crescentcityjewishnews.com/op-ed-steps-israel-should-take-to-control-its-destiny/.

11 Poll number 50, Palestinian Center for Policy and Survey, December 19-22, 2013.

12 Reut Institute, "Is One State Enough?" June 12, 2007, http://www.reut-institute.org/Publication.aspx?PublicationId=1753.

13 Brom, "Israel and the Palestinians."

14 Transcript from roundtable discussion "Going It Alone? Unilateralism vs. Negotiations," with Mazen Sinnokrot, Nazmi Ju'beh, Ron Pundak, Danny Rubinstein,

and Omar Karmi (moderator), *Palestine-Israeli Journal* 13, no. 2 (2006), http://www.pij.org/details.php?id=819.

15   Israel Ministry of Foreign Affairs, "Israel's Disengagement Plan: Renewing the Peace Process," April 20, 2005, http://mfa.gov.il/MFA/ForeignPolicy/Peace/Guide/Pages/Israels%20Disengagement%20Plan-%20Renewing%20the%20Peace%20Process%20Apr%202005.aspx.

16   "Going It Alone? Unilateralism vs. Negotiations."

17   A recent report by Molad ("The Settlers' Secret Slush Fund," Setember 14, 2014, analysis by Liat Schlesinger) shows that hundreds of millions of taxpayer shekels are transferred to the Settlement Division of the World Zionist Organization each year, and are used as a secret slush fund for the settlement movement. The analysis alleged that despite being fully funded by taxpayer money, the Division keeps its budget under wraps. Molad's report uncovers that the Division allocates 74.5 percent of its support to settlements in the West Bank. In fact, the single settlement of Beit El receives more than all 115 beneficiaries in the Negev and Galilee combined.

18   For example, see Local Authorities in Israel 2010, Publication No. 1498 of the Central Bureau of Statistics, June 28, 2012.

19   Yadlin and Sher, "Unilateral Peace."

Contributors

Editors

Gilead Sher is a senior research fellow at INSS, where he heads the Center for Applied Negotiations (CAN). Mr. Sher was the Head of Bureau and Policy Coordinator of Israel's former Prime Minister and Minister of Defense Ehud Barak. He served as Chief and co-Chief negotiator in 1999-2001 at the Camp David summit and the Taba talks, as well as in extensive rounds of covert negotiations. Mr. Sher is an attorney and senior partner in Gilead Sher, Kadari & Co. Law Offices. His professional career combines the practice of law, policy planning, academic research, and involvement in public bodies and civil society organizations. His book *The Israeli-Palestinian Peace Negotiations, 1999-2001: Within Reach* was published by Routledge in 2006. Mr. Sher was a visiting professor on Conflict Resolution and Negotiations at the Wharton School of the University of Pennsylvania (2001-2011) and taught at Tel Aviv University. He serves as chairman of the executive board of Sapir Academic College, the largest public college in Israel.

Anat Kurz is a senior research fellow and Director of Research at INSS. She has lectured and published extensively on various insurgency-related issues, the institutionalization process of organized popular struggles, Palestinian national movements, Israeli-Palestinian relations, and policy dilemmas of dealing with sub-state conflicts. Dr. Kurz has taken part in forums, conferences, and Track II meetings on strategic affairs, Middle Eastern security, and conflict resolution, and has taught courses at Tel Aviv University. She is the author *of Fatah and the Politics of Violence: The Institutionalization of a Popular Struggle* and *The Palestinian Uprisings: War with Israel, War at Home*; co-editor of the INSS annual volume *Strategic Survey for Israel*; and editor of *INSS Insight*.

Authors

Trond Bakkevig is a Dean in the Church of Norway. He is also the Convener of the Council of Religious Institutions of the Holy Land, consisting of the Chief Rabbinate of Israel, the Meeting of the Heads of Churches in Jerusalem, and the Supreme Judge of the Sharia Courts in Palestine. Dr. Canon Bakkevig has been the General Secretary of the Church of Council on Ecumenical and International Relations (1984-93), and was also the full time personal advisor to the Norwegian Foreign Minister (1987-88). He was a member of the Central Committee of the World Council of Churches (1997-2006) and Moderator of the Board of the Institute for Human Rights, University of Oslo. In 2011 he was made Commander of the Order of St. Olav, awarded by the King of Norway, and also received several other honors. In 1984 he defended his doctoral dissertation on Theology and Nuclear Arms and was made a Doctor of Theology at the University of Oslo.

Daniel Bar-Tal is Branco Weiss Professor of Research in Child Development and Education at the School of Education, Tel Aviv University. His primary research interest is political and social psychology, studying socio-psychological foundations of intractable conflicts and peace building, as well as development of political understanding among children and peace education. He has published twenty books and over two hundreds articles and chapters in major social and political psychological journals, books, and encyclopedias. He served as a President of the International Society of Political Psychology and received various awards for his work, including the Lasswell Award and the Nevitt Sanford Award of the International Society of Political Psychology and the Morton Deutsch Conflict Resolution Award of the Society for the Study of Peace, Conflict, and Violence (Div. 48 of APA).

Benedetta Berti is a research fellow at the Institute for National Security Studies, a member of the faculty at Tel Aviv University, and a post-doctoral fellow at Ben-Gurion University. Dr. Berti's areas of expertise include human security, internal conflict, integration of armed groups, and post-conflict stabilization, as well as democratization, civil society, social movements, and strategic nonviolence. Dr. Berti's work has appeared, among others, in *Foreign Policy, Foreign Affairs, Studies in Conflict and Terrorism,*

Mediterranean Politics, and the *Middle East Journal*. She is the author of the book *Armed Political Organizations: From Conflict to Integration* (Johns Hopkins University Press, 2013).

Byron Bland is senior consultant for the Stanford Center on International Conflict and Negotiation (SCICN), Lecturer in Law at the Stanford Law School, and Chaplain/Ombudsperson for Palo Alto University. He was recently appointed director of PAU's Program on Conflict Resolution and Community Mental Health. Dr. Bland retired from Stanford University in 2009 where he had served as associate director of SCICN and research associate at the Center for Democracy Development and the Rule of Law for twelve years. Having worked for just under 25 years in Northern Ireland and over ten years on the Israeli-Palestinian conflict, Dr. Bland continues his involvement in both conflicts. Dr. Bland is an ordained Presbyterian minister and, from 1976-1991, served as campus minister for Untied Campus Christian Ministries at Stanford. He is also an adjunct professor at the Center for Innovation in Ministry at San Francisco Theological Seminary.

Miriam Fendius Elman is associate professor of political science at the Maxwell School of Syracuse University, where she is a research co-director at the Program for the Advancement of Research on Conflict and Collaboration (PARCC). Dr. Elman received her Ph.D. in political science from Columbia University and completed her B.A. in International Relations at the Hebrew University of Jerusalem, Israel. An award winning scholar and teacher, she has published over forty articles and book chapters and is the editor of *Paths to Peace: Is Democracy the Answer?* (1997), and the co-editor of *Bridges and Boundaries: Historians, Political Scientists, and the Study of International Relations* (2001); *Progress in International Relations Theory: Appraising the Field* (2003); *Democracy and Conflict Resolution: The Dilemmas of Israel's Peacemaking* (2013); and *Jerusalem: Conflict and Cooperation in a Contested City* (2014).

Marc Finaud is a former French diplomat who was seconded to the Geneva Centre for Security Policy (GCSP) between 2004 and 2013 and now works for this institution to train diplomats and military officers in international and human security, and conduct research in those fields. During his career as a diplomat, he served in several bilateral postings (in the Soviet Union, Poland, Israel, Australia) as well as in multilateral missions (to the Conference on Security and Cooperation in Europe, the Conference on Disarmament, and the United Nations). He holds Master's degrees in International Law and Political Science. He is also Senior Resident Fellow (WMD Program) at the United Nations Institute for Disarmament Research (UNIDIR).

Patrick Hajayandi is currently working as a Senior Project Leader at the Great Lakes Desk of the Institute for Justice and Reconciliation based in Cape Town, South Africa. He previously held a teaching position at the Department of Political Science and International Relations of the National School of Administration in Burundi. He also worked as a Researcher for the Transitional Demobilization and Reintegration Program (TDRP) of the World Bank on a research project aimed at exploring the role of the family in the reintegration of ex-combatants. In 2010, Mr. Hajayandi worked for the NGO Radio Labenevolencija HTF where he was in charge of political analysis of the programs related to electoral processes in Burundi. He specializes in conflict transformation.

Eran Halperin is currently an Associate Professor and the Dean of the School of Psychology at the IDC, Herzliya. His research uses psychological and political theories and methods to investigate different aspects of inter-group conflicts. More specifically, he is interested in widening the understanding regarding the psychological roots of some of the most destructive political ramifications of inter-group relations – e.g., intolerance, exclusion, and inter-group violence and conflict. Most of his studies concentrate on the role of emotions and emotion regulation in determining public opinion toward peace and equality on the one hand, and war and discrimination on the other. Dr. Halperin is a strong believer in "bottom-up" processes, as well as in the power of the people to create social change. Hence, his entire work focuses on the peoples' perspectives, aspiring to uncover ways to set social change in motion toward democracy and peace. The unique case of Israeli society in general and of the Israeli-Palestinian conflict in particular, motivates his work and inspires his thinking, and, hence, most of his studies are conducted within the context of this "natural laboratory."

Ariel Heifetz Knobel is an international conflict practitioner and Northern Ireland specialist currently facilitating Track 1.5 and Track 2 initiatives in Israel and the West Bank. For the past four years, she has been working with Northern Irish peacemakers to bring best practices to the Middle East, having conducted fieldwork in Belfast through the Harvard Program on Negotiation. Heifetz Knobel served as Public Diplomacy Director at the Israeli Consulate to New England, and as a mediator in Boston's district courts. She holds an M.A. in International Negotiation and Conflict Management from The Fletcher School at Tufts University and a B.A. from Columbia University.

Louis Kriesberg earned a Ph.D. in sociology at the University of Chicago, and is Maxwell Professor Emeritus of Social Conflict Studies and founding director of the Program on the Analysis and Resolution of Conflicts (PARC) at Syracuse University. Dr. Kriesberg's books include: *Realizing Peace: A Constructive Conflict Approach* (2015); the 4th edition of *Constructive Conflicts*, co-authored with Bruce W. Dayton, published in 2012 – earlier editions were published in 1998, 2003, and 2007; *Conflict Transformation and Peacebuilding* (co-edited with Bruce Dayton, 2009); *International Conflict Resolution* (1992); *Timing the De-Escalation of International Conflicts* (co-edited, 1991); and *Intractable Conflicts and Their Transformation* (co-edited, 1989). In addition, he has published 165 book chapters and articles.

Alan J. Kuperman is Associate Professor at the LBJ School of Public Affairs, University of Texas at Austin, where he teaches courses in global policy studies and is coordinator of the Nuclear Proliferation Prevention Project (www.NPPP.org). His latest publications include *Constitutions and Conflict Management in Africa: Preventing Civil War Through Institutional Design* (University of Pennsylvania Press, 2014), and "A Model Humanitarian Intervention? Reassessing NATO's Libya Campaign," *International Security* (summer 2013). In 2013-2014 he was a senior fellow at the U.S. Institute of Peace, and in 2009-2010 a fellow at the Woodrow Wilson International

Center for Scholars, both in Washington, DC. He holds a Ph.D. in Political Science from the Massachusetts Institute of Technology.

Gallia Lindenstrauss, a research fellow at the Institute for National Security Studies, specializes in Turkish foreign policy. Her additional research interests are ethnic conflicts, Azerbaijan's foreign policy, the Cyprus issue, and the Kurds. She completed her Ph.D. in the Department of International Relations at the Hebrew University. During the years 2009-2010, Dr. Lindenstrauss was a postdoctoral fellow at the Davis Institute for International Relations at the Hebrew University. In 2007-2009, she was a Neubauer research fellow at the Institute for National Security Studies. Dr. Lindenstrauss lectures at the Interdisciplinary Center, Herzlia and has also lectured at the Hebrew University of Jerusalem.

Gary Mason is a Methodist clergy leader and has worked in peace building and conflict transformation for almost thirty years. He currently directs a conflict transformation organization called Rethinking Conflict, working locally, globally, and internationally. Prior to this Dr. Mason spent 27 years as a Methodist clergy person in Belfast and played an integral role in the Northern Irish peace process. He is a close advisor to Protestant ex-combatants on the civilianization efforts of paramilitaries. He was instrumental in facilitating negotiations with paramilitaries and government officials, and in 2007 his contribution was formally recognized by the Queen of England. In 2009, his church was the stage from which Loyalist paramilitaries announced their weapons decommissioning. He has lectured in political and academic forums throughout Europe, South Africa, the Middle East, and the U.S.A. on lessons from the Irish peace process. Dr. Mason is a Research Fellow at the Kennedy Institute for Conflict Intervention at Maynooth University in Ireland.

Robert H. Mnookin is the Samuel Williston Professor of Law at Harvard Law School, the Chair of the Program on Negotiation at Harvard Law School, and the Director of the Harvard Negotiation Research Project. A leading scholar in the field of conflict resolution, Professor Mnookin has applied his interdisciplinary approach to negotiation and conflict resolution to a remarkable range of problems; both public and private. Professor Mnookin has served as a consultant to governments, international agencies, major corporations, and law firms. As a neutral arbitrator or mediator, he has resolved numerous complex commercial disputes. Professor Mnookin has written or edited ten books and numerous scholarly articles. In his most recent book, *Bargaining with the Devil: When to Negotiate, When to Fight*, he explores how to make decisions in the most challenging disputes.

Ruthie Pliskin is a doctoral candidate at the School of Psychological Sciences at Tel Aviv University and the School of Psychology at the Interdisciplinary Center, Herzliya. Her interests lie in the psychology of intergroup relations, and her research focuses on the interrelations of emotional processes and ideology in intergroup conflict, and how these work together to influence the attitudes and behaviors of individuals involved in conflict. She has published work in *Personality and Social Psychology Bulletin, Journal of Conflict Resolution*, and *Advances in Political Psychology*, and has presented her research at various professional conferences, including the annual meetings of EASP, ISPP, APSA, and CERE. She completed her M.A. at Tel Aviv University and her B.Sc. at Boston University. While at BU, she was also awarded the College of Communication's prestigious Blue Chip Award for Academic Excellence and Leadership.

Lee Ross is the Stanford Federal Credit Union Professor of Psychology at Stanford University and co-founder of the Stanford Center on International Conflict and Negotiation. The co-author of two influential books, *Human Inference* and *The Person and the Situation* (both with Richard Nisbett), his research on attributional biases and shortcomings in human inference has been influential in social psychology and the study of human inference, judgment, and decision making. His more recent research has explored psychological barriers to conflict resolution, and he has participated in relationship building and public peace process initiatives in Northern Ireland and the Middle East. He was elected in 1994 to the American Academy of Arts and Sciences and in 2010 to the National Academy of Sciences.

James K. Sebenius is a professor at Harvard Business School, where he teaches advanced negotiation to students and senior executives. Formerly on the faculty of Harvard's Kennedy School, he serves as Vice Chair of the Program on Negotiation (PON) at Harvard Law School. At PON, he chairs the University's annual Great Negotiator Award program, which has engaged intensively with negotiators such as Richard Holbrooke, James Baker, Lakdhar Brahimi, George Mitchell, and Bruce Wasserstein. Professor Sebenius also directs the Harvard Negotiation Project, which currently focuses on China-related negotiations and PON's Middle East Negotiation Initiative. He wrote *Negotiating the Law of the Sea* (Harvard University Press) and co-authored (with David Lax) *3D Negotiation* (HBS Press, 2006) and *The Manager as Negotiator* (Free Press, 1986); he has also produced a large number of academic and popular articles, field case studies on negotiation, and multimedia teaching materials. He co-founded Lax Sebenius LLC, an ongoing negotiation strategy firm that advises companies and governments worldwide on their most challenging negotiations. Away from Harvard, he worked full-time for several years for the New York-based Blackstone Group, and has served with the United States State and Commerce Departments.

Erik Solheim was elected to chair the OECD Development Assistance Committee (DAC) in January 2013. He also serves as United Nations Environment Program's special envoy for environment, conflict and disaster, and he has contributed to peace processes in Burundi, Nepal, Myanmar, and Sudan. A member of the Socialist Left party (SV), from 2007 to 2012 he held the combined portfolio of Norway's Minister of the Environment, and International Development; he likewise served as Minister of International Development from 2005 to 2007. From 2000 to 2005, Mr. Solheim was the main negotiator in the peace process in Sri Lanka, party secretary from 1987 to 1997, and a member of the Norwegian parliament for twelve years.

INSS Memoranda, April 2014–Present